TRUTH IN ACCOUNTING

TRUTH

IN

ACCOUNTING

By

KENNETH MACNEAL, C.P.A.

SCHOLARS BOOK CO.

BOX 3344

LAWRENCE, KANSAS 66044

657

M16t

Reprinted 1970 by

SCHOLARS BOOK CO.

LAWRENCE, KANSAS 66044

MN

To

LAWRENCE E. JONES

whose share in this book is greater than he knows

EDITOR'S FOREWORD

THIS IS THE FIRST of a planned series of reissues of "Classics in Accounting." The purpose of the series is to make available certain out of print works that have made significant contributions to accounting thought. MacNeal's *Truth in Accounting* was selected as the first book to be reissued because it

(1) reaches conclusions similar to those reached by contemporary researchers, despite the fact that it was written over thirty years ago under the vastly dissimilar conditions of the Great Depression, and

(2) is so scarce that it is virtually impossible to purchase a copy.

The economics of publishing is such that the price of this volume would have been prohibitive had it not been for a grant from Arthur Andersen & Co. In keeping with their policy of encouraging the free flow of ideas, they have provided the funds necessary to make this book available at a reasonable price. In keeping with this same policy, they suggested that "all editorial decisions be made on campus by the editor." Therefore, the responsibility for such decisions, chiefly the selection of the books to be reissued, rests solely with me.

ROBERT R. STERLING

October, 1970
University of Kansas
Lawrence, Kansas

PREFACE

In this work it has been my aim to present a comprehensive analysis of modern accounting theory and practice, and at the same time to suggest a definitive remedy for many serious accounting imperfections. The facts disclosed herein lead unavoidably to a conclusion that the great majority of contemporary certified financial statements must necessarily be untrue and misleading due to the unsound principles upon which modern accounting methods are based. A revision of these principles is suggested. Throughout the work, a consistent effort is made to bring every accounting rule into line with the proven principles of economics and logic, without resort to the commodity dollar concept. A complete indictment is made of present accounting methods and a practical, easily intelligible procedure is offered as an alternative.

The discussion is of vital importance to students of accounting and to practicing accountants in both public and private work. For more than four hundred years, since the publication of Pacioli's book on double entry bookkeeping in 1494, accounting methods, and hence accounting reports, have been based on expediency rather than on truth. Financial statements today are composed of a bewildering mixture of accounting conventions, historical data, and present facts, wherein even accountants are often unable to distinguish between truth and fiction. The toll which this situation levies on business management, and on the general public, is beginning to be recognized. Signs are not lacking that accountants must shortly revise their methods if they are to maintain their place in the public esteem.

The subject dealt with is of particular concern to bankers, brokers, and investment counselors. The information supplied by accountants' reports is of paramount importance to those who lend money on the basis of financial statements or who advise investors relative to the merits of securities. If balance sheets are misleading, a determination of the net worth of a borrower is apt to be largely a matter of guesswork. If both earnings and net worth are in doubt, investment counsel must of necessity be based largely on hearsay and conjecture.

Much of the material presented should merit the attention of lawyers, legislators, and government officials concerned with the laws regulating financial practices. If such laws are to fulfill their purposes, the constitution of a truthful financial statement should be clearly understood. Under present conditions a full, honest disclosure of the facts in a set of financial statements is most improbable. If the management of a company desired such disclosure its accountant would in all probability feel compelled to refuse to certify the figures.

Business men would do well to familiarize themselves with this situation because it may affect them to a marked degree. Present accounting methods may often compel them either to overstate or to understate their earnings or their assets and may practically prohibit them from publishing important truths about their affairs. In some cases a certified public accountant's certificate can be obtained to the most flagrant overstatement, while in other cases the accountant may insist upon just as flagrant an understatement, depending entirely upon how the facts line up with accepted accounting practice. Hence, an honest management may be prevented from telling the truth, or may perhaps even be prevented from knowing it, while a dishonest management may find itself in a position to take full advantage of the distortion of facts.

An understanding of the historical reasons for this state of affairs and of the remedy therefor should be of great benefit to the investing public. Few individuals who fail to understand the limitations of contemporary financial statements can hope to avoid being deceived by them. Investors should know why the sincere and honest accountant of today is all too likely to be an unconscious purveyor of misinformation. They should learn to read financial statements, even from the most reputable sources, with the greatest caution, and should know why such statements can hardly be otherwise than untrue and misleading as long as present accounting methods remain unchanged.

In attempting a work such as this, which attacks the accepted practices of an honorable and respected profession, I am deeply sensible that I am exposing myself to charges of being an ingrate or worse. I acknowledge the justice of such charges from the viewpoint of a self-satisfied group, but I plead that it is precisely because of my high regard for the great probity of individual accountants and because of my belief in the disinterested public service viewpoint of the public accounting profession as a whole, that I have dared to write as I have. If the profession is to enhance or even to maintain its place in the public esteem, it must, in my opinion, offer more than individual honesty and passive willingness to be of service. It must offer mental equipment equal to the full requirements of the job, and that, it seems to me, means intellectual ability sufficient to enable it to determine and to present the truth, in so far as this may be possible.

The typical certified public accountant of today is, in actual fact, apt to be little more than a graduate bookkeeper. It is true that he knows something about law and a great deal about the theory and practice of bookkeeping. But he rarely knows anything to speak of about economics or about economic theory relating either to money or to value. He is not legally regarded as a valuer, nor does he so regard himself, and consequently the figures which he presents are in the main merely a bookkeeper's figures. For the most part he simply satisfies himself that the bookkeeping has been properly done and then uses book figures with an almost total disregard of how they may vary from, or omit to tell, the truth. As a result, laymen with no knowledge of accounting may be deceived or, if they know the truth, may tend to regard accounting as the weirdest of professions.

I believe that this condition may eventually engender one of two outcomes. If accounting principles and practice remain unchanged, it seems reasonable to predict that the number of individuals who mistrust published financial statements will increase until the entire accounting profession loses caste and its individual members are paid accordingly. On the other hand, if the intellectual horizon of the profession is broadened, if candidates for a C.P.A. degree are required to know the rudiments of political economy, if accounting principles are revised so that the public may be supplied with that thing which is of greatest

value to it, namely, the truth, then I do not think it is un-
reasonable to look forward to a time when the profession
will occupy a position of public respect and esteem of which
it does not dream today. It seems to me that this latter con-
summation is to be desired, not alone for the benefit of
individuals in the profession, but also because of the service
that they would then be able to render to a public which
as yet only partly understands economic realities.

Twenty-two years ago in Chicago, when I started my
accounting career as a very young member of the staff of
Price, Waterhouse & Co., I was warned that accounting was,
after all, "only common sense." Perhaps this warning was
meant as an antidote for undigested economic theories,
acquired from two universities, in which I had much faith.
Be that as it may, the intervening years of experience, in
both public and private work, have not tended to confirm in
me the idea that accounting is only common sense. During
these years I have discussed the matter with a large number
of accountants, economists, lawyers, and business men.
Many of these have been men of high intelligence who
keenly realize that accounting is not fully performing the
service which it might perform. Yet it has seemed to me
that some of them have failed fully to realize that the vital
defect in present accounting practice is its disharmony with
the simpler principles of economics and logic, commonly
called common sense.

This book is an outgrowth of those discussions. The
responsibility for its defects is all mine. Much of the credit
for whatever good it may accomplish should go to others,
many of whom may be completely unaware that their ideas
have been incorporated herein. My indebtedness to these

unnamed contributors is very real and very great. I am particularly indebted to those friends who read and criticized the entire manuscript. Among these are John S. Cowing, C.P.A., Thomas H. Carroll, C.P.A., Harold C. Stott, C.P.A., Herbert W. Hess, Ph.D., Thomas C. Ottey, A.B., Robert A. MacNeal, B.S., and W. L. Hathaway. Harry B. Whitney procured certain data for the chapter on money. Miss Frances McGlynn labored with me throughout many weary months in the typing and preparation of the entire book, and to her energy and intelligence is due in no small measure the fact that the work was finally completed.

I am conscious of many imperfections in the present volume. The discussion is not exhaustive, and many problems have been covered only by assertions of broad principle. I particularly wish that I had the ability to write without the occasional appearance of ill temper and sweeping denunciation which my friends tell me is my greatest fault. Apparently I have, in a literary sense, a low boiling point of which I am scarcely aware. I can only assure readers that my criticism is of principles, not persons, that I distrust methods, not motives. I shall gratefully receive any suggestions with which I may be favored by those who feel that this book is a sufficiently constructive addition to accounting literature to warrant their contribution to another edition, which I hope will appear in the course of time.

KENNETH MACNEAL

Alden Park
Philadelphia, Pa.
November 29, 1938

CONTENTS

Chapter   Page

PREFACE   vii

EXPLANATORY NOTE   xvii

I THREE FABLES   1
    The Fable of the Two Factories   2
    The Fable of the Two Flour Mills   6
    The Fable of the Two Investment Trusts   9
    Futility of Securities Laws   15
    Weight of Authority   18

II PRESENT ACCOUNTING PRINCIPLES   20
    Meaning of Accountant's Certificate   20
    Accepted Accounting Practice   22
    Theory of Balance Sheet Values   24
    Balance Sheet Values in Practice   28
    Inconsistency of Principles Relating to Balance
      Sheets   32
    Theory of Profit and Loss Statements   33
    Profit and Loss Statements in Practice   37
    Inconsistency of Principles Relating to Profit and
      Loss Statements   39
    Balance Sheets and Profit and Loss Statements Are
      Interdependent   40
    Why Financial Statements Deceive   42

III DEFENSE OF PRESENT ACCOUNTING
     PRINCIPLES   44
    Theoretical Justification of Present Principles   44
    The Original Theory of Going Values   46
    The Present Theory of Going Values   47
    The Harm Done by the Present Theory   48

Reductio ad Absurdum 49
"Conservatism" as a Justification of Present
Principles 50
Practical Justification of Present Principles 52

IV ORIGIN OF PRESENT ACCOUNTING
PRINCIPLES 58
Accounting—Eleventh to Fourteenth Centuries 59
Accounting—Fourteenth and Fifteenth Centuries 60
Evolution of Double Entry Bookkeeping 61
Accounting—Sixteenth to Nineteenth Centuries 63
Accounting—Nineteenth and Twentieth
Centuries 65
Early Accountants 67
Evolution of Accounting Principles 69
The First Era 71
The Second Era 72
The Present Era 81

V THE NATURE OF VALUE 85
Economic versus Philosophic Concept 85
Economic Value 87
The Element of Scarcity 88
The Element of Exchangeability 89
The Element of Utility 91
Supply and Demand 95
Faulty Concepts of Value 99

VI MONEY 103
Mediums of Exchange 103
The Gold Standard 105
The Value of Gold 107
Values Expressed in Money 109
The Commodity Dollar 111
Stabilized Accounting 115
Illustration of Stabilized Accounting 118
Criticism of Stabilized Accounting 123

VII MARKET PRICES 127
Markets 127
Free Markets 129

I

THREE FABLES

Accounting is the language of finance. Members of the accounting profession are interpreters upon whom the vast majority of people must rely for information relating to any business or project with which they are not intimately and personally familiar. If interpreters do not tell the truth, or do not tell the whole truth, or tell truths intermixed with half truths, many people may be deceived to their hurt.

Doubtless few accountants or business men would contend that present accounting principles are perfect, or that all financial statements prepared in accordance therewith state truly and without misrepresentation the facts that they purport to state. But it is to be doubted if many laymen, business men, or even accountants, realize how faulty present accounting principles are and how serious and far reaching are the evils for which they are responsible.

Not so long ago the truthfulness of the financial statements issued by a business was largely a matter that concerned only the owner of the business and its creditors. During the past twenty-five years, however, a great change has taken place in the ownership of business organizations. Almost every business of any magnitude now is incorporated, and it is extremely rare for a large corporation to be owned entirely by individuals active in its management. Such a corporation is very apt to be owned by hundreds, or thousands, or even hundreds of thousands of small stock-holders who know nothing at all about its affairs except the information contained in the financial statements issued periodically by its management.

In the quite recent past the owner of a business could not be deceived by an untruthful balance sheet or profit and loss statement pertaining to his own business because he ran the business himself and was familiar with every phase of it at first hand. But now an untruthful balance sheet or profit and loss statement may give stockholders a false impression which they have no means of correcting. If published financial statements overstate the assets or earnings of a business, hundreds of investors may be led into paying too much for its stock, or may be led into buying the stock of a company which is on the road to bankruptcy while under the impression that the company is really prosperous. On the other hand, if published financial statements understate the assets or earnings of a business, hundreds of disappointed stockholders may be led to sacrifice their holdings for only a portion of what such holdings are worth. Hence it can be seen that the truthfulness of financial statements has become an extremely important matter, not only to managements, creditors, and stockholders, but to the general investing public as well.

The following fables illustrate, in a very simple and purposely exaggerated fashion, a few of the situations that present accounting principles repeatedly cause to arise.

THE FABLE OF THE TWO FACTORIES. Once upon a time there were two little factories. These little factories were alike in all respects. Their design, condition, and equipment were identical. Both factories had just been built by a local builder and each was quite obviously worth the same amount, but only the builder knew exactly what it had cost to build them.

In this same locality lived a capable business man named John and a stupid business man named William. The builder of the two factories went to John and, by reason of skillful argument, succeeded in selling him one factory for $5,000. A few days later this builder went to William and, by reason of William's stupidity, succeeded in selling him the one remaining factory for $20,000.

John then formed a corporation so that he could sell stock to raise money for operating his factory. He sold his factory to this corporation for the same price that he had paid for it, namely, $5,000, and accepted stock to a par value of $5,000 in payment therefor. John then called in a reputable accountant and asked him to prepare a certified balance sheet for publication. The accountant found that John's company had bought a factory for $5,000, and prepared a certified balance sheet showing the factory to be worth $5,000. William, copying John, also formed a corporation so that he could sell stock to raise money for operating his factory. He sold his factory to this corporation for the same price that he had paid for it, namely, $20,000, and accepted stock to a par value of $20,000 in payment therefor. William also called in the reputable accountant and asked him to prepare a certified balance sheet for publication. The accountant found that William's company had bought a factory for $20,000, and prepared a certified balance sheet showing the factory to be worth $20,000.

Both John's company and William's company then sold

additional stock on the basis of their respective balance
sheets. A banker put $5,000 cash into John's company in
return for stock to a par value of $5,000. The banker thus
acquired a one-half interest in John's company in return
for his $5,000. A farmer invested his cash savings of $5,000
in William's company in return for stock to a par value of
$5,000. The farmer thus acquired a one-fifth interest in
William's company in return for his $5,000.

Now almost everybody in town, except the farmer, knew
that John's factory and William's factory were identical
and were worth the same amount, so it was not long before
William found himself arrested on a charge of defraud-
ing the farmer. William defended himself by putting the
sole responsibility for the balance sheet upon the accountant, whereupon the accountant was arrested and put on
trial.

The accountant defended himself by confessing that he
did not know the value either of John's factory or of
William's factory. He did not know what these factories
could be sold for, nor indeed, if they could be sold at all.
He did not know what it would cost to build and equip
them. In the absence of any inkling as to what they could
be sold for, or what they could be built for, he had used the
original cost price to John's company as the value of its
factory, and had used the original cost price to William's
company as the value of its factory. He claimed that this
was the best he could do and, while admitting that the difference between the values of the two factories was absurd,
he maintained, nevertheless, that the makeshift of adopting
original cost price as value was the only makeshift at hand.
He spoke of these original cost prices as constituting "going

concern values" and challenged the jurors to say what they would have done if they had been in his place.

When the jury retired to consider its verdict, it disagreed. Certain jurors thought that the accountant should have made numerous inquiries as to what the factories could be sold for, and should have adopted one of the resulting bids as the value of each factory. Some jurors thought that the accountant should have had a builder estimate what it would cost to build each factory, and should have used this amount as its value. Still others felt that the accountant did right in adopting the value of $5,000 for John's factory, and the value of $20,000 for William's factory because, they reasoned, no one could know what the factories could be sold for, and an accountant could hardly be expected to know what a factory could be built for. At the end of three days the jury was still in disagreement and the accountant was released.

But the farmer, nevertheless, because of his reliance on the accountant's balance sheet, received for his $5,000 only a one-fifth interest in the assets and earnings of William's company, whereas the banker, in reliance on the same accountant's balance sheet, had, for the same sum, received a one-half interest in John's company. Yet William's company had at no time been worth one penny more than John's company although the reputable accountant had certified one as having assets worth $20,000 and the other as having assets worth $5,000.

The accountant was anxious to do right but he himself did not know what to do. Therefore, although he was careful to keep away from twin factories in the future and was never arrested again, he continued to prepare balance sheets in the same manner that he prepared John's and William's. And reputable accountants still do the same down to this day.

THE FABLE OF THE TWO FLOUR MILLS. Once upon a time there were two corporations, each of which had just been formed. Each corporation had $150,000 cash in its treasury, had no other assets and had no liabilities. Thus the net worth of each corporation was exactly $150,000. All of the capital stock of one corporation was owned by a very competent business man named Henry. All of the capital stock of the other corporation was owned by a very incompetent business man named Bill.

Each corporation started operations on January 1 by leasing a small flour mill for an annual rental of $1,000, and each immediately paid one year's rent in advance in cash. Thus, at this point, each company had $149,000 cash remaining in its treasury.

On January 1, wheat was selling at $1.00 a bushel. Henry, who had studied the wheat market closely, decided that this was as low as wheat would be apt to go. Accordingly he invested $100,000 of his corporation's cash in wheat. Flour was then correspondingly cheap so he decided to hold the wheat until he could get a higher price for flour, after which he would convert the wheat into flour and sell it.

Bill, on the other hand, knew little about the flour business or about the wheat market. Accordingly he did not buy wheat in January when it was low but waited for it to go still lower. Meanwhile he put $100,000 of his corporation's cash out at 6% interest. Shortly thereafter wheat began to go up in price, but Bill left his money out at interest and waited for wheat to come down again. Finally a year passed and on December 31 wheat, which had risen steadily, sold at $2.00 a bushel. Then Bill became fearful that it would go still higher so he called in his money, amounting to $100,000 plus $6,000 interest, and put $100,000 into wheat at $2.00 a bushel. Of course Bill could only buy one-half as much wheat as Henry had bought because he paid twice as much per bushel for it.

Thus, on December 31, Henry and Bill each had $100,000 invested in wheat, but Henry had an unrealized profit of 100% on his $100,000, whereas Bill had earned only 6% interest on his $100,000.

At this point both Henry and Bill decided to sell one-half of their capital stock to the public. Henry employed the most reputable accountant in the town and asked him to prepare a certified balance sheet and profit and loss statement. The accountant prepared a balance sheet showing the remainder of Henry's original cash, namely, $49,000, and showing Henry's wheat at its original cost price of $1.00 per bushel, namely, $100,000. Thus Henry's balance sheet showed that his company now had assets valued at $149,000. The accountant also prepared a profit and loss statement showing that Henry's company had incurred, during the year, a net loss of $1,000 representing the rent which it had paid for its mill.

Then Bill employed the same accountant and asked him to prepare a certified balance sheet and profit and loss statement. The accountant prepared a balance sheet showing the remainder of Bill's original cash, namely, $49,000, and showing his wheat at its original cost price of $2.00 per bushel, namely, $100,000. In addition the accountant showed that Bill had $6,000 cash for the interest his money had earned during the year. Thus Bill's balance sheet showed that his company now had assets valued at $155,000. The accountant also prepared a profit and loss statement showing that Bill's company had, during the year, earned a net profit of $5,000 consisting of $6,000 interest less $1,000 rent.

Both Henry and Bill now mailed their certified financial statements to a wealthy farmer in a neighboring town. Henry offered to sell one-half of his $150,000 capital stock for $75,000 and Bill offered to sell one-half of his $150,000 capital stock for $75,000. The farmer knew very little about financial statements so he went to his bank for advice. The banker pointed out that a comparison of the net worths shown on the two balance sheets revealed that Bill's business was worth $6,000 more than Henry's business. The banker also pointed out that Bill's profit and loss statement disclosed that he had earned $5,000 during the year, whereas Henry's profit and loss statement disclosed that he had lost $1,000 during the year. The banker said that this indicated that Bill was a more capable business man than Henry. Accordingly the banker advised the farmer to purchase Bill's stock rather than Henry's stock. So the farmer bought Bill's stock and never ceased to regret it.

Of course the farmer and his banker were deceived because Henry's business was really worth $249,000 whereas Bill's business was worth only $155,000. Henry must therefore really have earned $99,000 during the year whereas Bill had earned only $5,000 during the year.

Henry converted his wheat into flour during January and sold it for $100,000 profit. Bill converted his wheat into flour during January and sold it for no profit at all.

Yet, when the reputable accountant was later questioned, he insisted that he had done right in refusing to "anticipate" the unrealized profit on Henry's wheat and in valuing both Henry's and Bill's inventories at "cost or market whichever is the lower." The accountant described his method of valuing these inventories as "conservative." And reputable accountants still value inventories in that manner down to this day.

THE FABLE OF THE TWO INVESTMENT TRUSTS. Once upon a time there was a small group of financiers. These financiers formed two investment trusts. One investment trust was called the American Trust and the other was called the National Trust. Each trust started business with a paid-in capital of one million dollars comprising its sole assets and net worth. Each trust had numerous small stockholders, but the management of each was controlled by the small group of financiers. Each trust proposed to operate by investing its capital in small amounts among a large number of listed securities, buying such securities when they were considered cheap and selling them when their market price had appreciated so much that they were no longer considered attractive. Dividends were to be immediately reinvested.

Very soon after the formation of the two investment trusts, a crash in the stock market gave each of them an opportunity to invest all of its capital in sound securities at low prices. This each did and the American Trust invested its capital in exactly the same securities at exactly the same prices as did the National Trust. The stock market then started up and continued to go up for the next four years.

Now the financiers who controlled each of these trusts not only understood the investment trust business but also understood accounting principles. They were keenly aware of the opportunities presented to financiers by modern accounting procedure and they decided to enrich themselves at the expense of the public by taking full advantage of these opportunities. They therefore laid their plans with this in view.

By December 31 of the first year of operation both the American Trust and the National Trust had fared exactly alike because their investments were the same. Dividends had not amounted to much because the securities purchased had very small yields, but the appreciation in the market value of these securities had amounted to an average of 20% of their cost. Accordingly on December 31 the American Trust was ordered to sell all of its securities in order to "realize" its profit and was ordered to reinvest the proceeds in other securities. The investment manager of the American Trust pleaded in vain that other securities could not be more desirable than those already owned, but the financiers were firm. The investment manager therefore had no choice except to obey orders, and the securities on hand were sold and other securities were purchased.

On January 1, the small group of financiers requested a well-known firm of certified public accountants to prepare a balance sheet and income statement for the past year for each of the two trusts controlled by it. This firm of certified public accountants was respected by everybody for its incorruptible integrity, and for the ability of its staff. Financial statements certified by it were accepted without question by bankers and individuals all over the world. This firm of certified public accountants made an audit of both trusts, and a certified balance sheet and a certified profit and loss statement for each trust were prepared by it and delivered to the financiers.

The profit and loss statement of the American Trust disclosed that it had earned $30,000 from dividends and had earned $200,000 from realized profits on the securities it had sold. This amounted to $230,000 or 23% on its capital stock. Its balance sheet disclosed that it had securities to a value of $1,230,000 and no liabilities. These securities were described as being valued at "cost or market whichever is the lower."

The profit and loss statement of the National Trust disclosed that it had earned $30,000 from dividends and that it had no other earnings whatever. Its earnings as certified therefore amounted only to 3% on its capital stock. Its balance sheet disclosed that it had securities to a value of $1,030,000 and no liabilities. These securities were described as being valued at "cost or market whichever is the lower." It is true that there was a footnote on the balance sheet stating that the present market value of these securities was $1,230,000, but most of the public did not pay much attention to this and looked chiefly at the total of the assets which was distinctly shown as $1,030,000 and at the surplus which was distinctly shown as $30,000. The few people who did see and understand the footnote disregarded it because, they said, the appreciation of $200,000 was only a paper profit and could not be considered until it had been realized by being converted into cash, because a decline in the security market might wipe it all out in no time. Also, earnings were clearly shown in the profit and loss statement as only $30,000 without any qualification whatever.

Now, of course, as soon as the certified financial statements of the American Trust and of the National Trust were mailed to stockholders and printed in the newspapers, everybody learned that the American Trust had earned 23% on its capital stock during the year whereas the National Trust had earned only 3% on its capital stock. The price of the American Trust stock therefore rose sharply as many investors rushed to buy it, and the price of the National Trust stock dropped sharply due to selling by disappointed stockholders.

But the small group of financiers knew that, although the American Trust had earned 23% on its capital stock, the National Trust had also really earned 23% on its capital stock. It was intelligent enough to see that a decline in the security market which would wipe out the 20% unrealized profit of the National Trust would also wipe out the 20% realized profit of the American Trust and that therefore the unrealized profit was just as safe as the realized profit. So the small group of financiers sold a large part of its holdings of American Trust stock at high prices and bought additional stock of the National Trust at very low prices.

By December 31 of the next year both trusts had earned an additional $30,000 from dividends and each had a further unrealized profit of $200,000 in its securities. So this time the National Trust was ordered to sell all of its securities and to invest the proceeds in the same securities that the American Trust owned. This was done and the profit of $200,000 for the current year plus the profit of $200,000 for the previous year was duly realized. The assets of the National Trust were now identical with those of the American Trust. The market value of each was $1,460,000. The two trusts were exactly alike and each owned exactly the same quantities of the same securities with a total market value of $1,460,000.

On January 1 the same widely known and trusted firm of certified public accountants was requested to prepare balance sheets and profit and loss statements for the past year for each of the two trusts. When this had been done the profit and loss statement of the American Trust disclosed that it had earned $30,000 from dividends and that it had no other earnings whatsoever. Its earnings as certified therefore amounted only to 3% on its capital stock. Its balance sheet disclosed that it had securities to a value of $1,260,000 and no liabilities. These securities were described as being valued at "cost or market whichever is the lower."

The profit and loss statement of the National Trust, however, disclosed that it had earned $30,000 from dividends and had earned $400,000 from realized profits on the securities it had sold. This amounted to $430,000 or 43% on its capital stock. Its balance sheet disclosed that it had securities to a value of $1,460,000 and no liabilities. These securities were described as being valued at "cost or market whichever is the lower."

Now, of course, as soon as the certified financial statements of the American Trust and of the National Trust were mailed to stockholders and printed in the newspapers, everybody learned that the American Trust had earned only 3% on its capital stock during the past year whereas the National Trust had earned 43% on its capital stock during the same period. The price of American Trust stock therefore dropped sharply due to selling by disappointed stockholders and the price of National Trust stock rose sky high as investors rushed to buy it.

But the small group of financiers knew that the American Trust had really earned 23% on its capital stock during the past year although its earnings were certified as only 3% and it also knew that the National Trust had earned only 23% on its capital stock during the past year although its earnings were certified as 43%. Also, it was intelligent enough to realize that a decline in the security market which would wipe out the 20% unrealized profit of the American Trust would also wipe out the same amount of the realized profit of the National Trust because each trust owned exactly the same quantity of exactly the same securities. Therefore the unrealized profit of the American Trust was obviously just as safe as the realized profit of the National Trust. In fact there was no difference whatever between them. It was clear to the small group of financiers that each trust now possessed exactly $1,460,000 of the same securities, and that each had started with exactly $1,000,000 in money two years ago. Neither trust had received anything except profits earned in the ordinary and usual course of its business. Therefore, each trust must have made exactly the same amount of money since its formation, and the practice of the accountants in recognizing realized profits as earnings but in refusing to recognize un-realized profits as earnings must have been pure hokum. So the small group of financiers bought back at low prices the American Trust stock it had sold at high prices a year ago and bought more in addition. Then it sold at high prices the National Trust stock it had bought at low prices a year ago and sold more in addition.

The profits to the financiers on these transactions were far greater than they could have hoped to make merely from dividends on their stock. So they continued the process year after year and never failed to make a killing be-cause they knew that the accounting firm would always maintain that unrealized profits were not earnings. And they have become exceedingly wealthy and respected, and no one has ever ventured to criticize them because the trusted firm of accountants has certified every one of their financial statements and everyone is convinced that such a firm would never certify a fraudulent or deceptive profit and loss statement or balance sheet.

Yet it is obvious that year after year small stockholders were deceived and defrauded because of their confidence in the trusted firm of accountants. And down to this day this firm and other accounting firms still maintain that realized profits are earnings and that unrealized profits are not earnings and, of course, the small group of financiers and other groups of financiers enthusiastically agree.

FUTILITY OF SECURITIES LAWS. Business throughout the country is now laboring under the Amended Securities Act of 1933 and the Securities Exchange Act of 1934. It has been charged that these acts are contrary to American ideals of government because they invade the rights of the States and individuals and because the commission created by them acts, in a very practical sense, in the multiple rôle of law maker, prosecutor, witness, judge, and jury. However, quite apart from this, it is relevant to the design of this book to note that the chief purposes for which the acts were passed can probably never be more than partly realized as long as present accounting principles remain unchanged.

Virtually the entire purpose of the Securities Act of 1933, and at least an important part of the purpose of the Securities Exchange Act of 1934, is to exact reliable information from the issuers of securities so that investors may be enabled to form dependable opinions regarding the value of present or prospective investments. The most important exhibits in the required information, and indeed the only exhibits which pretend to give a comprehensive picture of the value of the securities offered, are the financial statements of the issuing company. If these financial statements are false and misleading, it must necessarily follow that many investors will be deceived, regardless of the multiplicity of other data furnished to them.

It seems a pity that the present complicated laws, with their vast and ramified government machinery and the great expense, delay, and uncertainty which they necessarily cause to business, should in a large part be so clearly futile from the outset. This is the more to be regretted because, if accounting principles were changed, perhaps most of the objectives of the Acts might be achieved without the Acts themselves, and without their intricate and expensive machinery, merely by permitting the preparation of truthful financial statements and by educating investors to demand them. Under such circumstances the laws governing fraud might alone be sufficient to cope with such dishonesty as might occur, entirely without the aid of the dozens of security laws now on the statutes of the individual states and also entirely without the numerous blue-sky commissions now functioning in the individual states.

Most of the machinery of government regulation of security issues, as typified by the numerous state blue-sky commissions, and finally by the enormously burdensome Federal Acts, has originated in the conviction of the public that it was not being treated fairly by the sellers of securities. The public knew that its purchase of securities was largely a hazardous gamble, and it quite naturally concluded that the cause of this was deliberate dishonesty on the part of business men. Accordingly, over a long period of years, blue-sky laws have been passed and blue-sky commissions have been set up in most of the forty-eight states. These commissions have passed upon new security issues after minute and onerous investigations without any noticeable reduction in the hazards of investing except as regards the most flagrant type of security crook. After the financial collapse of 1929 it was realized that these blue-sky commissions were of little value, but it was manifestly not realized where most of the fault lay. The Federal Government therefore superimposed upon the state blue-sky commissions a national blue-sky commission with the duty of regulating security issues throughout the entire country.[1] It was apparently hoped that this would serve the

[1] Originally the Federal Trade Commission. Later the Securities and Exchange Commission.

purpose which the state blue-sky commissions alone had failed so signally to perform.

The writer ventures to predict that the national commission will be scarcely more successful in safeguarding investors than have the individual state commissions. It seems evident that this must be so as long as the figures relating to the securities offered are false and misleading. What is needed is a revision of those figures, not a multiplication of administrative machinery. If the principles of accounting could be corrected so that accountants could prepare truthful balance sheets and profit and loss statements, then the figures presented would speak for themselves and no amount of verbal or written comment could effectively serve to deny them.

The problem is intellectual, not moral. The accounting profession is not corrupt. Its individual members are, on the whole, as honorable as any group of men in the country, and they are faithfully following principles that have been expounded and developed by accounting authorities over many years. Nor does bad faith on the part of business men, nor on the part of investment bankers, cause the trouble. For the most part these publish faithfully the figures prepared by independent accountants. The real difficulty lies in the sophistry, illogic, and untruth of accounting principles which produce figures deceiving accountants, business men, and the public alike.

WEIGHT OF AUTHORITY. Yet these faulty accounting principles are tenaciously defended by the overwhelming majority of contemporary accounting, banking, and business authorities. There is hardly a practicing accountant,

banker, or business man in the country who does not regard
them with respect or reverence. Unquestionably the weight
of authority is on their side. The young business executive
who may indulge in some clear thinking and attempt to
question them finds himself immediately against a stone
wall of opposition. His firm of certified public accountants
will courteously refuse to be shown. His banker will question his business judgment. Older business men will smile
at his impetuous ignorance.

II

PRESENT ACCOUNTING PRINCIPLES

ACCOUNTING procedure is governed by a number of laws, or customs, on which there is rather general agreement. It is common for these laws to be variously described as rules, conventions, practices, methods, or customs. Taken together they serve to indicate the theoretical generalizations, or principles, upon which accounting procedure may fairly be said to be based.

MEANING OF ACCOUNTANT'S CERTIFICATE. Prior to 1933, the usual form of unqualified certificate employed by auditors read, with minor variations, as follows:

We certify that the above balance sheet is, in our opinion, a correct statement of the financial condition of the Company as of December 31, 1931, and that the accompanying profit and loss statement is correct.

In this usage Webster's *Unabridged Dictionary* defines "correct" as meaning "conforming to fact or truth." In 1933 a Securities Act was passed by Congress, and this Act made accountants responsible with the issuers of securities for false and misleading statements which they might make relative to a material fact. The original regulations under which the Act was administered, promulgated July 6, 1933, by the Federal Trade Commission, required accountants to certify that after reasonable investigation they believed their financial statements to be true. This requirement caused great agitation in accounting circles, and efforts were made both within and without Congress to have it modified. On April 5, 1934, Senator Hastings of Delaware told the United States Senate: "An audit is not a statement of facts and an accountant should not be required to certify that the statements contained in a balance or profit and loss statement are true. Such a certificate is really misleading."

On April 7, 1934, subsequent to conferences with representatives of the American Society of Certified Public Accountants, the Federal Trade Commission announced that its original regulations had been amended and that accountants need not thereafter certify to a belief in the truth of their statements. The accounting profession thereupon changed its form of unqualified certificate, with minor variations, to the following:

We have, after reasonable investigation, reasonable grounds to believe, and do believe, at the date of this certificate, that the statements contained in the attached balance sheet and in the attached profit and loss statement, truly and fairly reflect the application of accepted accounting practices to the facts disclosed by our investigation.

It is the purpose of this chapter to examine some of the reasons why such a complete change of front was necessary. The accounting profession is not dishonest. Its individual members probably possess as high a degree of personal integrity as the members of any calling in the world today. Yet, upon the passage of a law which would make accountants responsible for material untruths, their profession, without a single important exception, felt impelled to change its form of certificate from one which states that its financial statements are true, to a form of certificate which omits any mention of truth but merely states that such financial statements *truly and fairly reflect the application of accepted accounting practices to the facts disclosed.*

This is a humiliating confession for the profession to make, and many individual accountants must feel deep chagrin that the work which they produce with so much care for strict accuracy cannot, even in a legal sense, be considered truthful. It seems obvious that all accountants would gladly label their financial statements "true and correct" if in their opinion this were the case, despite any law which might make them responsible for untrue statements. The accounting profession has not been timid in its defense of truth and accuracy, and surely every accountant would jump at the chance to demonstrate the probity of his profession by boldly continuing to state that in his opinion his work was correct, if he could honestly do so. The simple fact of the matter is that, regardless of how honest or accurate or conscientious an accountant may be, he must almost of necessity prepare false and misleading financial statements if he follows accepted accounting practice. Every thoughtful accountant must at some time have realized this. Surely it is worth while to conduct a serious search for sound accounting principles which may enable every accountant, who finds himself in a position to sign an unqualified certificate, to state honestly that, in his opinion, the facts set forth are entirely true.

ACCEPTED ACCOUNTING PRACTICE. Accepted accounting practice prescribes in general that balance sheet asset values be stated at original cost, except in the case of current assets with a determinable market value which are valued at "cost or market whichever is lower," and except in the case of cash or current collectible claims for cash which are valued at face value. As regards earnings, the necessary corollary of this procedure is embodied in the rule: "Never anticipate a profit but provide for all losses." This rule serves to prevent the recognition of unrealized profits arising in connection with both current and fixed assets. Accepted accounting practice also permits the profit and loss statement to exclude large realized non-recurrent profits and losses which have not been earned in the ordinary and usual course of the business under review.

Hence land, buildings, and fixed assets generally, are valued at original cost without reference to whether that cost is above or below market value. On the other hand, current assets, such as inventories, are valued at original cost only if this cost is below market value, and are valued at market value only if this is below original cost. Large realized profits or losses not incurred in the usual course of business, such as profits or losses arising from the sale of fixed assets, are frequently not permitted to show in the profit and loss statement but are placed directly in some balance sheet account, preferably surplus or some subdivision of surplus. Unrealized profits or losses on fixed assets are frowned upon in theory, although as a matter of practice they may be allowed, provided that they are not exhibited in the profit and loss statement. Unrealized profits on current assets, such as inventories, are absolutely taboo. Unrealized losses on such current assets are virtually always insisted upon, however, and such losses are generally allowed to find their way into the profit and loss statement exactly as though they had been realized.

If a factory is sold at a large profit, this profit is commonly credited directly to surplus and is not shown in the profit and loss statement. If the management of a business should insist upon writing up to its market value some fixed asset which would otherwise be exhibited at a lower cost figure, the accountant may allow this but will insist that the resulting profit be not shown in the profit and loss statement both because it is non-recurrent and because it has been "anticipated," i.e., it has not been realized in cash or in a collectible claim for cash. However, if the management of a business should insist upon writing up to its market value some current asset such as inventories, which would otherwise be exhibited at a lower cost figure, the accountant will in all probability feel compelled to refuse to certify the figures, regardless of whether the resulting profit is placed in surplus or in the profit and loss statement.

THEORY OF BALANCE SHEET VALUES. In England it seems to be well established that a public accountant is not a valuer and that balance sheets prepared and certified by him may misrepresent the facts to any extent, provided that they confine this misrepresentation to understatement. In a famous English case, the Court formally stated: "The purpose of the balance sheet is primarily to show that the financial condition of the company is at least as good as there stated, not to show that it is not or may not be better."[1] One is tempted to ask how, if the accountant is not a valuer, he may determine the point at which undervaluation stops

[1] *Newton* v. *Birmingham Small Arms Co.* (1906) 2 Ch. 378.

and overvaluation begins and how he may be sure that his valuation is not in fact an overvaluation.

In this country there is evidence that the accounting conscience does not wholly accept the English view. American accounting authorities seem, in theory at least, to incline to the view that the aim of accounting should be to supply truthful balance sheet values which will exhibit the real net worth of a business and will enable a true profit and loss statement to be presented.[2] Thus Henry Rand Hatfield, a well known accounting authority says:

In all the foregoing discussion it has been assumed that the purpose of accounting is to present the facts fully and without reservation; but argument is sometimes made that the statement set forth in the balance sheet does not even profess to be true; indeed, that a variation from the truth, provided only that it understates the wealth of the concern, is really a merit rather than a fault. . . .

This view is frequently supported by theoretical writers and has the further sanction which comes from the precedent set by conservative corporations in all lands. . . . For precedents may be cited the Bank of England which omits from its statement its land and building, which are certainly worth many millions; the practice common among German companies of listing their real estate and sometimes their other fixed plant at the nominal sum of one mark; and the tendency among American railways to mark down the

---

[2] The four accounting works quoted in this chapter may be mistakenly assumed by some to be out of date inasmuch as the first edition of each was published over twenty years ago. In the writer's opinion, these books still constitute the most representative works on accounting in this country. Hatfield, Montgomery, Dickinson, and Esquerré have exerted a dominating influence on the formation of current American accounting thought. The quotations cited undoubtedly represent the great preponderance of contemporary American opinion. Taken together they furnish an accurate general exposition of the reasoning underlying present accounting theory and practice. For a discussion of recent pronouncements indicating the beginning of an altered concept of the accounting function, see Chapter XV.

valuation placed on the road whenever large earnings make that possible. . . .

But to state that an absolute understatement is praiseworthy neglects the fact that fraud may surely be perpetrated in that manner; and while the reaction against overvaluation is but natural and in general healthful, it seems a mistake to overlook the value of accuracy and to cease to hold it up as the goal of accounting . . . certain notorious bear operations in the stock exchanges show that the unforeseen has frequently happened, and the undervaluation of assets, with its accompanying understatement of profits and establishment of a secret reserve, if the lesser of two evils, nevertheless falls far short of the ideal standard of accounting.[3]

Robert H. Montgomery, in his admirable book *Auditing Theory and Practice*, says:

If purchases have been made on a falling market, it is not conservative to place a higher value on an inventory item than the price at which the same thing can be duplicated in the open market. It deceives the banker, creditor, and stockholder, who have a right to believe that the values stated are real values as of the date of the balance sheet.[4]

The author differs from those who maintain that an auditor, *not* being a valuer, has no right to attempt to pass upon physical valuations, including stock-in-trade and plant; his opinion is that an auditor's duty is not properly performed unless he does all that his experience and skill enable him to do.[5]

It might not be a bad idea to urge every stockholder proposing to sell his stock to call for a professional auditor's report upon the accounts and affairs of the corporation before the sale is consum-

[3] Henry Rand Hatfield, *Modern Accounting*, New York and London, D. Appleton & Co., 1913, pp. 83, 84, 85.
[4] Robert H. Montgomery, *Auditing Theory and Practice*, New York, The Ronald Press Co., 1913, p. 104.
[5] *Ibid.*, p. 106.

PRESENT PRINCIPLES 27

mated. . . . When a man buys a horse he wants it examined by an expert on horses; so he calls in a veterinarian. He knows less about accounts and values than he does about horses, but he does not think of calling in an expert on values or accounts when he buys or sells a share of stock . . . he does not know that the absence of an auditor's certificate from a balance sheet may indicate that the assets shown therein are improperly stated, and that if he decides to sell because the business does not appear to be as prosperous as he thought it would be, his action is exactly in line with the intention of the insiders, who promptly buy out all those who have become discouraged.

The fact of the matter is that an auditor is taking big chances when he passes a balance sheet which conceals or understates assets. Good faith may be only apparent, the real purpose of the management being to buy the interests of the misinformed.[6]

Arthur Lowes Dickinson, discussing the valuation of fixed assets and of inventories, says:

It is necessary to recognize that there are causes at work, particularly in young and growing communities, which may render a statement prepared on the basis of cost of capital assets misleading and even prejudicial to the proper interests of present owners. Over a period of years changes in value due to rise or fall in prices may be sufficiently permanent to render it unfair to one business to maintain original cost values as compared with another whose assets have been created at widely varying costs. . . . In fact, there are well-known cases in which by far the larger part of the ultimate profits of a corporation over a long series of years has been due not to the results of its activities but to the large unearned increment on its capital assets.[7]

. . . a balance sheet is required to show the true financial position

[6] *Ibid.*, p. 146.
[7] Arthur Lowes Dickinson, *Accounting Practice and Procedure*, New York, The Ronald Press Co., 1914, pp. 80, 81.

as a going concern. The inventory at actual cost may represent more or less than the market value, and, therefore, overstate or understate the assets. . . .[8]

Paul-Joseph Esquerré has the following comment to make about the truthfulness of balance sheet values:

A manufacturer of prominence in the City of New York once stated to the writer, in a tone indicative of deep-rooted pride, that his capital assets had been "bodily knocked down into the pit of secret reserves," and that their book value, as it stood at the time, was preposterous. Since the said manufacturer was the president of a corporation, the questions at issue were: Did he want to deceive the stockholders, the government, the public, or himself? Did he wish to submit to the directors, the stockholders, the banks, and the public, financial statements with a mental footnote to the effect that things were not in truth what they showed on their face?[9]

BALANCE SHEET VALUES IN PRACTICE. The above quotations clearly give the impression that, in the opinion of the authorities quoted, a balance sheet should show real values actually existing as of the date of the balance sheet. But, although accounting authorities may at times seem to agree that the values which they exhibit should be truthful values, almost without exception they advocate rules which make the consistent exhibition of such values nearly impossible. Thus Hatfield says:

In general it is considered legitimate to continue fixed assets at their cost despite a subsequent decline in their value.[10]

What has been previously said in regard to fixed assets generally,

[8] Dickinson, op. cit., p. 94.
[9] Paul-Joseph Esquerré, The Applied Theory of Accounts, New York, The Ronald Press Co., 1915, p. 377.
[10] Hatfield, op. cit., p. 81.

applies preëminently to land where that is held for the uses of the company. The rule here is that land for permanent holding may be held at its cost despite a decline or rise in its market value.[11]

The conservative rule, generally adopted, is that merchandise is to be inventoried at cost except where there is a decline in value, in which case the lower value is to be used.[12]

The general practice of conservative American accountants, especially in banks, insurance companies and other fiduciary institutions, is in line with German law, and favors marking down the investments when the market price is below the cost price, but opposes taking recognition, except in an explanatory footnote to the balance sheet, of the appreciation due to a rising market.[13]

The following quotations are taken from Montgomery's *Auditing Theory and Practice:*

Raw materials, and Stock Purchased to be Resold in the Same Form: . . . The basis of value should be cost or market whichever is the lower.[14]

Land should appear in the balance sheet at cost, and should not be written up, although it may be clearly established that values have increased. . . .

Similarly, if the land has apparently depreciated in value, custom justifies the carrying of this item at cost until realization. . . .[15]

Where the purchase and sale of securities is part of the regular business of the firm or corporation, an inventory thereof should be taken as with the stock-in-trade of other concerns.

It is usually easier to ascertain market values than is the case with other inventories, but greater care must be taken with the individual items. The rule of cost or market, whichever is the

[11] *Ibid.,* p. 86.
[12] *Ibid.,* p. 102.
[13] *Ibid.,* p. 92.
[14] Montgomery, *op. cit.,* p. 104.
[15] *Ibid.,* pp. 120, 121.

lower, also applies and governs each item rather than the aggregate.[16]

The valuation of buildings opens up the question of depreciation, which is discussed fully in Chapter XXI. Following the suggestions there made, buildings should appear on the balance sheet at cost. . . .[17]

In discussing fixed assets Dickinson seems to take for granted that they will be valued only at original cost. Although this is implied very clearly, the writer has been unable to find where Dickinson has stated a definitive rule. The following quotations relative to inventories and to investments are, however, of interest:

It is accordingly generally recognized as a correct accounting principle that if the cost value of the inventory exceeds the market value, a reserve should be created to bring it down to the latter value, while, on the other hand, if the market value exceeds the cost, no credit should be taken for the profits until they are realized by an actual sale.[18]

Investments should be carried on the balance sheet at cost unless the market value is below cost, when they should be written down to market value.[19]

Paul-Joseph Esquerré agrees in the main with other authorities except for his rule that inventories and speculative securities should always be stated at cost, regardless of whether their market value is above *or below* their cost. He says:

The inventory of a trading concern should be valued at cost. It has been held that it is proper to compute it on the basis of the

---

[16] Montgomery, *op. cit.*, pp. 113, 114.
[17] *Ibid.*, p. 122.
[18] Dickinson, *op. cit.*, p. 94.
[19] Dickinson, *op. cit.*, p. 117.

market value, if such a value is smaller than cost; but it is generally denied that a market value higher than cost can be used. If the lower value is allowed, there is no reason why the higher one should not be. There is, however, a good reason why market values should not be used at all. Accounting is not interested in what would have happened "if," but in what has actually happened; and since the goods unsold were purchased at a certain price, the profits realized are to be measured by comparing that price with the proceeds. To reduce the inventory to a value lower than cost, is to add to the cost of the goods sold during the period; and to raise the inventory to a value greater than cost, is to reduce the cost of the goods during the period. In either case, the result is contrary to the truth.[20]

In connection with land and buildings there often arises the question of increased valuation due to favorable conditions in the real estate market. . . . The accountant is very likely to have in connection with this kind of profits the same opinion as the average lawyer has about all kinds of gains. To the lawyer, nothing is profit which has not been realized in cash. To the accountant, nothing brings profits which has not been sold. He instinctively objects to all kinds of estimates and inflations of capital assets on the basis of market values.[21]

Securities purchased for speculative purposes should be carried on the books at their original cost, that is to say, at their market value on the day of the purchase, plus fees required by law or custom, and charges for services rendered by the agents who attended to the purchase.[22]

It apparently did not occur to Esquerré that his rule with reference to inventories only makes it more probable that the inventory value will be misstated, that the net worth of

[20] Esquerré, op. cit., p. 171.
[21] Ibid., p. 229.
[22] Ibid., p. 262.

the concern will be misrepresented, and that the profits shown will include profits and losses from previous periods. This subject is discussed in detail in Chapter XIV.

INCONSISTENCY OF PRINCIPLES RELATING TO BALANCE SHEETS. From the foregoing pages it will have become evident that the appearance of truthful present values in a balance sheet is a great deal more apt to be a matter of accident than of design. This is so because, although accounting authorities do at times seem to give lip service to the idea that balance sheets should exhibit real values as of the date of the balance sheet, they advocate methods which make the exhibition of such values almost impossible.

Thus Hatfield holds accuracy up as the goal of accounting, and deplores both undervaluation and overvaluation as falling far short of that goal. Yet he teaches that land should be carried at original cost despite a decline or rise in its market value, and that neither merchandise nor investments should be valued above original cost in recognition of an appreciation in their value.

Montgomery states that the banker, creditor, and stockholder "have a right to believe that the values stated are real values as of the date of the balance sheet." Yet he proclaims that inventories, investments, and land should appear in the balance sheet at original cost and "should not be written up although it may be clearly established that values have increased." He also affirms that fixed assets such as land and buildings should be carried at cost even though their value may have depreciated below this.

Dickinson points out that "a balance sheet is required to show the true financial position as a going concern," and that "the inventory at actual cost may represent more or less than the market value and therefore overstate or understate the assets." Yet he then proceeds to direct that inventories and investments be carried at cost when this is less than their market value.

And Esquerré reproaches a manufacturer for submitting financial statements "with a mental footnote to the effect that things were not in truth what they showed on their face," while on another page he rules that inventories, land, buildings, and securities be shown at original cost whether this be above or below their market value.

Theory of Profit and Loss Statements. A profit and loss statement, sometimes called earnings statement, statement of income and expenses, statement of profits and income, or some similar name, is popularly supposed to analyze and set forth the profits earned, or losses incurred, by a business during a specified period. To an economist, profits are all increases in net wealth and losses are all decreases in net wealth. The following definition is quoted by Montgomery:

> . . . from an economist's point of view profit consists of the surplus remaining over from the employment of capital after defraying all the necessary expenses and outlays incurred in its employment, and after the capital has been replaced or provision made for its replacement. If there are not sufficient assets left to replace the capital, the result of the venture or employment is a loss and the amount by which the capital is diminished is the measure of this loss. Profits are arrived at by means of balance sheets showing the true financial position of the concern, supplemented, where the books are properly kept, by a profit and loss account.

For example, the profit of a company for the first year would be the excess of assets over liabilities (including in the latter the paid up capital), while there would be exhibited in the profit and loss account the sources from which the profits have arisen. The profit for any period is the difference between the surplus of assets over liabilities at the beginning of the year and the surplus as shown at the close.[23]

This is the ordinary common sense definition of profits and losses, and is the one instinctively used by laymen in contemplating their personal affairs. It is probably the only definition of profits whose truth is susceptible of mathematical proof. It is as simple as saying that if a person has one dollar and adds another dollar to it, he will then have two dollars. Or, if a person had one dollar a minute ago and has two dollars now, he must have acquired the net sum of one dollar during the minute in question.

For example: If a boy starts out on a Saturday morning with a capital of twenty marbles and, by a skillful morning's play, adds to this capital the net number of thirty marbles, he will then have fifty marbles. Or, if a boy starts out on a Saturday morning with a capital of twenty marbles and by skillful playing winds up at noon with fifty marbles, he must have added the net number of thirty marbles to his capital during the morning. If the marbles were instantly saleable at one cent each, the boy would probably calculate that he had started out with twenty cents' worth of marbles and had won an additional thirty cents' worth during the morning. He would be incredulous if an accountant attempted to tell him that he had not profited to the extent of thirty cents by the morning's play because he had not yet sold his winnings of thirty marbles. Yet this is precisely

[23] Montgomery, *op. cit.*, pp. 183-84.

the view that many strictly orthodox accountants would be apt to take, although the same accountants would be certain to insist that the boy's opponent had lost thirty cents during the same morning. The boy might win exactly thirty marbles on each of five consecutive mornings and, on the sixth morning, instead of playing marbles, he might sell his accumulated winnings of one hundred and fifty marbles for a dollar and a half. If an accountant were to audit the boy's books each afternoon, he might duly certify on each of the first five days that the boy had won nothing, after which he would certify that on the sixth morning the boy had won one dollar and a half. Yet to an economist and to most laymen it is obvious that the boy had won thirty cents on each of the first five mornings and that on the sixth morning he had won nothing.

There is at least some evidence that accountants would like to make the accounting definition of profits and losses conform to self-evident economic principles if they could see a way to do so. Thus Montgomery says:

If an absolutely accurate balance sheet could be prepared at the beginning and end of a period, the difference would represent the net profit or net loss for the term, but the valuation and revaluation of capital assets involves too much speculation to permit such a practice being recognized as satisfactory.[24]

Hatfield says:

The Profit and Loss Account, called also Revenue, Income, Loss and Gain and other similar names, is a temporary, collective account, recording the changes in net wealth due to the business operations of a stated period.[25]

[24] Montgomery, op. cit., pp. 184, 185.
[25] Hatfield, op. cit., p. 195.

The valuation of assets (the problem of the inventory) is clearly a question as to Profit and Loss, for changes in the book value of assets mean corresponding changes in the net wealth.[26]

And Dickinson says:

In the widest possible view, profits may be stated as the realized increment in value of the whole amount invested in an undertaking; and conversely, loss is the realized decrement in such value. Inasmuch, however, as the ultimate realization of the original investment is from the nature of things deferred for a long period of years, during which partial realizations are continually taking place, it becomes necessary to fall back on estimates of value at certain definite periods, and to consider as profit or loss the estimated increase or decrease between any two such periods.

This method would permit any business concern to revalue periodically the whole of its assets and liabilities, and to record the difference between its surplus so ascertained at the commencement and the end of the year as its profit or loss, respectively; and provided that this estimate were fairly and reasonably made, there would be no objection to such a course. In other words, every appreciation of assets is a profit, and every depreciation a loss; and in many private concerns this method, technically known as "single entry," of ascertaining profits has been regularly adopted for years without bad results.[27]

If the balance sheets at the beginning and end of a period are theoretically and practically accurate, and show the true financial position at those dates, the increase or decrease of the surplus, after allowing for distributions of profit during the interval, represents the true profit or loss for the period, subject always to the factor of "estimate" necessarily present in the valuation of assets and liabilities.[28]

[26] Hatfield, *op. cit.*, p. 197.
[27] Dickinson, *op. cit.*, pp. 67, 68.
[28] *Ibid.*, p. 74.

PROFIT AND LOSS STATEMENTS IN PRACTICE. However, as much as accountants would like to make earnings statements conform to obvious economic truths, the principles of present accounting practice prevent them from doing so. The rules relating to the balance sheet valuation of assets at original cost rather than at market value, and the rule prohibiting the recognition of unrealized profits, often serve to make both balance sheets and earnings statements vary from or omit to tell these truths. Montgomery says:

> If a public accountant were asked to define the term "net profit" he would probably reply: "The net profit of a business is the surplus remaining from the earnings after providing for all costs, expenses, and reserves for accrued or probable losses."[29]

Clearly the meaning of the above definition is dependent upon the meaning given to the word "earnings." If unrealized profits and losses are not to be considered as affecting earnings, although such profits and losses obviously increase or decrease net wealth, then it becomes evident that neither an earnings statement, nor a balance sheet, nor the two combined can avoid being at times false and misleading. The following quotations illustrate how present accounting practice constantly prevents the recognition of indisputable facts. Montgomery says:

> There may be in exceptional cases an obvious rise in value of an item of fixed assets, but a footnote on the balance sheet is all that is required to secure the benefit of an increased credit rating, and any adjustment of the account in the books by increasing the asset and crediting surplus is rarely permitted by good accounting practice.[30]

[29] Montgomery, *op. cit.*, p. 184.
[30] *Ibid.*, p. 194.

Hatfield says:

> More delicate is the question of unrealized profits. In the discussion of the Inventory in Chapter IV, it was shown that mere fluctuations in value may be disregarded; and that even permanent appreciation, if it is of assets whose nature is such that the gain cannot be realized by the going concern, should similarly be left out of account. Thus an estimated appreciation in the value of the factory site should be left out of account, even though the estimation have every element of certainty. The prohibition of thus marking up assets precludes any credit in the Profit and Loss account, or elsewhere. But where the appreciation is in merchandise, or in what are commony called circulating assets, there is less uniformity. It has been seen that German law distinctly prohibits the taking of profits due to appreciation of unsold merchandise, even where the increased value is evidenced by quoted prices in produce or stock exchanges. But on the other hand, Austrian law authorizes the taking of such profits. . . . The opinion of accountants, always siding toward wise conservatism, is well-nigh unanimous against taking profits on unsold goods.[81]

Dickinson says:

> On practical, if not on theoretical, grounds, the principle must be accepted that a decrease in value of fixed assets not of a wasting character, arising otherwise than in the process of earning profits, need not be provided for. It is true that in the long run all shrinkage of these assets is a loss, and that no profits can be earned unless the capital, both fixed and circulating, is maintained intact. But the changes in actual values of capital assets due to a lower range of prices, the introduction of improved processes of manufacture, etc., may be so great and at the same time so indefinite, and the actual realization thereof is as a rule deferred to such distant periods, that

---

[81] Hatfield, *op. cit.*, p. 224.

it becomes quite impracticable to provide for shrinkage in value due to such causes as a direct charge against profits.[32]

INCONSISTENCY OF PRINCIPLES RELATING TO PROFIT AND LOSS STATEMENTS. From the foregoing pages it will have become evident that the publication of a profit and loss statement which is complete and truthful in an economic sense must be a rare accident. This is so because present accounting principles are out of harmony with economic principles and because accounting authorities seem unable to harmonize the two, although they appear to recognize the incontrovertible status of the latter.

Thus Hatfield points out that the profit and loss account "is a temporary collective account recording the changes in net wealth due to the business operations of a stated period," and calls attention to the fact that the valuation of assets "is clearly a question as to profit and loss, for changes in the book value of assets mean corresponding changes in the net wealth." Yet, a little later, he writes that "German law distinctly prohibits the taking of profits due to appreciation of unsold merchandise, even where the increased value is evidenced by quoted prices in produce or stock exchanges. ... The opinion of accountants, always siding towards wise conservatism, is well-nigh unanimous against taking profits on unsold goods."

Montgomery states that "if an absolutely accurate balance sheet could be prepared at the beginning and end of a period, the difference would represent the net profit or net loss for the term." Yet, a few pages later, he declares that, even in cases involving an obvious rise in value of an item

[32] Dickinson, *op. cit.*, p. 73.

of fixed assets, "any adjustment of the account in the books by increasing the asset and crediting surplus is rarely permitted by good accounting practice."

And Dickinson, who seems more aware of the inconsistency of accounting principles, makes contradictions follow in rapid succession upon assertions of economic principle. On one page he states: "In other words, every appreciation of assets is a profit and every depreciation a loss." Yet, on another page, he writes this contradiction: "On practical, if not on theoretical, grounds, the principle must be accepted that a decrease in value of fixed assets . . . need not be provided for." Then, in the following sentence, he asserts again: "It is true that in the long run all shrinkage of these assets is a loss, and that no profits can be earned unless the capital, both fixed and circulating, is maintained intact." After which, in the next sentence, he again writes a contradiction: "But the changes in actual values of capital assets . . . may be so great . . . that it becomes quite impracticable to provide for shrinkage in value . . . as a direct charge against profits."

BALANCE SHEETS AND PROFIT AND LOSS STATEMENTS ARE INTERDEPENDENT. It has been seen that accounting authorities appear to acknowledge in theory that every appreciation in the value of assets is a profit and that every depreciation in such value is a loss, although they are unable to adhere to this theory in actual practice. However, all accounting authorities stress the fact that the proper valuation of assets is necessary to the proper statement of profits. This has been amply evidenced by the foregoing quotations.

If an asset is undervalued, other things being equal, total profits will be understated by the same amount. If an asset is overvalued, other things being equal, total profits will be overstated by the same amount. It matters not that some profits or losses may be placed in the profit and loss account to appear in the profit and loss statement, whereas others may be placed directly in some subdivision of surplus or in some other proprietary account on the balance sheet. The fact will remain that the net worth will have been incorrectly stated, and if the net worth is incorrectly stated then the total profits, as shown by the financial report as a whole, will be incorrectly stated. An exception to this rule may occur when two incorrect balance sheets, one at the beginning and one at the end of a period, both vary from the truth in the same amount. In this case net worth will be misrepresented but net profits during the period in question will be stated correctly. However, at the time the error was first made in the balance sheet, the net profits for the period then ending must of necessity have been incorrect to the amount of the error.

At this point the harm done by present accounting principles becomes clearly apparent. If the undervaluation or overvaluation of assets not only understates or overstates net worth but understates or overstates profits by the same amount, the correct valuation of assets becomes fully as important to the correct statement of profits as it does to the correct statement of net worth. If it is assumed, as will be argued later, that every profit and loss statement should disclose, in proper classification, *all* of the profits or losses of a business during the period covered, it becomes obvious that if assets are not correctly stated, both balance sheets and profit and loss statements must of necessity be contrary to the truth.

WHY FINANCIAL STATEMENTS DECEIVE. Present accounting principles prescribe that most fixed assets be carried at original cost although this cost may be clearly more than or less than the market value of such fixed assets. Present accounting principles also prescribe that most current assets be carried at original cost provided that this cost be less than the market value of such current assets. In each of these cases the net worth will be misrepresented. In many cases similar assets acquired at different costs may be carried in the same balance sheet at different values although these assets may in every practical sense be identical.

As a corollary of the above, present accounting principles prescribe that no profits be "anticipated," and vigorously maintain, in defiance of economic principle, that a profit is not a profit until it has been realized, i.e., until the asset has been sold for cash or for a collectible claim for cash. This seems merely to reinforce and to describe, as regards earnings, the necessary result of the valuation of assets at original cost when that cost is below market value. Its effect is to sanction the misrepresentation of profits and to conceal from stockholders profits of which they should be informed.

But the accounting rule "never anticipate a profit but provide for (i.e., anticipate) all losses" also contains the injunction to reflect losses in the balance sheet and in the profit and loss statement, whether such losses have been realized or not. The rule is enforced, however, only with reference to current assets such as inventories. Thus, if original cost is above market, the value of the inventory is marked down to market and the resulting loss is usually allowed to appear in the profit and loss statement as a part of the cost of goods sold. This seems effectively to establish a rule that unrealized losses are losses in contradistinction to the rule that unrealized profits are not profits. Yet when unrealized losses on fixed assets are involved, this rule seems no longer to hold, because the writing down of fixed assets is frowned upon. In other words, present accounting principles appear to maintain that unrealized losses on current assets are losses, but that unrealized losses on fixed assets are not losses. The effect of this incongruous situation is to misrepresent both net worth and profits whenever unrealized losses on fixed assets exist.

Present accounting principles generally permit large realized non-recurrent profits and losses to be excluded from the profit and loss statement and to be placed directly in one of several subdivisions of surplus on the balance sheet. The practical effect of placing realized non-recurrent profits or losses directly in a balance sheet account is partially or wholly to conceal them. It would seem that there could be no valid argument against, and that there are very good arguments for, presenting a statement of such profits or losses to those who have a right to know about them. This may be done by exhibiting them in a separate section of the profit and loss statement. This subject will be discussed in detail in the chapter relating to profit and loss statements.

III

DEFENSE OF PRESENT ACCOUNTING PRINCIPLES

WHEN THE origin and development of accounting methods is examined in Chapter IV, it will be seen how the principles governing the valuation of assets originated and how indeed they could hardly have taken any other form. With the advent of modern conditions, however, accounting authorities have apparently felt the need for justifying methods of valuation which were apt to be so widely at variance with the facts. The arguments used have ranged from purely theoretical ones to practical arguments based entirely on expediency. The theoretical arguments most often advanced hold that original cost valuations are real values from the standpoint of a going concern, or claim that the undervaluation of assets and the consequent concealment of unrealized profits is "conservative" and is often an aid to the management of a business. The practical arguments commonly point out the expense and "impracticability" of determining economic values. It is the purpose of this chapter to review some of these arguments.

THEORETICAL JUSTIFICATION OF PRESENT PRINCIPLES. The most ingenious theoretical justification of the use of asset valuations based on original cost consists of an extension of the "going concern" theory of value. Hatfield states the theory admirably:

Having accepted the principle that the original valuation of assets should not exceed the cost price, and having noticed the practical and theoretical difficulty in determining the exact cost price, there remains the more important question as to subsequent revaluations of assets. Shall they be put down at the original acquisition price or at some other valuation? If at some other value, shall it be the current market price, the present value to the concern, or the price they would bring in liquidation? The general principle which, with various applications, is now universally accepted, is: The inventory should be on the basis of the value of the assets to the present holders as a "going concern." The proper value is that which they have to the holding concern, and not that which they might have to other persons, whether these persons are ordinary customers, or those who might bid in the assets at a liquidation sale.[1]

A piece of land, for instance, is purchased at a fair price for the purpose of erecting a factory. Its services are presumably perpetual and undiminishing; the value to the company was, in the first instance, represented by its full cost price; its services, and hence its value to the going concern, are the same as before. It is therefore proper to continue in the inventory the cost price of the land quite irrespective of changes in its market value whether that be greater or less than the cost. The market price, evidently, can never be realized so long as the land is still used as a factory site, the abandonment of the factory means ordinarily that the enterprise ceases to be a going concern. To be sure the factory site might conceivably be sold and a less expensive one be bought in its stead, but this implies recognition of a double set of unrealized conditions and is too vague for embodiment in formal accounts. Changes in the market value of an absolutely fixed asset, such as land, railroad bed, or water rights, may be ignored on the principle that such changes do not affect the value of the going concern. This is most clearly seen in the case of land, but is equally applicable to any form

[1] Hatfield, *op. cit.*, pp. 80, 81.

of fixed asset provided, of course, that allowance is made for its necessary maintenance and renewal.[2]

This theory does, at least on the surface, seem reasonable, logical, and true, although it contains a subtle fallacy which will be discussed in detail in the chapter on value. Some practical aspects of the theory, however, may be reviewed here.

THE ORIGINAL THEORY OF GOING VALUES. The theory of "value to a going concern" or, as it is called herein, the "going value" theory, was originally a very sensible, necessary, working hypothesis in the preparation of financial statements. Its chief present fault is that it has been distorted to make virtue out of necessity, and consequently has become a defense for misrepresentation. Fundamentally the "going value" of an asset is the value that that asset may possess as part of an operating business as opposed to the value that it would have as part of a liquidating or bankrupt business. Thus a flourishing bank might be able to sell its building for a large figure if it desired to move into larger quarters. Should it fail, however, no other bank would be apt to regard its building as a propitious residence, and the building might not be suitable for most other types of business. Under such circumstances the building might be worth very little. Obviously it is the correct and sensible thing to carry the building at its reasonable value as part of a going business, in other words, at its "going value." This is right because the business is actually going. The management, creditors, and stockholders are actually dealing with a going business, and a balance sheet

[2] Hatfield, *op. cit.*, p. 82.

purports to tell them what that business *is* worth, not what it *would be* worth if it failed.

THE PRESENT THEORY OF GOING VALUES. However, accountants soon found that they needed some justification for the incongruous situations which arose through their practice of accepting the original cost of an asset as its value. An example is cited in "The Fable of the Two Factories" in the first chapter of this book. John pays $5,000 for a factory and William pays $20,000 for an identical factory. The accountant values each at cost because he does not know what each is worth and he does not know, at the time, that they are identical. When challenged he says that $5,000 is the "going value" to John of John's factory, and that $20,000 is the "going value" to William of William's factory. He reasons that the original value of each factory to its purchaser must presumably have been what the purchaser paid for it. He further reasons that the original value of each factory must have been predicated upon the value of its services to each purchaser, and that since these services cannot change unless a change takes place in the physical condition of the factories themselves, it must necessarily follow that the values of the factories to their respective owners cannot change. The accountant further reasons that each factory will be depreciated over its life and that meanwhile John's business will reap the advantage of John's acumen through smaller charges for depreciation. "We must assume," the accountant says, "that both John's and William's judgment of the value of the factories to themselves was correct, and if it turns out not to be so, the error will be adjusted in their respective earnings statements over the life of the factories."

THE HARM DONE BY THE PRESENT THEORY. The faulty premise underlying this reasoning is the tacit assumption that John and William are the only persons interested, that each will continue to own his respective business throughout the life of the factories and that, therefore, neither can ultimately lose or profit through the adoption of the "going values" in question. This assumption ignores all consideration of creditors and inactive stockholders. Creditors are obviously misled in either one case or the other, although they have usually learned through experience that they can place little reliance on the valuations of fixed assets in a balance sheet and as a matter of practice ordinarily ignore them. Bankers commonly use only current assets in computing their security, and mortgagees are invariably contemptuous of balance sheet values and insist upon appraisals of market value or replacement cost.

But uninformed, temporary stockholders are hopelessly deceived, not only as to the value of the assets behind their stock, but also as to the earnings of their company. If John's factory is valued at $5,000 and William's factory is valued at $20,000, the depreciation charged against earnings each year will be four times as much for William as for John. Consequently William's earnings will be shown by the accountant as less than John's although, after the initial profit or loss occasioned by the purchase of the factories, both may be earning exactly the same sum. In other words, the accountant will first exhibit two balance sheets showing William's factory to be more valuable than John's, and then he will exhibit two earnings statements showing the earnings from this valuable factory to be less than John's. Both exhibits will be false and misleading. Neither exhibit will afford any sane comparison of the value of John's business with that of William's. A stockholder might just as well flip a coin as to attempt to decide from these exhibits whether a one-fifth interest in John's company is more valuable than a one-fifth interest in William's company, or vice versa. If he looks at asset values he will conclude that William's company is worth more and that its normal earning power is logically greater. Here, of course, he will be badly misled. If he looks at earnings, he will conclude that John's company is worth more. Here again he will be badly mislead. For the truth is that both companies possess the same asset values and that both are earning the same amounts, despite the accountant's certified statements to the contrary.

REDUCTIO AD ABSURDUM. Suppose, for example, that a group of financiers decide to make some money through the promotion of a new company. Certain members of the group purchase privately the required assets for, let us say, $1,000,000 in cash. Then other members of the group form a corporation which repurchases these assets for $5,000,000 in cash, and a certified audit is had exhibiting these assets at their cash cost of $5,000,000. After this the public is invited to buy $5,000,000 in stock at its book value, whereas it may actually be worth less than one-fifth of this amount. How reliable is the book value? Of what use is the accountant except as a sort of accessory in a confidence game?

Almost every large consolidation starts out with water in its balance sheet, i.e., with stated values which do not exist. The United States Steel Corporation is considered a model of frankness with the public in its published financial statements. Yet when it was formed it was believed to have carried some $500,000,000 of water in its balance sheet. Throughout many years, by understating its earnings, a consolidation may succeed in replacing its water with real value, perhaps even to the extent that its balance sheet may eventually contain secret reserves in place of water. But does anyone believe that accounting methods worthy of confidence would permit such misrepresentation? What purpose is served thereby? Surely creditors, stockholders, and the public are not benefited by being placed in a position where informed insiders may take advantage of their ignorance.

"CONSERVATISM" AS A JUSTIFICATION OF PRESENT PRINCIPLES. Present accounting principles are often defended upon the ground that they are conservative. The accounting rule for conservatism is: "Never anticipate a profit but provide for all losses." The observance of this rule with respect to current assets causes them to be valued at "cost or market whichever is lower." "Conservatism" is the common justification used for valuing assets below their market value when the theory of "going values" cannot be made to apply and when the arguments of "expense" or of "impracticability" can obviously have no standing. Hence, when Hatfield attempts to justify the valuation of inventories at less than market values, he is forced to relinquish the going value theory and to fall back on conservatism, as follows:

General usage prescribes that merchandise on hand shall be inventoried at cost rather than at selling price. Prudence further demands that merchandise which evidently cannot be sold except at a loss, be marked down even below the cost price. If one could count not only on good faith but as well on unbiased judgment in making inventories, the taking of the present market value, instead of the cost price would not be objectionable, but rather to be commended. Indeed, the first principle of valuation laid down above, that of the "going concern" in strict logic demands that merchandise for sale be valued at the present selling price, with a reduction to cover selling expenses. A real change having taken place in selling value the original cost is of no effect, for whether bought at a high or low cost its value to the concern is determined at the normal price at which it can now be sold. But the German commercial code, in many respects a guide to those whose accounting practices are so free from legal control, in attempting to prevent overvaluation prescribes that the cost price of merchandise must be taken, except where there is a publicly quoted price—as for instance for grain in a produce exchange—which is lower than the cost price. Logic perhaps demands that the quoted price should be taken as well when over as when below the cost price, but this is not permitted by German law, although the Austrian law allows it to be done.

American practice agrees with German law. In one important decision the Massachusetts court, on the contrary, stated that depreciation or advance in the value of the stock unsold must be taken into account. But in this particular case there had been a loss of merchandise by fire instead of an appreciation in value; and it is to be hoped that this obiter dictum is not considered authoritative. In any event the judgment of accountants is adverse to such treatment of the inventory. The conservative rule, generally adopted, is that merchandise is to be inventoried at cost except where there is a decline in value, in which case the lower value is to be used.[3]

For an accountant to justify an untruth on the ground that it constitutes conservatism is scarcely a strong argument. An undervaluation may be very conservative and

[3] Hatfield, *op. cit.*, pp. 101, 102.

praiseworthy from the standpoint of a creditor or of a management eager to add some cheap stock to its holdings, but the same undervaluation may seem outrageous and far from conservative to a stockholder desiring a just price for his stock. In the "Fable of the Two Investment Trusts" related in the first chapter of this book, the accounting firm mentioned therein undoubtedly defended its procedure on grounds of conservatism but the practical result was, none the less, deplorable. Conservatism will not appeal to intelligent individuals as a valid argument when it is used in defense of untruths which may cause widespread injustice.

PRACTICAL JUSTIFICATION OF PRESENT PRINCIPLES. A pamphlet dated August 2, 1934, was issued by the United States Department of Commerce entitled "Reports to Stockholders." The pamphlet contains a report made to the Business Advisory and Planning Council and signed by a committee of three, namely: Walter S. Gifford, Pierre S. duPont, and William A. Harriman. The committee states that the report was developed by its research secretary, T. H. Sanders, Ph.D., professor of accounting in the Harvard Graduate School of Business Administration, and states that it "reflects the conclusions reached after several months of careful research as well as conferences with the leading professional accountants and others interested in the problem with which the report deals." The foregoing is mentioned to show that the report emanates from the very highest business, banking, and accounting authority.

The report commences with an introduction containing the following statements:

The financial reports made by corporations to their stockholders, consisting primarily of a balance sheet, income statement and statement of surplus, are the principal means by which interested persons endeavor to appraise the position and accomplishments of large corporations. In a country in which the ownership of corporations is distributed among millions of stockholders and the savings of additional millions are invested in bonds of such corporations directly or through savings banks, insurance companies, and other fiduciary institutions, the amount of reliance placed upon corporate financial reports is very great; they are matters of considerable public concern. Indeed, it appears that these public financial reports, since they are most readily available to the general public, are the key to the solution of the basic problem of protecting the small investor.

This is an enlightened statement and shows a keen realization of the facts. It would seem that, with such an appreciation of the importance of financial statements, the committee would condemn their one overwhelming, glaring defect, their fundamental mendacity. Yet no such thing is done. Instead, the committee enters its defense of this untruthfulness in the following words:

But to regard every amount appearing on these statements as indisputable fact is to attribute to the statements a greater degree of certainty than they can possess.

This may be made clearer by considering the origin of the amounts usually placed upon the two principal groups of assets shown in any balance sheet, namely, the fixed assets and the current assets. In an ordinary operating business the property accounts, representing real estate, plant and machinery, are shown in the balance sheet at the historical cost of the property. This is the permanent record of what the owners invested in tangible property and it is important for many reasons; but the heading of the balance sheet,

containing the words "as at December 31" may lead a person uninformed of the general rule to suppose that the amount given opposite the plant item is its present value, whereas no balance sheet
that follows the accepted conventions of accounting attempts to
show *present* values for these assets. It would in most cases be impractical and expensive to re-value the fixed assets every year on an
appraisal basis; and even if it were possible it would not necessarily
be significant information, since there are other factors entering
into the determination of the value of a going industrial concern,
including the capitalized present worth of its estimated future earnings.

Current or working assets present an entirely different problem.
. . . The probable cash value of all of these assets is a matter of
dominant importance from the viewpoint of the credit of the company, and no more than this probable value is supposed to be shown
in the balance sheet. . . . For inventories of a going concern, therefore, the lower of cost or market is the common rule. . . .

In other words, even though financial statements are the
principal means of appraising an investment, even though
they are relied upon by millions of stockholders, and even
though they appear to be the key to protecting the small
investor, yet balance sheets are not to be permitted to show
present values of fixed assets because this might be impractical and expensive and because other factors, such as
estimated future earnings, should also be considered by a
stockholder. Furthermore, although the cash value of inventories "is a matter of dominant importance from the
viewpoint of the credit of the company" yet this cash value
may not be shown when cost is below it because such procedure is "the common rule." Such arguments seem so
weak that they hardly appear sincere.

In a later chapter it will be shown that the revaluation of

fixed assets every year, on an appraisal basis if necessary, is not only apt to be far from impractical but that, after the initial appraisal has been made, it is apt to be inexpensive as well. If accountants possessed the necessary knowledge and training, it is probable that they would frequently be able to make such revaluations in less time than it usually requires to draw up an insurance schedule or to attend to some other minor detail of an audit.

The statement that a balance sheet containing present values instead of original costs would not necessarily give significant information because future earnings should also be considered, is almost too feeble to require comment. It is the equivalent of saying that a truthful balance sheet and profit and loss statement would not be of advantage to an investor because these would truthfully describe only the past and present status of a business, whereas estimated future conditions must always be taken into account. This can only imply either that misleading statements are of greater value than truthful statements, or that both are of little value. If the latter meaning is intended, then it is indeed hard to visualize financial statements as "the key to the solution of the basic problem of protecting the small investor."

It will be noted that no defense at all is advanced for the undervaluation of current assets except that this is the "common rule." It cannot be said that the valuation of these assets at market would be impractical or expensive, because accountants themselves exhibit these assets at market value when this is below cost. It is not said that such market values are of little significance. On the contrary, it is asserted that they are of "dominant importance."

Why then should they not be shown fully and honestly?

With further reference to the report, one finds its main conclusions in the following paragraphs:

But, regardless of how conscientiously the statements have been prepared, it will still remain true that no reader can fully understand them who has not informed himself of the accounting principles which underlie them. If acquaintance with these principles leads him to realize what dependence he can place upon the statements, he is then in a much better position to understand the true significance of the figures presented.

. . . The American Institute of Accountants, through a committee on coöperation with stock exchanges, has suggested that every company make available to stockholders an authorized summary of its accounting principles and practices. If this were done it would be desirable that every report published include a statement in effect as follows:

The books of account from which these statements have been prepared have been kept in accordance with the accounting rules and principles set forth in. . . .

. . . These statements of accounting principles should be sufficiently explicit that any interested person could ascertain what accounting practices the company followed. A procedure of this kind would constitute a long forward step toward clearing up the entire problem of public financial reporting.

This is commendably frank, but it does seem a hopeless task to attempt to educate millions of stockholders regarding present accounting principles, to the end that they may realize what dependence they can place upon financial statements. Even if this were possible, the net result would merely be to cause stockholders to read financial statements with increased caution. Knowing wherein such statements might fail to tell the truth, they would still be in ignorance regarding the truth. They would be more suspicious but no wiser than before.

Financial statements are undoubtedly the principal means by which investors are informed. They are undoubtedly relied upon by millions of investors. But they can never become the key to the solution of the basic problem of protecting the small investor until the faulty accounting principles underlying their preparation are changed to permit a presentation of simple truth as it is instinctively understood by laymen everywhere.

IV

ORIGIN OF PRESENT ACCOUNTING PRINCIPLES

IT IS probable that accounting in some form has been practiced by mankind since the dawn of human intelligence. The earliest reference to accounting in the Library of Congress in Washington is an exhibit of Sumerian administrative documents dating from 3945 B.C. An exhibit of Babylonian cuneiform tablets dating from 2474 B.C. is also contained in the Library as well as various other exhibits of later dates. Coincident with the growth of civilization and the expansion of trade and governmental authority, the importance of primitive accounting to the ancient peoples of the Mediterranean steadily increased, reaching its peak under the Roman Empire. Beginning with the disintegration of the empire after the death of Theodosius the Great in 395 A.D., however, the cumbersome accounting methods formerly in use were progressively altered until they disappeared entirely in the confusion of the fifth and sixth centuries. From the sixth to the eleventh centuries accounting, in a formal sense, may be said to have been almost non-existent.[1]

[1] For a detailed study of the long history of accounting see: *Accounting Evolution to 1900*, by A. C. Littleton, American Institute Publishing Co., Inc. New York. 1933. Also *History and Survey of Accountancy*, by Wilmer L. Green, Standard Text Press. Brooklyn. 1930. Also *History of Accounting and Accountants*, by Richard Brown. Edinburgh. 1905. These three volumes cover the subject admirably.

ACCOUNTING: ELEVENTH TO FOURTEENTH CENTURIES. To a modern accountant, accounting methods prior to the fourteenth century were unbelievably crude. For the greater part they consisted of descriptions of property or of simple reports of transactions stated in narrative form. The use of journal and ledger was unheard of. England supplies the chief examples of accounting efforts during this period, and here most records were written in Latin or Norman French and the use of Roman numerals was universal.

The Domesday Book, compiled in two volumes from the great survey of England made in 1086 by order of William the Conqueror, is the first known English effort at accounting. It was primarily a list of the crown lands and of the taxes and proceeds due therefrom to the crown. The Pipe Rolls, started in 1130 and prepared annually until 1834, were a continuation of the information contained in the Domesday Book, revised in accordance with yearly records kept by the sheriff of each county.

In the twelfth and thirteenth centuries certain lords of large English manors and certain English religious orders found it advisable to keep records of property owned and income derived therefrom. These records were not formalized, nor were similar items even grouped together. For the most part they were merely explanations written in Latin and Roman numerals without any effort at tabulation.

There is evidence that in Italy bookkeeping methods during this period had advanced much further than in England. Records have been discovered of a thirteenth-century Florentine banking house which describe various business transactions during the year 1211. The entries in these records were of the cross entry type which later gave rise to double entry. They constitute the first known beginning of the modern double entry technique.

ACCOUNTING: FOURTEENTH AND FIFTEENTH CENTURIES. At the beginning of the fourteenth century a slight improvement in English accounting skill was noticeable. Items began to be classified and values in money began to be arranged in columns. The accounts of the City of London for the year 1334 were written in columns with the narrative at the left and money values at the right. It is interesting to note that these accounts were written in Latin and in Norman French, that Roman numerals were used throughout, and that, although the pages were totaled, no total was carried forward to a following page. Roman numerals continued to be used both in England and in Scotland until the latter part of the seventeenth century, when they were superseded by Arabic numerals. It was apparently not until the early part of the eighteenth century that English bookkeepers learned to carry page totals forward and to record them on the next page.

On the European continent the earliest known fourteenth-century bookkeeping records are those of Herman and Johann Wittenborg of Lubeck, Germany. They describe business transactions occurring from 1329 to 1360, but seem to have embodied no striking improvements over the English methods of the same period.

This period, however, again gave evidence of the leadership of Italy in the development of modern bookkeeping technique. Books of account at Genoa for the year 1340

constitute the first known complete system of cross entry
so far discovered. Later a Venetian firm named Soranzo
and Brothers kept accounting records covering its business
operations from 1406 to 1434. These accounts were not
only kept in cross entry but contained Capital Accounts and
Profit and Loss Accounts as well. A ledger kept by the firm
of Barbarigo in Venice in 1430 supplies the first known
example of a ledger equipped with an alphabetical index.

At this time it was customary to balance the ledger and
ascertain profits at the conclusion of each venture. However, there is evidence that in some cases ledgers were
balanced only after they were completely filled. Andrea
Barbarigo of Venice apparently did not balance his ledger
from 1440 until 1449, and his son Nicola started a ledger
in 1456 which seems not to have been balanced until it
became full in 1482. Not until the seventeenth century did
business men generally begin to close their books and ascertain profits on an annual basis.

In 1458 an Italian named Benedetto Cotrugli wrote the
first known treatise on double entry bookkeeping, entitled
*Della Mercatura e del Mercante perfetto della Mercan-
tura,* which means "Concerning Merchandising and the
Perfect Merchandiser of Merchandise." This treatise was
in part the foundation of the famous later work of Pacioli.
It not only contained an exposition of the use of debits and
credits, but gave directions for closing the books and carrying all profits and losses to the capital account.

EVOLUTION OF DOUBLE ENTRY BOOKKEEPING. As far
as is known, modern double entry bookkeeping was first expounded by Frater Lucas Bartolomes Pacioli dal Borgo,

a Franciscan monk. Pacioli's book, *Summa de Arithmetica, Geometria, Proportioni et Proportionalita,* was published in Venice on November 10, 1494, and was the first printed work on bookkeeping and the first European treatise on algebra. An English translation of the title of this book reads "Everything about Arithmetic, Geometry and Proportion." Virtually everything since written on the subject of double entry bookkeeping has been based on Pacioli's work, and the methods he advocated are, with but few changes, the ones now in almost universal use.

Pacioli's system provided for the use of three books: the memorial, the journal, and the ledger. The memorial was used as a daybook to describe transactions and to record calculations reducing to a common denominator the different moneys involved. The journal and ledger were used substantially as they are today, save that only one journal was used and that neither closing entries nor transfers were journalized. It is interesting to note that Pacioli justified the use of the cumbersome Roman numerals by praising their beauty and that he directed that merchants "must begin all their transactions in the name of God and put His Holy Name on every account." Pacioli directed that all assets, except cash, be stated at their original cost. He apparently knew nothing of accruals, appraisals, or depreciation, and such subjects were not mentioned by him.

Although Pacioli was the first writer to expound a complete system of double entry, he made no claim to having invented it. He clearly stated at the beginning of his treatise that he was using the method of Venice, which he considered to be superior to all others. It is probable that the method had evolved gradually over a long period and that Pacioli was merely the first to describe it comprehensively in writing.

ACCOUNTING: SIXTEENTH TO NINETEENTH CENTURIES. Following the notable work of Pacioli, several additional Italian works appeared early in the sixteenth century, modeled closely after the Pacioli pattern. The tide of trade then swung northward, chiefly to England, and with it passed leadership in accounting. In 1531 Johann Gottlieb of Nuremberg, Germany, published the first treatise on bookkeeping to use Arabic figures in its text in place of Roman numerals. The first English book on bookkeeping was written by Hugh Oldcastle and published by John Gowghe of London in 1543. This book was entitled *A Profitable Treatyce called the Instrument or Boke to Learn to Knowe the Good Order of Kepying of the Famous Reconynze, called in Latin, Dare and Habere, and in Englyshe, Debitor and Creditor.* In the same year Jan Ympyn Christoffels of Holland published a treatise on bookkeeping which originated the trial balance. Nicolaus Petrie of Holland published a treatise in 1588 originating the compound journal entry. Before the end of the century Passchier-Goessens of Germany had improved the ledger by captioning each ledger page with the name of its account.

Prior to the seventeenth century it was the general custom to ignore the calendar and to close the profit and loss account at the conclusion of each venture. Simon Stevin of Holland helped to alter this custom in 1605 when he published his book *Hypomnemata Mathematica,* meaning "Mathematical Traditions." He also was the first to recommend the keeping of a separate cash book. It is interesting to note that Stevin's book was apparently written for the sole purpose of instructing his royal pupil, the Prince of Orange. Richard Dafforne published in England in 1636 a well written treatise on bookkeeping entitled *Merchant's Mirror*. This treatise was based largely on the work of Stevin, whom Dafforne described as "our master." The first Scottish work on bookkeeping was a book by Robert Colinson published in 1683 and entitled *Idea Rationaria, or the Perfect Accomptant necessary for all Merchants and Trafficquers; containing the True Form of Bookkeeping According to the Italian Method*. By 1685 the use of Roman numerals in England had been superseded by the use of Arabic numerals. Probably the earliest extant example of bookkeeping in the modern style is a ledger in the Advocates Library at Edinburgh. This ledger bears the date 1697 and is ruled by hand.

The eighteenth century witnessed nearly two hundred works on bookkeeping, few of which were oustanding. In 1719 a book by John Vernon was published in Dublin entitled *The Compleat Capital Countinghouse; or the Young Lad taken from the Writing-school and instructed in the mysteries of a Merchant*. The most successful eighteenth-century text was published in 1741 by John Mair of Edinburgh and entitled *Bookkeeping methodiz'd, or A Methodical Treatise of Merchant-Accompt, according to the Italian Form*. The eighth edition of this work was published in 1765. Toward the end of the century Edward Thomas Jones of Bristol, England, published a system of bookkeeping under the bombastic title *Jones' English System of Bookkeeping by Single or Double Entry, in which*

*it is impossible for an error of the most trifling amount to
pass unnoticed. Calculated effectually to prevent the evils
attendant on the methods so long established and adapted
to every species of trade. Secured to the Inventor by the
King's Royal Letters Patent.* William Mitchell of Philadelphia published in 1796 what seems to be the first American treatise on accounting, entitled *A New and Complete
System of Bookkeeping.*

ACCOUNTING: NINETEENTH AND TWENTIETH CEN-
TURIES. Few works of unusual merit dealing with accounting subjects appeared during the nineteenth century. In
1801 Dr. Patrick Kelly published a work in London called
The Elements of Bookkeeping. A book called *A Complete
Treatise on Practical Bookkeeping* was published in 1803
by James Morrison of Scotland. A Portland, Maine,
teacher of bookkeeping named Thomas Turner published
in 1804 a work called *An Epitome of Bookkeeping by
Double Entry.* In 1814 James Bennett of New York
brought out his *The American System of Practical Bookkeeping by Double Entry.* In 1817 there appeared a work
by Charles Gerisher of New York called *Modern Bookkeeping, Double Entry.* In 1828 a volume writen by J. H.
Goddard was printed in New York called *The Merchant,
or Practical Accountant.* C. C. Marsh's *Science of Double
Entry Bookkeeping Simplified* appeared in 1831.

Perhaps the best texts of the middle nineteenth century
were written by Thomas Jones, a New York school teacher.
His volume *The Principles and Practice of Bookkeeping*
was published in New York in 1841 and was followed in
1859 by a second work entitled *Paradoxes of Debit and*

Credit Demolished. These books, for the first time, taught that debits and credits were arbitrary conventions, and did not attempt to personalize them as all former texts had done. During the final fifty years of the nineteenth century scarcely any writings of note made their appearance. It seems plain that accountants, having spent the centuries from 1494 in perfecting a double entry bookkeeping technique, were temporarily resting on their oars without realizing the magnitude and importance of the job ahead.

Around the beginning of the twentieth century three notable works appeared in England which are still used as standard texts. These were: *Auditing* by L. R. Dicksee, *Accounting in Theory and Practise* by George Lisle, and *Auditors and their Liabilities* by F. W. Pixley. In these works, for almost the first time, serious consideration was given to such subjects as depreciation and the proper valuation of assets. It is to be regretted that, except for a recognition of the importance of depreciation, the result of this consideration took the form of condoning and justifying the practice of the past four centuries rather than of making a sharp break with the past by insisting that accountants acquire the knowledge to become valuers and thus place themselves and their profession far above the plane of expert bookkeepers.

In America a number of excellent volumes have appeared during the past several decades. Standard among these are: *Modern Accounting* by Henry Rand Hatfield, *Accounting Practice and Procedure* by Arthur Lowes Dickinson, *Auditing Theory and Practice* by Robert H. Montgomery, and *The Applied Theory of Accounts* by Paul-Joseph Esquerré. These works admirably cover almost every phase of accounting work, but follow the English lead in condoning the faulty method of asset valuation used in the past. Some of these authors have brought out revisions of their work within the past few years but, although they devote more space to a discussion of valuation principles, they still use the defensive arguments cited in the last chapter to justify the basic fact that accountants are not valuers, and are not equipped to state values accurately. The proper valuation of assets is the very basis of truthful financial statements.

EARLY ACCOUNTANTS. Very little is known of the work of early accountants. However, it is significant that until modern times accountancy was understood to mean the same thing as account-keeping or bookkeeping, and the terms "accountant" and "bookkeeper" were interchangeable. The earliest association of accountants on record is the Collegio dei Raxonati which was founded in Venice in 1581, but it is probable that the members of this association were not public accountants but were employees of governmental units. It has been claimed that George Watson, born in Edinburgh in 1645, was the first Scottish professional accountant, but it is known that he conducted a sizable private banking business and it seems doubtful that he was able to devote much of his time to other peoples' books. In England in 1670 it is recorded that John Dafforne, son of the author of the *Merchant's Mirror*, agreed to accept a fee of £100 a year to write up books of account.

It is known that about 1720 a London accountant by the name of Charles Snell was employed by Parliament to make an investigation into the transactions of a director of the South Sea Company who had been dealing in that company's stock. The report was apparently the first ever rendered by a public accountant. It was entitled *Observations made upon examining the books of Sawbridge and Company, by Charles Snell, writing master and accountant in Foster Lane, London*. At Milan in Italy a scale of fees for accountants was established in 1742, based upon the amount of mistakes or frauds discovered. In the latter part of the eighteenth century it was not unusual to find Scottish lawyers combining the practice of accounting with their practice of law. It is interesting to note that in 1799, when Holden's *Triennial Directory of London, Westminster and Southwark* was first published, eleven individuals were described therein as accountants. In the same directory in 1811, the number was twenty-four.

It seems plain that little progress was made by professional accountants in Great Britain, and virtually none at all elsewhere, before the middle of the nineteenth century. The first European society of accountants was incorporated by royal charter in Edinburgh in 1854 and was called "The Society of Accountants in Edinburgh." In 1870 the "Institute of Accountants" was formed in London, but it did not receive a royal charter until 1880, when it combined all of the existing societies in England and Wales under the name "Institute of Chartered Accountants in England and Wales." Apparently no societies of accountants existed outside the United Kingdom, except in British colonies, prior to 1895 when a society was formed in Utrecht for Dutch accountants called "Nederlands Instituit van Accountants."

Although modern accountancy originated in continental Europe, but little development has yet taken place there, and in most European countries professional accountants are literally unknown by the general public. Only in recent years have a number of European associations of accountants been formed in the hope of educating the public to the advantages of accountancy. In South America, Africa, and Asia, outside the British Empire, professional accountancy is virtually non-existent. In the British Empire and in the United States alone have professional accountants acquired broad recognition and public esteem.

The first society of accountants in the United States was The New York State Society of Certified Public Accountants, which was formed in 1896. At the beginning of 1938 it was estimated that approximately 13,000 certified public accountants and approximately 26,000 non-certified accountants were engaged in public accounting work in the United States.

EVOLUTION OF ACCOUNTING PRINCIPLES. It is probable that none of the early accountants or writers mentioned above were greatly concerned with the correctness of accounting principles as these are now understood. Up to the beginning of the twentieth century, accounting practice was concerned primarily with the development of its own bookkeeping technique. This technique was difficult, and it is probable that it absorbed the attention of most accountants to the entire exclusion of speculation upon such fine points as the truth or untruth, in an economic sense, of the figures produced. Early books on accounting seem to have been concerned exclusively with methods of making bookkeeping entries. Not only did they fail to discuss accounting principles, in the sense in which the word is now used, but they failed completely to mention such related subjects as the use and calculation of depreciation. During this period it seems probable that accounting principles originated spontaneously as an unconscious and direct outgrowth of conditions then existing. In other words, like Topsy, they just "growed."

In order, therefore, to make an effort to trace the development of accounting principles, it seems necessary to endeavor to reconstruct conditions as they existed from medieval times and to attempt to deduce therefrom the probable development of these principles in the light of those conditions. After this has been done, it will become more apparent how present principles may have originated and how they have come to have such a hold upon the business world. It will be manifest that these principles were adopted naturally and almost automatically, and that for many generations they were well suited to the conditions that then existed. It will also be evident that these principles have merely perpetuated themselves unchanged while the conditions for which they were designed have changed radically. Like all human institutions, they have tended to remain static while conditions have been steadily changing.

From one point of view the evolution of modern accounting may be divided into three eras. During the first era, the accountant or bookkeeper was concerned only with his employer, who was the sole owner and manager of the business. During the second era, the profession of public accounting originated due to the entrance of a creditor upon the scene and due to the insistence of this creditor upon an independently prepared financial statement. In this second era there were therefore two parties at interest, namely:

the owner of the business, who was also its manager, and the creditor. During the third era, which has commenced only during the last few decades, the individual owner tends to disappear and his place is taken by hundreds or hundreds of thousands of uninformed stockholders. In this third and present era there are three parties at interest: the stockholder, the management, and the creditor.

THE FIRST ERA. During the Middle Ages it is probable that the function of early accountants was limited strictly to "counting the cost" of a project or venture. In the case of public projects this enabled a King or a feudal lord to keep watch over his treasury. Small shopkeepers and tradesmen did not require or employ the services of accountants, if indeed they kept records at all in the modern sense. Great private businesses, in the continuing forms that now obtain, probably did not often exist. During the Middle Ages a big business transaction was more apt to be a venture or an adventure than an ordinary prosaic affair. Large businesses which required the services of accountants were necessarily hazardous and probably consisted for the most part of a series of ventures which, if successful, might be extraordinarily profitable or, if unsuccessful, might result in total loss.

Thus an Italian merchant might own a ship sailing from Venice to India with Venetian goods to be traded for perfumes, spices, and silks. These acquired articles might be brought back to Venice and sold, or the ship might be wrecked and everything on board lost. Each venture was apt to be a separate affair, and until its conclusion the chief thing that mattered was its cost to date. If the cost were known, the loss or profit could be determined upon the conclusion of the venture and a new venture embarked upon. Christians were forbidden to charge interest, and the extension of credit as we now know it was probably very rare. Such creditors as lent the merchant money presumably did so upon specific security or with the full realization that repayment of their money depended upon the success or failure of a specific venture. There were, in all likelihood, no inactive owners or stockholders in the enterprise. In any event, the merchant's bookkeeper was employed solely by the merchant and was responsible only to him. Any outsider who might desire to know about the business would have to rely upon his own wits or believe what the merchant told him.

It therefore appears probable that early accounting was utilized almost solely for the purpose of giving information to the owner-manager of a business, and that this owner-manager was, by the nature of his business, interested only in "counting the cost." In other words, all values except cash were in all likelihood computed solely on the basis of original cost. A bookkeeper had only his employer to consider, and if he kept the books as his employer desired his full duty was discharged. As yet the creditor and the absentee stockholder had not entered the picture. It seems necessary to admit that the use of original cost as a measure of value was almost ideally adapted to this era.

THE SECOND ERA. As modern times approached, however, the situation changed. The charging of interest by Christians was legalized in England in 1839. Business became safer, and creditors, consisting of bankers and tradesmen, found that it was possible to lend money or to extend credit on the basis of the worth of the owner, with the knowledge that huge unexpected losses were improbable. The practice arose of requiring the owner to submit a statement of his net worth and of his earnings so that the creditor might be informed before extending credit. To make sure that he received an honest statement, the creditor insisted upon its being prepared by an independent accountant not in the employ of the owner. Thus the profession of public accounting was born.

During this era, few corporations were in existence. Public ownership of corporate securities on a large scale was, except for a few outstanding exceptions, almost unheard of. Virtually every business was owned outright by a single man or at most by two or three partners who were active in its management. The only outside parties interested were creditors, such as bankers who might have loaned the business money, or individuals who might have sold it goods on time. Therefore, an accountant who prepared the financial statements of such a business had an obligation to only two interested parties, namely: the owner, who also managed the business and who knew all of its details, and the creditor who was interested only in the ability of the owner to pay his accounts or loans when due.

Obviously an accountant could carry out his obligation to both of these parties by preparing the sort of profit and loss statement and balance sheet the owner desired, provided that there was no overstatement of earnings or of net worth. The creditor was interested only in knowing that earnings and net worth were at least as great as represented. Any understatement of earnings and net worth merely meant that he had more security than he thought he had, which of course was to his advantage. On the other hand the owner was fully conversant with his own business and, if he desired to understate the value of his own property, this could hurt no one.

As a matter of fact business men were quick to see that credit could more easily be obtained were they known to be in the habit of understating their earnings and net worth, exactly as a man is looked up to for "being better than his word." Hence successful business men made understatement a practice, and such understatements became a mark of success and stability. Creditors came to look with great esteem upon those who understated their earnings and net worth, and accountants came to feel that the prevention of overstatement was their sole duty. This was very natural and entirely honest. Understatement harmed no one and it provided a margin of safety for creditors in case of misfortune. Secret reserves became, and still are, widely approved. Businesses which possessed huge undisclosed assets, and consequently must have made huge undisclosed profits, were looked upon with envy, and still are. Successful bankers carried their land and buildings at one dollar or omitted all mention of them, and still do. Immensely valuable assets were carried at a tithe of their value; securities, instantly saleable at double their cost, were shown at cost or less; and the world applauded, and still does.

With this state of public opinion all around him let us see how an accountant of fifty years ago may have reasoned as he prepared a balance sheet and profit and loss statement. First, he was faced with the problem of valuing fixed assets, such as land, buildings, machinery, or equipment. There was probably no ready market for such property. He did not know what it could be sold for or if it could be sold at all. He did not know what it could be built or bought for. He only knew what it had originally cost the owner. Therefore, the only expedient possible for him was to value it at its original cost to the owner.

But the next day this property might be sold to a new owner for one-half of its original cost and thus its value might decline fifty per cent over night. Or it might be sold for twice its original cost and thus its value might double over night. The accountant had to be prepared to explain this possibility. So to describe and to justify his original cost value, he invented the "going value" theory, which was a very serviceable fiction, although it had the weakness of considering only a permanent owner's viewpoint and overlooked entirely the viewpoint of a temporary owner or a creditor. It may have occurred to the accountant that he could find out how much such assets could be built or bought for. However, such appraisals of replacement cost would require the services of an appraiser. This would cost the owner an extra fee, and the accountant probably had an instinctive fear of the appraiser as a competitor and also was afraid that there might not be any audit at all if it were to entail too much expense. So he asserted his "going value" theory, which seems to justify either over-valuation or undervaluation, depending upon who does the buying and upon whether capital stock, other "going values," or money is given in exchange for the purchase. A pyramid of "going values," one exchanged for the other, could make a bean shooter take on the value of a seventeen-acre plant or vice versa, but the accounting mind of fifty years ago would apparently rather have faced even this possibility than admit that an accountant alone was unable to state correctly all of the values in a balance sheet.

However, the accountant probably did realize that in adopting "going values" he might be overvaluing assets from the standpoint of a creditor. If, therefore, the owner wished to write down the value of these assets to a figure below their original cost, the accountant was apt to be quick to commend such conservatism and to allow the revaluation. On the other hand, if the owner wished to write up the value of these assets to a figure above their cost, the accountant would be far from quick to approve this. If he allowed such a write-up at all it would probably be only after having received incontestable proof of the increase in value, and after having done everything in his power to dissuade the owner. The resulting profit would, of course, not be allowed to appear in the profit and loss statement and, before crediting this profit to surplus, the accountant would in all probability use all of the arguments at his command to persuade the owner to credit it to a reserve account to offset a possible overvaluation of some other asset.

When the accountant faced the problem of valuing current assets, such as inventories, he was quite naturally apt to be on the alert to prevent both their overvaluation and the inclusion of any unrealized profits in the profit and loss statement. If the inventories had no recognized market he could value them only at their original cost. If the market price of the inventories was below their original cost, he would value them at market. If, on the other hand, the inventory were wheat bought at $1.00 a bushel and if the current market price were $2.00 a bushel, the accountant would, did, and still does, proclaim it to be worth only $1.00 a bushel, and so value it in the balance sheet. As a concession to the owner he might add a footnote to the balance sheet that the market price was $2.00 a bushel, or he might include this in brackets in the balance sheet itself, but in any event he would actually use only the value of $1.00 a bushel in arriving at the net worth and earnings of the business. Called upon to explain by the owner, he would say that the $2.00 a bushel would not be realized until the wheat was made into flour and sold, and that meanwhile the price might drop. The owner might then point to an impending world shortage and contend that wheat was much more likely to rise than to decline in price. To this the accountant would reply that inventories should always be valued at "cost or market whichever is the lower" because "conservatism" was the best policy and because it was always unwise to "anticipate" a profit.

The business man could be pardoned if at this stage he became perplexed. On one hand he saw the accountant perhaps obviously overvalue certain of his assets. Then he saw him just as obviously undervalue others. He might have borrowed $1.50 on every bushel of his wheat and he might know that the lender was a hard-headed business man, yet the accountant would only concede him a value of $1.00 a bushel for it. He may even have known that his competitor had recently purchased a similar shipment of wheat at $2.00 a bushel and that this same accountant had shown this wheat in his competitor's balance sheet at $2.00 a bushel. Why did the accountant apparently think that his competitor's wheat was worth $2.00 a bushel and that his own wheat was worth only $1.00 a bushel, although both shipments of wheat were identical?

When the wheat was converted into flour the business man fared no better. The accountant still insisted that the flour be carried at original cost until it had been sold. The flour may have been instantly convertible into cash, may in fact have been sold on the morning of January 1, but the accountant who arrived in February to prepare a balance sheet as of December 31 would not add a penny to its original cost for balance sheet or for profit and loss statement purposes. This, of course, was sheer dogma shielded by sophistry. History does not record the efforts of the first accountant for a gold mine to convince the owner of the mine that his gold bullion should be valued at original cost until it had actually been coined. However, there is little doubt but that he made the attempt.

The reason for the accountant's action was plain. Certain assets have no free and active market, so the accountant was forced, when dealing with this type of asset, to use some index of value other than market price. Only two indices were available, replacement cost or original cost. The accountant might know that present replacement cost would probably be much nearer to the truth than would the original cost, but he alone did not know how to compute present replacement cost. That would require engineering or technical knowledge far beyond his ability to command. He would have to request the owner to authorize an appraisal of present replacement cost, which would be tantamount to admitting that an accountant alone was unable to draw up correct financial statements. The owner might then decide that an audit coupled with an appraisal would be too expensive and might dispense with both. Why should the accountant voluntarily accept such humiliation and risk? Quite naturally he decided to follow in the footsteps of his predecessors and to use original cost as value, although he might know that this could be vastly greater or vastly less than a reasonable present value. Also, quite naturally, he then resolved to do his best to undervalue the remaining assets and the earnings in order to be on the safe side with regard to the banker or the trade creditors.

The accountant did not think of small stockholders who knew nothing of the business and might be left in ignorance of the value of their equity. There were none. Also he gave scant thought to the man who held a mortgage on the fixed assets. The mortgage lender had never paid any attention to balance sheet values but had always made his own independent appraisals. Small bondholders, who might be ignorant enough to rely on balance sheet values, had not yet come into existence. As regards the owner, the accountant recited his theory of "going values" to defend his valuation of fixed assets at cost and called attention to the advantages of "conservatism" to justify his valuation of current assets at the lower of original cost or market. The accountant probably did not realize that the theory of "going values" applied only to a permanent owner and was wholly unjustifiable from the standpoint of a banker, a creditor, a possible bondholder, or a temporary stockholder. Nor did it occur to him that his argument in favor of conservatism applied only to the owner in his capacity as a manager and might some day serve as a justification for the deception of thousands of inactive temporary stockholders.

So the owner was made to swallow the accountant's theories and, although they may have been fallacious and untrue, yet at that time they probably did the owner more good than harm. In the first place the owner could hardly be hurt, no matter what the accountant did. He was a permanent and sole owner of the business, and the last thing that would occur to him would be to sell out on the basis of the accountant's figures. The accountant may at times have kept him from borrowing as much at the bank as he would like to have, but in his heart the owner knew that this was a measure of protection to himself. In fact he argued with the accountant only when he was young and had insufficient capital for which he wanted to compensate by borrowing. Later, after he had built up a successful business, he never allowed himself to borrow as much as the bank was willing to lend, and thus he acquired a supreme indifference to what the accountant did. When the accountant refused to sanction a profit unless it were "realized," the owner adopted an attitude of unconcern. Whatever the accountant did would not change the facts, and the owner knew very well that there was many a slip 'twixt cup and lip and he realized that perhaps he would work harder and be more careful if he imagined himself worse off than he really was. So, as he grew older, the owner came to approve the methods of the accountant as an aid to managing a business; and young business men, who knew the owner to be rich and successful, adopted his ideas until today almost every business man has the same ideas and is scarcely conscious that conditions are no longer the same as they were when the owner lived.

Thus present accounting principles were fairly well

suited to the second era, although they were in no sense correct or true. The owner was not deceived because he knew his business intimately. The banker and trade creditors disregarded all balance sheet values except those for current assets, and rested secure in the knowledge that these assets were worth at least as much as represented and perhaps a great deal more. The man who lent the owner money and took a mortgage on the fixed assets disregarded the accountant's valuations altogether and made his own independent appraisals. The small stockholder or bondholder who might place confidence in the entire balance sheet and profit and loss statement did not yet exist. Hence nobody was hurt. Each party looked after his own interest in his own way and the system worked, after a fashion.[2]

THE PRESENT ERA. In the latter part of the nineteenth century a profound change began to take place in the ownership of business. Businesses grew larger, and large numbers of them became corporations. The owner-manager of such a business ceased to exist and his place was taken by a multitude of small stockholders on the one hand and by a hired management on the other. Mortgages on fixed assets were split into bonds and sold in small amounts to people of moderate means. Later many mergers and consolidations were made and corporate security holders grew more and more numerous until today almost every business of any magnitude is a corporation, literally owned out-

[2] To adapt this system to modern needs, Professor Bonbright suggests the simultaneous preparation of a variety of "single purpose" balance sheets and earnings statements, each prepared in accordance with different standards. See *The Valuation of Property*, New York, 1937, pp. 253, 254.

right by small security holders who know little or nothing about it except information contained in financial statements sent out by the paid management. Today there are a number of large corporations, each of whose stockholders are counted in the hundreds of thousands. It is not unusual for the largest stockholder in a big corporation to own less than 1% of its stock. Frequently the entire management, including the Board of Directors, owns only an insignificant fraction of a company's securities. It is reliably estimated that in the United States alone there are not less than twenty million corporate security holders.

Clearly, therefore, the old owner-manager has gone a long way on the road to oblivion. *Today the most important party at interest in modern business is the small uninformed security holder who virtually did not exist when the present principles of accounting originated.* Many large businesses of today carry huge cash reserves and are lenders of money, not borrowers. In a multitude of instances bankers have ceased to be at interest at all. Trade creditors commonly have total claims amounting to less than the cash on hand, and their interest in a company is at most usually only a fraction of that of the security holders. The old mortgage on the fixed assets has been split into a great number of small mortgage bonds which have been sold to the public. Debenture bonds, preferred stock, and common stock have been issued and sold to a legion of investors. Compared with the interest of these security holders, that of bankers or trade creditors is apt to be insignificant.

What do present accounting principles do for the small security holder who must rely almost entirely upon them for information regarding his property? In the first place they give him a balance sheet which may often be seriously false and misleading. In the second place they give him a profit and loss statement which may be quite as far from the truth as any dishonest management could wish. This profit and loss statement will be quite certain to ignore unrealized appreciation in the value of current assets and will be apt to exclude both capital gains and capital losses relating to fixed assets, whether realized or not. However, the same profit and loss statement will be quite sure to include depreciation in the value of current assets whether realized or not. The result is that the small security holder may be told that his company is losing money year after year and may finally conclude that the business is hopeless and may sell his holding at a large loss, only to learn shortly thereafter that his company has sold its old plant at an enormous profit and has cut a huge mellon for its stockholders. Or he may, as in the case of the "Fable of the Two Investments Trusts," purchase the stock of a company because of its splendid reported earnings, only to see these reported earnings drop almost to nothing in the following year. He may then be forced or frightened into selling his stock at a great loss, meanwhile remaining in total ignorance of the fact that the actual earnings of the company were the same for both years.

In other words, the millions of small investors who own the great industries of this country, and of other countries, are unable to learn the truth about their own properties and are left at the mercy of individuals with inside information who may care to prey on them, largely because the accounting profession sees fit to turn out reports which, in many cases, are misleading and untrue, and whose preparation is in accordance with principles suited only to conditions existing many years ago. The simple truth of the matter is that an accountant's present knowledge and training do not wholly qualify him to prepare correct financial statements. If accountants would complete their educations, to the end that they might adopt sound accounting principles and might be fitted to value those assets whose economic values are not immediately apparent, they would be so qualified. Accountants must either become valuers, or must employ valuers, if they are to prepare truthful financial statements. Financial statements purport to deal with present economic values, and they are apt to be useful only to the extent that they do so. They are extremely apt to be mischievous to the extent that they do not do so.

V

THE NATURE OF VALUE

VALUE is one of the most common words in modern use, and one of the least understood. In its wider aspects it enters the fields of psychology, theology, ethics, logic, aesthetics, and metaphysics. In its different concepts it has been studied by Plato, Aristotle, Kant, Lotze, Nietzsche, and a host of modern thinkers. None of these has fully succeeded in defining it. Plato called it the most difficult question of all science. The modern recognition of its importance has been called "the greatest philosophical achievement of the nineteenth century." It has assumed such a large field in psychological and philosophical study that the search for its true nature has come to be a separate science called axiology. Yet its true nature is still unknown. No one has so far succeeded in evolving a fully satisfactory general theory concerning it.

ECONOMIC VERSUS PHILOSOPHIC CONCEPT. But, although this is true concerning the meaning of value in its universal aspect, it is emphatically not true concerning the meaning of value in its economic aspect. The nature of economic values has long been fairly well known, and the economic theory of value is sufficiently complete to serve most practical purposes. It is because accountants and laymen allow their minds to leap from an economic concept of value to a psychological or philosophical concept that meaningless, misleading financial statements are possible. People speak of "intrinsic value," "real value," "actual value," when they wish to quarrel with the market price of something. What do they mean? Air to breathe is perhaps the most valuable possession of any of us because without it life would cease in a few minutes. Do they mean that every man, in submitting a balance sheet to his banker, should list air as his most valuable asset? Should he list his health, his intelligence, his personality, his happy home life, his grace with God? All of these things are commonly considered to be of value. Evidently some values have no fit place in a balance sheet or in a profit and loss statement.

In axiology every thing, thought, or act has a value, either positive or negative. Every act or thought involves a conscious or subconscious judgment of values. Life is made up of alternatives, of decisions, conscious or subconscious, of judgments of value. All things have value, whether religious, ethical, logical, aesthetic, or economic. From this point of view philosophy itself tends to become a study of values. Axiology has not yet discovered how to measure these values, or to compare them, or even to define them.

A balance sheet and a profit and loss statement purport to state values. In order to fulfill their purpose, they must state values according to economic concepts, commonly called economic values, because these are the only values that anyone knows how to state. No accountant can hope to express values if he strays from the comparatively restricted concepts of economics and thereby finds himself in the intellectual mazes of axiology. Yet this is precisely what he will be very apt to do unless he thoroughly understands the economic theory of value.

ECONOMIC VALUE. Economic value is a measure of the relative importance which a community, exhibiting its collective preferences through the market process, attaches to a particular good in comparison with other goods. In other words, the economic value of anything is its "power in exchange" which, measured in money, is its market price. The market price of a thing is the price at which it *is actually being bought and sold*. Economic value is not necessarily the price at which a thing *could* be sold, nor is it necessarily the price at which at thing *could* be bought. Economic value is not a prophecy. It is a fact. It does not relate only to selling or only to buying, but relates to both simultaneously under conditions that *actually exist*. It affords to both buyers and sellers a reliable basis of actual present fact upon which each can base his own estimate of the future.

In the absence of an actual market price, the economic value of a thing may be estimated by calculating or imputing what its market price would be if existing potential buyers and sellers were brought together. Such an imputed market price does not mean the price that would be realized at forced sale nor does it mean the price that would have to be paid at a forced purchase, for both of these presume a disturbance of the existing ratio of supply and demand. It means merely the price that presumably would obtain were potential buyers and sellers brought together with no accelerating of either supply or demand, and with no effort made by either buyers or sellers to influence each other,

other than in the announcement of their bids and offers. Methods of imputing market prices will be examined later. It is advisable to emphasize at this point, however, that in any community the economic value of a thing is its market price or is evidenced by its imputed market price. In other words, the economic value of a thing is its market price and that alone. The definition and meaning of market price will be discussed in a following chapter.

Many valuable things, perhaps most things of value from the axiologist's standpoint, have no economic value whatever. Thus ordinary air has no economic value, although without it we could live only a few minutes at best. A mother's love, faith in God, immunity from smallpox, all may be worth a great deal to us, yet they have no economic value. A consideration of what differentiates economic values from other values uncovers the fact that all things having economic value possess three specific elements, whereas all other things are lacking in one or more of these. The three elements which everything having economic value must possess might be called, respectively: scarcity, exchangeability and utility. Nothing which does not possess all three of these elements can possibly have economic value nor can it have any fit place in a balance sheet or in a profit and loss statement.

THE ELEMENT OF SCARCITY. Scarcity may be defined as that quality of a thing which causes its actual or potential supply to be less than the demand for it, or which gives rise to some difficulty or expense in obtaining it. Hence scarcity has an effect upon the economic value of a good by affecting its supply. Wheat may be superabundant. There may be a present supply greater than the present demand for it, even were it given away. Still it possesses the element of scarcity because the growing of wheat occasions difficulty and expense, and growers will not tend to give it away but will tend to obtain as much as possible for it and to store it or to stop producing it if they cannot sell it. Ordinary air, on the other hand, is also superabundant, but the obtaining of it occasions no difficulty or expense, hence it does not possess the element of scarcity and has no economic value. Water is superabundant, but perhaps not where it is needed. Water in a desert town may possess the element of scarcity due to the difficulty or expense of bringing it there, whereas water in a house boat colony on Lake Michigan would not possess the element of scarcity and would have no economic value.

A man may find a large natural diamond quite by accident. He may incur no difficulty or expense in obtaining it. Yet the supply of diamonds is not equal to the demand for them, consequently his diamond possesses the element of scarcity. It is obvious that anything which is superabundant and free to everybody, without expense or difficulty, will have no economic value. On the other hand, anything which is scarce, or is difficult or expensive to obtain, will have economic value provided that it also possesses the two remaining elements of value, namely, exchangeability and utility.

THE ELEMENT OF EXCHANGEABILITY. Exchangeability may be defined as that quality of a thing which enables it to be exchanged or transferred from one person to another so that this other person may enjoy the utility it possesses. Exchangeability has no effect upon the economic value of a good because it has no influence upon either the supply of, or demand for, that good, save that where it is lacking it makes the possession of any economic value by that good impossible. Exchangeability takes no cognizance of legal restrictions or indeed of physical impediments to transfer unless they are part of the very nature of the thing itself. Thus a contract for another man's services may not be assignable without his consent, but this contract possesses the element of exchangeability in an economic sense because by its nature it is exchangeable. A man may own a large machine located on a farm which is surrounded by high mountains. There may be no way to get the machine over the mountains in case the man wished to sell it to some other farmer. Yet the machine possesses the element of exchangeability because by its nature it is exchangeable.

On the other hand, a man's brain is by its nature not exchangeable and hence can have no economic value. But the work of his brain may possess the element of exchangeability and have great economic value. So with health, intelligence, personality, a happy home life, religious belief, a mother's love, or immunity from smallpox. By their very nature none of these things are exchangeable and they thus can possess no economic value. The direct or indirect product of their use or enjoyment, however, may be exchangeable and may possess great economic value. A good that lacks exchangeability must lack economic value because its purchase or sale must forever remain impossible, and thus no market price for it can ever exist. Human beings cannot conceive how a man could sell his good health to another man and, although they can imagine potential buyers or even potential sellers, they will always decline to enter into transactions that to them appear inconceivable.

Yet the average individual considers good health to be worth much. He knows men possessing it who would not sell it for large sums, and he knows other men who would buy it if they could for any sums within their ability to pay. To the philosopher or to the axiologist good health has value. To the economist it has none. If the axiologist knew how to measure his values, two balance sheets might be prepared which would compare all the values possessed by each of two men, including their respective cash balances, their religious beliefs, foresight, intelligence, good health, and a hundred other things of value which they might possess. But the axiologist does not know how to measure his values, or even how to define them, and so the accountant must confine himself to stating economic values which possess the element of exchangeability along with scarcity and utility. Good health and a multitude of other things, although valuable from a philosophical concept, do not possess economic value and hence cannot be included among the values exhibited in financial statements.

THE ELEMENT OF UTILITY. Utility, sometimes called "value in use" or "subjective value," may be defined as the usefulness or desirability of a thing to an individual consumer. Because men's needs, likes, and dislikes differ, the utility of a given good at a given time may be vastly different for one man than for another. Utility is ordinarily divided into three types called respectively: form utility, place utility, and time utility. Form utility is the usefulness or desirability that attaches to a thing because of its composition, shape, or appearance; in short, because of what it is. Place utility is the usefulness or desirability that attaches to a thing because of its location. Time utility is the usefulness or desirability that attaches to a thing because of the time at which it may be used or enjoyed.

Utility has an effect upon the economic value of a good by affecting the demand for it. Thus a bushel of wheat may have value, even in a well-fed community, because it possesses form utility as food. The same bushel of wheat, however, would have a greater value, other things remaining equal, were its location changed to a wealthy community that was starving for lack of food. Moreover, this wealthy community would probably pay more to have the bushel of wheat immediately than to have it after thirty days. Interest rates tend to express the time utility factor with regard to money. Thus a note payable in one year without interest is not worth as much as a similar note payable immediately.

The extent by which the utility of a good to an individual exceeds the price which he must pay to obtain it is called the consumer's surplus. A small boy may run an errand in exchange for an ice cream soda. This soda may possess for him a high utility, so high in fact that it may afford him a large profit in satisfaction over the inconvenience and effort involved in running the errand. The boy may then run a second errand in exchange for a second soda. In all probability, however, this second soda will not taste as good as the first one. In other words, its utility, and hence the consumer's surplus which it yields, will be less. If the boy continues to consume sodas, sooner or later a point will be reached where the utility or satisfaction to be obtained by him from an additional soda will be so low that it will not compensate him for the running of an errand and will thus yield him no consumer's surplus at all. The general tendency for additional quantities of a good to yield lower utilities as the point of satiety is approached, is known as the law of diminishing utility. Consumer's surplus is the personal gain which each purchaser receives through the purchase of a good. It is the extent by which the utility to him of that good is more valuable than the utility to him of the good with which he parts in exchange. The utility of a good at any one time clearly varies according to the likes and needs of different consumers, and varies as well from time to time with the changing circumstances of each individual consumer. It is the consumer's surplus part of the utility element in a good that gives rise to a demand for it and creates buyers willing to pay for it.

No good can possess economic value unless it has utility. No one would pay for it unless its ownership could fill a want of some kind. Yet it is evident that the economic value of a good is not in proportion to its usefulness or utility. This must be so because utility is an individual subjective thing, varying with each different consumer, whereas economic value is a community affair involving the collective judgment of many buyers and sellers, and being affected fully as much by the influence of scarcity upon supply as by the influence of utility upon demand. Economists have, however, devised the terms "marginal vendibility" and "marginal utility" which serve in theory to co-relate economic value with a restricted concept of utility relating to a group of buyers and sellers. Suppose a farmer to have driven a wagonload of apples to a retail market place. He wishes to price the apples so that he will sell all of them that day. If he fixes the price per apple too high, some purchasers may buy but perhaps not enough of them to take his whole stock. In order to accomplish his purpose, he must lower his price per apple to a point where it will not exceed the value of the utility of an apple to the least eager purchaser that he will require in order to dispose of his whole stock. The marginal vendibility of any unit in a stock of goods thus means merely the price which must obtain in order to sell the whole stock at a fixed price per unit.

Conversely with reference to an individual purchaser, marginal utility means merely the satisfaction received from the purchase of the last unit of a stock of goods possessed by the purchaser. This satisfaction must be precisely equal to the satisfaction received from the ownership of *any one unit* of the stock owned. The law of diminishing utility causes each additional unit purchased and added to the stock to have less utility for the purchaser. The purchase of the last unit must therefore have yielded the least satisfaction or utility to the purchaser. The value of this utility to the purchaser must be at least equal to the price paid, otherwise the last unit would not have been purchased. Yet, since the units are all alike, any one of them, *after* having been purchased, must possess the same economic importance to its owner as any other one owned by him. If he were to part with one, its utility to him would be the utility of the last one purchased. This would be the marginal utility of that good to that owner at that time. The concept of marginal utility is important to theoretical economists. It probably possesses little practical importance for accountants.

Obviously, utility is a necessary element in economic value because, if a thing were neither useful nor in any way desirable, no one would want it and there would be no actual or potential demand for it at any price. With no demand existing or possible, there could be no market price or imputed market price. Common mosquitoes have no economic value. Honey bees do have economic value. On the other hand, it matters not that a thing may in reality be useless or undesirable if people think it useful or desirable. A rabbit's foot as a good luck charm may in reality be entirely useless and even totally undesirable because of the disease germs that it may carry. If, however, people desire rabbits' feet, then rabbits' feet possess utility from the economic viewpoint and, provided the other two elements of economic value are also present, namely, scarcity and exchangeability, such rabbits' feet will possess economic value.

SUPPLY AND DEMAND. So far it has been affirmed that economic value is market price or is evidenced by imputed market price, and that all things having economic value must possess the three elements of scarcity, exchangeability, and utility. The element of scarcity as herein defined means the existence of an effective supply less than the effective demand at zero price. The element of utility as herein defined means the existence of an effective demand at something more than zero price. The element of exchangeability as herein defined means the actual or potential existence of a market to bring supply and demand together.

Thus the discussion has been narrowed down to the two opposing factors of supply and demand, whose counter-action results in market price. In the final analysis, therefore, it can be said that the ratio of supply and demand determines economic value.

Suppose wheat to be selling at $1.00 a bushel. The corn crop fails, compelling a large number of corn consumers to turn to wheat for their requirements. Naturally the price of wheat will rise because now the ratio of supply and demand has changed to the advantage of sellers. The supply of wheat remains the same but the demand for it has increased. Wheat now has utility for a large number of corn consumers which it did not possess before the failure of the corn crop. This utility is the usefulness of wheat as a cheaper food or fodder than corn. As long as corn sold for less than wheat this utility did not exist. When corn rose in price, or became non-existent, this new utility of wheat came into existence. And yet the wheat, which may now sell at $2.00 a bushel, is the same wheat that formerly sold at $1.00 a bushel. Its utility to a housewife is doubtless exactly the same.

Suppose a man to have purchased for personal consumption a supply of wheat at $1.00 a bushel. After wheat has risen to $2.00 a bushel an accountant undertakes to prepare the man's balance sheet. The accountant values the wheat at $1.00 a bushel and says to the man: "You purchased the wheat at $1.00 a bushel which was its value to you then. You do not intend to sell it. The wheat has not changed. It is the same wheat. Its utility for you has not changed. Therefore its value to you cannot have changed, but is still $1.00 a bushel. The wheat should therefore be shown in your balance sheet at $1.00 a bushel, which is its value to you." This is the way the accountant usually reasons, not only with reference to wheat for personal consumption, but with reference to land, buildings, machinery, and other assets. How does the accountant know that $1.00 a bushel is now, or ever was, the value of the utility of wheat to the man? Perhaps if the man could have secured wheat in no other way he would have paid $10 a bushel for it. Perhaps he would have paid $100 a bushel for it rather than starve.

Surely it must be evident that the original cost of $1.00 a bushel was not the value of the utility of wheat to the man. The $1.00 value was not determined alone by the usefulness of the wheat either to the man or to other consumers. It was merely the price at which the effective supply counterbalanced the effective demand at that time. Thus the $1.00 value was the product of the two opposing forces of supply and demand. Utility or usefulness cannot be valued alone without reference to supply. Philosophers have been trying to do that for many years with no practical success whatever. When an accountant attempts it he is allowing his mind to leap from an economic concept of value to a philosophical and psychological concept of value. If his training had qualified him to deal with these concepts he would realize the untenability of his position.

Again suppose wheat to be selling at $1.00 a bushel. An enormous crop is harvested and the market price drops to 50¢ a bushel. Here the utility of wheat remains the same; it is just as useful as ever, the demand for it is just as great as ever. But the scarcity element of its value has changed. The supply is much greater in comparison with the demand, and hence the ratio of supply and demand has changed to the advantage of buyers. Consequently the value of wheat has declined. A former purchaser may say: "I bought my wheat at $1.00 a bushel because it was worth that much to me. It is still the same wheat so I am going to value it in my balance sheet at $1.00 a bushel." This purchaser is only attempting to fool himself. He did not buy wheat at $1.00 a bushel because it was worth that much to him. He bought it at $1.00 a bushel because that was its market price and because he then thought it was worth more than that much to him.

The worth of a thing to an individual is not measured by what he pays for it. Air is worth our very lives to us and yet no one pays anything for it. And the worth of a thing to an individual is no more dependent solely upon the thing itself than is its economic value. The element of scarcity and the changeableness of utility with the varying circumstances of the individual must be considered. Ten minutes after the above purchaser bought his wheat at $1 a bushel, someone may have made him a present of a large quantity of flour. If he had possessed the flour ten minutes earlier he probably would not have been willing to pay anything for the wheat. After possessing the flour he may be glad to sell his wheat for anything he can get. He may even give it away to the neighbors to make room for the flour. Thus in ten minutes his wheat may have become worthless to him, even a nuisance. Yet it is still the same wheat, it will perform the same service as before.

How then can anyone substantiate a claim that the value of a thing, even to an individual, will remain constant as long as the thing remains unchanged? Economic value is dependent upon the forces of supply fully as much as upon the forces of demand. Any attempt to value the utility of a thing irrespective of its supply and demand merely plunges one into a maze of philosophical abstraction where no one knows truth from fiction. Yet this attempt is constantly made by accountants when they expound their theory of "going values" in an effort to justify the valuation of fixed assets at original cost.

FAULTY CONCEPTS OF VALUE. It has been seen that there are two broad concepts of value. One is a concept of the absolute worth of a thing irrespective of its demand or supply, either as respects an individual or as respects a community. The other is a concept of value as the result of the counterplay of the forces of supply and demand within a community. The first concept is philosophical and presumes values that no one in the world knows how to measure, compare, or define. The second concept relates to economic values upon which the entire business world relies, and which in many cases can be stated with mathematical accuracy. It would seem reasonable to assume that everybody would naturally use economic values in his business affairs since these are the only values that anyone knows how to measure. But this is not so. Accountants and laymen alike are constantly rebelling against economic values which do not please them, are throwing the law of supply and demand to the winds, and are setting up values of their own which can have no justification save in the desires of their inventors.

A man buys a listed stock at $20 per share. Its market price promptly declines to $10 per share. The man doesn't like that. It seems inconceivable to him that the value of the stock could change so quickly when there has been no change in the utility to him of the stock itself. Therefore he says that the market price of the stock is below the stock's "actual" value and he refuses to recognize the $10 value. He says that the stock must eventually "come back" to its "actual value" of $20 per share. He may be right and he may be wrong. The present value of the stock is $10 per share and the man is hoping that in the future its value may be $20 per share. But it may fall to $5 per share and remain there.

Another man buys a listed stock at $50 per share. Its market price promptly rises to $100 per share. The man's accountant doesn't like that. It seems inconceivable to him that the value of the stock could change so quickly when there has been no change in the utility to the man of the stock itself. Therefore, the accountant says that the market price of the stock is above the stock's "conservative value" to the man, and he refuses to recognize the $100 value. He uses $50 per share as the stock's value and says that the market price may fall to $50 per share. He may be right and he may be wrong. The present value of the stock is $100 per share and the accountant is fearful that in the future its value may be $50 per share. But it may rise to $200 per share and remain there. One is tempted here to ask why the accountant is fearful that the market price will fall to $50 per share. Why is he not fearful that it will fall to $40, or $30 or $10? Why does he not use one of these figures as its value?

A man buys some land and buildings comprising an industrial plant. A city grows up around it. The market price of the plant is clearly many times its original cost. The accountant continues to exhibit the plant at its original cost and calls this cost its "going value." He says that the value of the plant to the man has not changed because neither the land and buildings nor their usefulness have changed as regards the man's going business. The accountant is merely attempting to value the utility of the plant apart from the external factors of supply and demand. He is trying to apply a philosophic concept to an economic situation. But he is not so modest as the philosopher. He claims success where the philosopher admits failure. And to complete his unconscious burlesque he uses as his axiologic value a former economic value which was created by the very law of supply and demand which he now discredits.

People constantly speak of "intrinsic value," "real value," "actual value," when they wish to differentiate between the market price or economic value of a thing and their opinion of what the economic value should be, or their expectation of what the economic value will be at a later date. In doing this, they unconsciously fall back on the philosophic concept of an absolute value for a given utility irrespective of supply or demand. They forget that values are not determined by usefulness or desirability alone. If they were, water would be more valuable than diamonds and a pound of flour would be worth many pounds of truffles. People also instinctively discredit sudden changes in economic values. If the change is gradual they become accustomed to it and accept it, probably because they are thereby enabled to reconcile it with their philosophic concept of value by concluding that there must be some change in utility of which they are unaware. But if a large change in economic value suddenly occurs, they refuse to believe it, deny that it has occurred, call it a market fluctuation, talk about "intrinsic," "real," or "actual" value, and assert that sooner or later market price must return to such "actual" value. In such prophecies they may be quite as often wrong as right. Our economic life is replete with large sudden changes in economic value which not only do not for years retrace their rise or fall but which are likely to remain permanent in a very practical sense. Someone discovers a use for platinum and its value soars, permanently. Someone discovers a process for synthesizing indigo. Most of its value vanishes, permanently. A railroad is built through a town and land values soar, permanently.

People, and most of all accountants, should recognize and remember that we are living in a world of kaleidoscopic changes in economic values, many of which are apt to be permanent. No accountant should undertake to prophesy the future of any economic value. No accountant has a right to use a fictitious value in place of an economic value because he thinks that the economic value may rise or fall in the future. It matters not whether his fictitious value be above or below the economic value. All that he can be certain of is the present economic value and if, knowing it, he does not use it, he should be held to be faithless to his trust, for his action is almost certain to deceive people to their disadvantage. Stockholders and creditors have a right to believe that the figures given to them state values, not private prophecies, and the only values that any one knows how to state are economic values.

VI

MONEY

In communities where a state of barter and exchange exists, market prices are quoted in terms of different commodities instead of in terms of a common medium of exchange such as money. Hence the value of a cow might be fifty bushels of wheat, or five pigs, or twenty yards of cloth. A given quantity of any one thing might have a value expressible in terms of scores of different commodities. This system of direct exchange without the use of money exists in some few places in the world today and, indeed, has not been entirely eradicated even in the most advanced communities. Thus the Sunday newspaper may carry large numbers of advertisements offering to exchange property such as a radio or a house for an automobile or what have you.

Mediums of Exchange. Barter is, however, a very complicated way of doing business. Suppose a large department store attempted to adopt it. The price tag on each of the articles carried for sale would have to list hundreds, if not thousands, of equivalent prices, each expressed in terms of a different commodity. A complete catalogue of prices would fill a municipal library. Certain commodities would not be divisable to make the price desired, with a result similar to that of tendering a street car conductor a hundred dollar bill. Swift, frictionless trade, as it is now known, would be impossible.

Even primitive peoples have recognized the disadvantages of barter as a system of exchange and have set up some sort of a medium of exchange to facilitate their reckoning and their trade. This medium of exchange, whatever form it may take, is money. Among certain Arab tribes, camels are money. Among the North American Indians, wampum was money. Among many African tribes cowrie shells are money. In China silver is money. In the United States and Europe gold is money.

Governments may issue, as money, pieces of paper or coins made of metal other than the one designated as money. Such paper and coins are known as representative money, and the maintenance of their face value depends upon the real money securing them or upon the taxing power of the issuing government in relation to the wealth of its people, i.e., its credit. When a government does not hold real money sufficient to secure its outstanding representative money, and when its credit also declines, the value of its representative money tends to fall. Under such conditions representative money tends to lose the value which it possessed by virtue of its representation of a given quantity of real money and tends, instead, to revert to its economic value as a commodity. In postwar Germany, paper marks fell to about their value as baled paper.

When money comes into existence, values tend to be expressed in terms of money alone. An individual may know perfectly well that a dollar bushel of wheat is worth ten pounds of copper but he will say that wheat is worth $1.00 a bushel and that copper is worth 10¢ a pound. This reduces all values to the common denominator of money and enables them to be more readily compared, as well as more readily exchanged. In all civilized communities, values are expressed or measured in terms of some one commodity designated by the existing government as money, rather than in terms of many different commodities. The commodity selected for use as money is known as a money standard, or as a standard of value.

THE GOLD STANDARD. Why did gold come to be the money standard of most of the civilized world instead of camels, wampum, or sea shells? Probably because, after much experiment, gold was found to possess to a superior degree the combination of qualities desirable in any commodity which is to be used as money. The three most important of these qualities may be said to be durability, convenience, and stability of value. Under the heading of convenience must be included such qualities as plentifulness, distinctiveness, divisibility, portability, small bulk, and in general those qualities which go to make up the physical convenience of a money standard.

Durability is essential. Camels die, sea shells break, wampum deteriorates. If these were used for money they would hardly represent a very permanent form of wealth upon which to base a governmental paper money issue. Plentifulness is highly desirable. Radium would be unsuitable because one government might corner the supply. High value and small bulk are desirable. Many ships would be necessary to transport wheat, lead, or copper of a value equal to an ordinary gold shipment, to say nothing of the storage space necessitated upon its arrival. Stability of value is perhaps the most important quality of all because without it money is an ever changing measure of value somewhat comparable to a rubber tape measure, or to a scale that weighs differently every time it is used.

Gold has survived as a money standard because it embodies the combined qualities of durability, convenience, and stability of value as well as, if not better than, any other one commodity. Silver is still widely used as a money standard but it is not so convenient as gold, due to the larger bulk and weight necessary to make up a given value. But even though gold is as suitable as a money standard as any other one commodity, it is still far from ideal. With reference to durability and convenience, it will not rust but it is so soft that it wears easily, and it is so heavy that large sums cannot be carried about without the employment of men and conveyances. The defects of gold as regards durability and convenience are, however, largely avoided by the use of representative money or instruments of credit such as checks or bills of exchange. These defects do not, therefore, constitute important obstacles. They occasion expense and inconvenience, and in a sense levy a small overhead on the business world, but the overhead is neither great nor burdensome.

It is in relation to the third quality of money, called stability of value, that the evil chargeable to gold assumes major proportions. This evil is so enormous, so destructive, and so pernicious, that it constitutes one of the most serious and costly defects of our present economic system. Failures, bankruptcies, strikes, unemployment, hard times, depressions, and bread lines follow in its wake. Yet it is so concealed, so hidden from the lay mind, that probably not one man in a hundred even knows that it exists. Every accountant should be familiar with its nature, its causes, and its possible cure. Otherwise he can only imperfectly understand the absurdities of present accounting principles and only imperfectly grasp the compelling reasons for changing them.

THE VALUE OF GOLD. Gold has a value determined by the action of supply and demand just as have other things. In the United States the value of other things is expressed in terms of gold dollars, each gold dollar now being 1/35th of an ounce of gold. Prior to the revaluation in 1933, each gold dollar was approximately 1/20th of an ounce of gold. It is obvious that the value of things expressed in terms of gold will vary either as their value varies, or as the value of gold varies. If gold should fall to half its present value, the value of everything else, expressed in gold dollars, would be double. But if gold is valued in terms of itself, its stated value can never change except by government decree. One thirty-fifth of an ounce of gold is always worth one dollar because 1/35th of an ounce of gold *is* one dollar. There would be as much sense in saying that sixteen ounces of butter were worth a pound of butter. This would be true, whatever the value of the butter, for sixteen ounces of butter *are* one pound of butter.

In order to show changes in the value of gold, therefore, its value must be expressed in terms of commodities other than itself. Gold might be valued in terms of wheat except for the fact that then changes in value might be ascribed as much to the wheat as to the gold. If a gold dollar is now worth two bushels of wheat, whereas it was previously worth one bushel of wheat, one person might say that the value of gold had doubled and another person might say that the value of wheat had halved. The best way to settle this difficulty is to value gold in terms of a combination of all other commodities because changes of value can occur only in the relation of one commodity to another. The total value of all commodities combined must inevitably remain the same, for it comprises a universe of itself with which there is nothing else to compare. To borrow a phrase from mathematics, it is the only "frame of reference" that is available. If the value of gold changes, as expressed in terms of all other commodities combined, one may be sure that the value of gold itself has changed to the precise extent, and in the opposite direction, that the value of all the other commodities combined has changed in terms of gold.

An index made up of all commodities other than gold would comprise thousands of items, many of small importance, and would be impracticable to compile. The result of such an index can, however, be approximated by the periodic compilation of an index composed of leading commodities, weighted according to their importance. A number of such indices are in current use and have been available to the public for many years. There are indices of wholesale prices relating to so-called raw material, and there are indices of retail prices which are intended to reflect the cost of living for the ordinary consumer. All of these indices are constructed differently, and yet all of them show a remarkable degree of uniformity in their fluctuations.

An examination of these indices discloses the following

gyrations in the value of the United States dollar. Using the 1913 dollar as a base, the dollar at the beginning of 1865 was worth about 48¢, the dollar in 1896 was worth about $1.50, the dollar in 1920 was worth about 44¢, and the dollar in 1932 was worth about $1.05. The value of a dollar rose from 44¢ in 1920 to 77¢ in 1921, an appreciation of about 75% in one year. This means that a commodity which was worth $1.00 in 1920 would be worth only 57¢ in 1921, due entirely to a change in the value of gold and without there being any change whatever in the commodity itself, its supply, its demand, or its value as compared with all other commodities except gold. A plant worth one million dollars in 1920 would be worth a little more than half a million dollars in 1921. An inventory worth $100,000 in 1920 would be worth $57,000 in 1921. Yet the stated value of money, expressed in terms of itself, would of course remain unchanged.

Gold is not more stable than silver in its value. If anything, silver is probably more stable than gold. But neither gold nor silver are suitable for money as regards stabilization of value. The United States dollar and the Chinese yuan dollar are both rubber tape measures. The simple fact is that neither are units of value any more than an expanding and contracting rubber band is a measure of length. Both are fixed weights of a given metal, but there is little that is fixed about the value of either.

VALUES EXPRESSED IN MONEY. What would intelligent individuals think of a primitive savage who calculated that his hut was worth one elephant, his clothes worth ten rabbits, his spears and shields worth five dogs, his bows and arrows worth sixty cats, and who then announced that his possessions had a value of seventy-six animals, without stating which animals he had in mind? Intelligent individuals would probably laugh and advise the savage that they were no wiser than before. Yet, when a modern certified public accounting firm does very nearly the equivalent of this, they are extremely apt to accept its figures in all seriousness and to assume that they are fully informed regarding the value of the possessions in question.

When an accounting firm makes up a balance sheet it has in mind many different-sized dollars with which to measure values. It has little dollars worth about 44¢ each in terms of 1913 dollars, and it has big dollars worth about $1.50 or almost four times as much. It also has in mind dollars of various sizes worth different amounts in between. If it finds that a man bought his land in 1920 it values this land in little 44¢ dollars, and of course it takes a lot of them because the dollars are worth so little. If, on the other hand, it finds that the man bought his land in 1896 it values this land in big $1.50 dollars, and it doesn't take many of these dollars because they are worth so much. If the man bought property in 1921, this property is valued in dollars almost twice as big as they would be if the man had done his buying in 1920, and is thus valued at about half as many dollars. After the accounting firm gets through, it will add up its figures and inform the man and his banker that the man is worth so many dollars. This is supposed to be accurate information, and the banker will probably lend the man dollars of a still different size because of the accountant's figures.

Comedy of this sort is going on all the time, and yet nobody laughs or even smiles. Bankers spend weeks deliberating whether a bond issue shall bear 4¾% or 5% interest and never give a thought to the kind of dollars the bond will be paid in at maturity. Perhaps half of the principal will be wiped out, perhaps the principal will be doubled. A business operates profitably for a number of years and then the value of gold almost doubles, as it did between 1920 and 1921. The business may still sell as many goods as before but, measured in double-value dollars, the dollar volume of sales is only half as big. Yet the concern goes on paying out the same number of dollars for wages, rent, and bond interest as it did when those dollars were worth only half as much. It does this as long as it can and then it suspends operations or goes into bankruptcy. As a result unemployment ensues, people talk of overproduction, and misery and distress stalk the land.

THE COMMODITY DOLLAR. The cure for most of this seems to lie in the stabilization of the money standard, or standard of value. In his famous book *The Money Illusion,* Irving Fisher states that stabilization could be accomplished by basing the value of our dollar upon a representative commodity index instead of upon a fixed *weight* of gold. His plan provides that coinage of gold coins be discontinued and that gold be issued by the government in bullion only. The weight of gold in a dollar would then be made to vary as the commondity index varied, and each dollar of representative money would be payable in the amount of gold representing a dollar at the time of redemption. The plan contemplates that few people would be aware of any change and that business would function as usual, but without most of the troubles now caused by periodic depressions. The man in the street would notice only that his cost of living did not rise or fall and that his salary sufficed for his needs as well in one year as in another. The working man would not be caught between the high cost of living in one year and unemployment in another, as he now is. Professor Fisher indicates that all of this could be accomplished by the passage of one money stabilization bill by Congress. The Fisher plan is a highly controversial subject, and some authorities believe that it would produce results contrary to those contemplated. Without reference to any particular plan, however, students of finance generally acknowledge that money stabilization is one of the most important advances possible in the economic world today.

With reference to accounting practice it seems evident that, in preparing financial statements, every accountant should endeavor to use economic values as of the date of the balance sheet, expressed in dollars as of the date of the balance sheet. Present accounting procedure tends to put the informed insider in a position to deceive the uninformed outsider, be he stockholder, bondholder, banker, or creditor. After what has been said, the fallacy of using original costs in place of present economic values should be at once apparent. Values should be revised at least each year, and should express present economic values in terms of present dollars. Stockholders would then be informed of the vast changes that now periodically bewilder them, and might come to appreciate the importance of money stabilization. They would be advised of the facts, in startling clarity, instead of having these facts concealed from them.

It has been suggested that accountants invent a fixed commodity dollar of their own and translate the figures from each set of financial statements into terms of this commodity dollar. This would express financial statements solely in terms of purchasing power, and would show the profit or loss for each period minus the influence exerted by changes in the value of gold. For example, a balance sheet as of December 31, 1921, of a given business, exhibiting December 31, 1921, values expressed in December 31, 1921, dollars, would probably show the assets of the business to be worth approximately one-half as much as the assets exhibited by the same business as of December 31, 1920, expressed in December 31, 1920, dollars. In other words, the 1921 financial statements would show an enormous loss. On the other hand, this loss would be due almost entirely to the change in the value of gold and would affect all commodities except gold almost equally. Consequently, in terms of purchasing power, i.e., in terms of a fixed commodity dollar, the business would probably have suffered very little actual loss in the value of its assets although it probably would have suffered a diminution of most of its asset values as compared with most of its liabilities, and also it probably would have suffered a diminution of its gross earnings as compared with its fixed expenses. The actual extent of its loss, therefore, is rather to be measured by the appreciation in the purchasing power of its liabilities and fixed expenses than by a depreciation in the purchasing power of its assets and gross earnings. If the liabilities and fixed expenses of the business were large in relation to its assets and gross earnings, it is probable that the business would be forced into bankruptcy. On the other hand, if these liabilities and fixed expenses were very small or non-existent, it is probable that the business would suffer no loss at all.

It is true that the expression of financial statement values in terms of a fixed private commodity dollar would eliminate changes in values due to the fluctuations of our present medium of exchange. It is to be doubted, however, whether such a procedure can be seriously considered at this time. In the first place, such financial statements would probably be wholly unintelligible to laymen and, in the second place, it is likely that even experts would encounter difficulties due to the fact that liabilities as well as assets would have to be expressed in terms of this commodity dollar. During booms and depressions, most asset values would tend to remain stable but most liability values would tend to decline and rise. Thus, unless legal dollars as of the date of the balance sheet happened to be identical with the commodity dollar employed, it would be necessary to make a calculation before such a simple thing as the debt of a business could be ascertained in present money. Also, both net worth and earnings would have to be retranslated into present dollars before a creditor or stockholder could determine the value of his holdings in current money. Under the circumstances, it seems far better to delay the preparation of financial statements in terms of a fixed commodity dollar until the Government shall have made such a commodity dollar legal or shall have otherwise stabilized our medium of exchange. The preparation of financial statements in terms of a fixed legal commodity dollar would, of course, be a far different matter than their preparation in terms of a fixed private commodity dollar, because liabilities as well as assets would then be unaffected by fluctuations in the value of gold.

Business men and laymen instinctively feel that they have lost money if the number of dollars which they possess declines, even though this smaller sum of dollars may have the same purchasing power as the former larger sum. When accountants prepare financial statements showing changes in money values rather than changes in purchasing power, they are only doing what people generally do, and the change in financial condition that they exhibit is the same change in financial condition that almost every individual would compute for himself were his personal resources involved. The date at the top of a balance sheet is sufficient information to enable an expert to translate the present values shown into terms of any commodity dollar that he may wish to invent, and thus this expert could translate a series of financial statements into fluctuations of earning power if he desired. The public and the business world, however, are far from familiar with such a theory, and accountants must, if their figures are to be understood, prepare financial statements in accordance with a concept comprehensible to laymen.

STABILIZED ACCOUNTING. The problem offered to accountants by changes in the value of money has been attacked in a somewhat different fashion by Henry W. Sweeny in his able work *Stabilized Accounting*.[1] Sweeny's view is that the purpose of accounting statements should be to exhibit changes in purchasing power. To accomplish this purpose he attempts, through a system of grouping and averaging, to translate *every entry on the books* into terms

[1] Henry W. Sweeny, *Stabilized Accounting*, New York and London, Harper & Brothers, 1936.

of a commodity dollar equal in purchasing power to the legal medium of exchange existing at the date of the balance sheet. Changes in the value of money are computed by means of a commodity index intended to show fluctuations in general purchasing power. Changes in the value of specific assets may be computed from three different sets of data, stated in the order of their preference: From market prices or appraisals of replacement cost, from individual commodity indices for individual localities, and lastly, from the general purchasing power index mentioned above. It is emphasized that market prices and appraisals of replacement cost are more desirable as valuation bases than are original costs modified by commodity indices.

The balance sheet results obtained from this rather complicated treatment of the accounts are strikingly similar to those obtained more simply by the methods outlined in this book, although there are differences in detail due to the different concept employed. Thus, if market prices and replacement costs are used, the two balance sheets would be identical as regards assets, liabilities, and total net worth. The only difference would be in the allocation of net worth as between capital and surplus. If the general commodity index doubled during a year, Stabilized Accounting would show both the original capital account and surplus account at twice their former amounts and would omit the amount of this increase from earnings, whereas the writer would exhibit the capital account and surplus account unchanged and would show the entire increase in net worth as earnings. Similarly, if the commodity index halved, Stabilized Accounting would halve the capital account and surplus account and would automatically credit the amount of this decrease to earnings.

A simple illustration will suffice to show how confusing Stabilized Accounting might be to business men. Assume a business with only $2,000 cash, $1,000 capital, and $1,000 surplus. No transactions take place during the year and, at its end, the business still possesses the same $2,000. The commodity index, however, has doubled during the year. The writer would exhibit the balance sheet at the end of the year unchanged with no profit or loss. Stabilized Accounting, however, would exhibit a balance sheet showing the capital as $2,000 and the surplus wiped out. It would also exhibit an earnings statement showing that the business had lost $2,000, or all of its former capital and surplus during the year. Regardless of how correctly such figures may interpret the concept employed, they clearly do not talk the language of business men and the public in general.

With reference to the profit and loss account, both the net and detailed results obtained by Stabilized Accounting are strikingly different from those obtained by the methods recommended in this work. The entire difference in the net result, however, is accounted for by the fact that Stabilized Accounting automatically omits from the profit and loss statement that portion of the profits or losses which are reflected in the adjustment necessary to restate net worth on the basis of the general commodity index level existing at the date of the balance sheet. Thus if a business possessing $1,000 capital and $1,000 surplus earned $4,000 during a period when the general commodity index doubled, Stabilized Accounting would show the net earnings for the period as only $2,000, and the other $2,000 earnings would be regarded, not as earnings, but as a normal increment necessary merely to maintain the purchasing power of the net worth as it was at the beginning of the period. Stabilized Accounting does not regard profits as an increase in money value. It regards them solely as an increase in purchasing power, i.e., an increase in the number of fixed commodity dollars which a business is theoretically worth. This viewpoint is apt to change almost every book figure used in the detail of a profit and loss statement, as shown in the example immediately following.

ILLUSTRATION OF STABILIZED ACCOUNTING. Assume a corporation which started business on January 1 with $2,000 cash, $500 capital stock, $1,000 notes payable, and $500 surplus. Orthodox accountants, the writer, and Stabilized Accounting would all exhibit its balance sheet as follows:

BALANCE SHEET—JANUARY 1

Assets		*Liabilities*	
Cash	$2,000	Notes Payable	$1,000
		Capital Stock	500
		Surplus	500
	$2,000		$2,000

During the year ended December 31, the corporation made sales of $2,000 for cash. These sales were made steadily throughout the year. The corporation also incurred, steadily throughout the year, expenses of $1,000 which were immediately paid in cash. During the year the general commodity index rose steadily from 100 to 200.

Orthodox accountants and the writer would both exhibit the year end balance sheet and profit and loss statements as follows:

BALANCE SHEET—DECEMBER 31

Assets	*Liabilities*	
Cash $3,000	Notes Payable $1,000	
	Capital Stock 500	
	Surplus	
	Balance Jan. 1 . . . $ 500	
	Profit for year 1,000	
	Balance Dec. 31 . . 1,500	
$3,000	$3,000	

PROFIT AND LOSS STATEMENT FOR YEAR ENDED DECEMBER 31

Sales $2,000
Less Expenses 1,000
Profit for Year $1,000

Stabilized Accounting, however, would exhibit the year end balance sheet and profit and loss statement as follows:

BALANCE SHEET—DECEMBER 31

Assets	*Liabilities*	
Cash $3,000	Notes Payable $1,000	
	Capital Stock 1,000	
	Surplus	
	Balance Jan. 1 . . . $1,000	
	Profit for year . . . none	
	Balance Dec. 31 . . 1,000	
$3,000	$3,000	

PROFIT AND LOSS STATEMENT FOR YEAR
ENDED DECEMBER 31

Sales	$2,666.66
Less Expenses	1,333.33
Profit on Operations	1,333.33
Add Profit on changes in money value:	
Notes Payable	1,000.00
	2,333.33
Deduct loss on changes in money value:	
Cash	2,333.33
Profit for Year	none

It will have been seen that the only difference between the two year-end balance sheets lies in the composition of the net worth, whose total is identical in both instances. The two profit and loss statements, however, vary so greatly that not a single item is alike in both instances. This disparity is caused because, unlike the writer, Stabilized Accounting is not content merely to express present existing values in terms of present money and to compare them with previous values stated in terms of previous money, but attempts to translate every figure on the books into terms of a private commodity dollar equal in purchasing power to present legal money. In addition it insists upon ascribing a profit or a loss to every asset or liability, whether now existing or not, which did not, during the period of its existence, fluctuate in value exactly as did the general commodity index.

For explanation, the sales figure of $2,666.66 shown in the stabilized profit and loss account is merely the book figure of $2,000 restated in terms of a commodity dollar equal in purchasing power to the year-end legal dollar. Sales were made steadily throughout the year and the commodity index rose steadily from 100 to 200 throughout the year. Therefore the average of all sales must have been made when the commodity index averaged 150. The purchasing power of $2,000 at a commodity index level of 150 is equal to the purchasing power of $2,666.66 at a commodity index level of 200. Therefore $2,666.66 is the figure which expresses the purchasing power value of the sales in terms of year-end money.

Similarly the expenses were incurred steadily throughout the year and therefore the average of all expenses must have been incurred when the commodity index averaged 150. Restated in terms of dollars at a commodity index level of 200, the $1,000 expenses becomes $1,333.33 expenses.

Notes payable remained unchanged during the year while the commodity index rose steadily from 100 to 200. A note payable is a money value liability, i.e., it always represents the same number of present legal dollars regardless of how the value of those dollars may fluctuate. Therefore, the item of notes payable represented at the end of the year a liability of one thousand year-end dollars, whereas at the start of the year it represented the equivalent of a liability of two thousand year-end dollars. This is true because the purchasing power of $1,000 at a commodity index level of 100 is equal to the purchasing power of $2,000 at a commodity index level of 200. Therefore, in terms of purchasing power, the business profited from the change in the commodity index by the sum of one thousand year-end dollars.

Cash is a money value asset, hence a change in the commodity index level always occasions a profit or a loss in purchasing power to the possessor of cash. The business in question possessed $2,000 cash at the start of the year and increased this steadily throughout the entire year to $3,000. Therefore $2,000 of the year-end cash was held throughout the entire year, and the balance of $1,000 was acquired when the commodity index averaged 150. This is true, even though we use the Stabilized Accounting technique of considering cash to be disbursed always in the order of its receipt, because it was assumed that both sales and expenses were cash transactions and that both were consummated steadily throughout the year. Hence the disbursement of cash must invariably have been accompanied by the receipt of cash. The business lost purchasing power to the extent of two thousand year-end dollars in connection with the $2,000 cash which it held throughout the year, because $2,000 at a commodity index level of 100 is equal in purchasing power to $4,000 at a commodity index level of 200. Also the business lost purchasing power to the extent of 333.33 year-end dollars in connection with the $1,000 cash which it acquired at an average commodity index level of 150, because $1,000 at a commodity level of 150 is equal in purchasing power to $1,333.33 at a commodity level of 200. Thus the business had a total loss of purchasing power equal to 2,333.33 year-end dollars by virtue of its possession of cash during a period of rising commodity prices.

For purposes of comparison, Stabilized Accounting each year revises all previous financial statements so that they express their information in terms of a private commodity dollar equal to the legal dollar as of the date of the last balance sheet. The same result could be secured with less effort through the use of a permanently fixed private commodity dollar, but apparently it is thought that the labor of constant revision does not outweigh the advantage of making at least the final balance sheet intelligible to laymen by causing it to express values as of its date, in terms of money as of its date. The final profit and loss statement fails fully to meet this requirement because all transactions, expressed by the books and understood by laymen in terms of money as of the dates of the transactions, are restated by Stabilized Accounting in terms of money as of the date of the balance sheet.

CRITICISM OF STABILIZED ACCOUNTING. It seems evident that an unbiased criticism of Stabilized Accounting must give great credit to its originator. Sweeny has clearly seen the glaring faults of accepted accounting principles. Furthermore he has undertaken to remedy these faults in a very definite and final manner by refusing to express business facts in terms of a fluctuating legal medium of exchange, and by expressing them instead in terms of a commodity dollar representing a given amount of purchasing power. The result is, within the limits of accuracy of the data available, an exhaustive and mathematically impregnable system for displaying changes in purchasing power. Whether or not one approves the concept employed by Stabilized Accounting, he must admit that it completely achieves its announced purpose.

It appears to the writer that there are two important objections to the general use of Stabilized Accounting. The first of these is that the concept employed may be far beyond the comprehension of the ordinary man or woman who would have to depend for financial information upon the figures presented. The purpose of accounting is to supply information, and it must not be forgotten that data of any character, however accurate, ceases to be information if it is expressed in terms which the recipient cannot understand. One can imagine the difficulty of explaining to a group of stockholders, or even to a board of directors, why actual sales of $2,000 are stated to be $2,666.66, or how a loss of $2,000 was sustained in connection with $2,000 cash which never left the company's treasury. Such data would not inform the ordinary stockholder or the ordinary director. It would merely make him doubt the accountant's sanity. Very few people are familiar with even the rudimentary theories of political economy. Stabilized Accounting would require them not only to be familiar with economic theory, but would also require them to possess the ability to discard concepts which have become second nature to them, and automatically to regard commonplace facts from the viewpoint of a different concept. This is an extremely difficult matter, as anyone who has attempted to understand Einstein will appreciate, and it is to be doubted whether many of us could successfully accomplish it without years of constant and determined practice.

The second important objection to Stabilized Accounting derives from the fact that, even if stockholders and business men could understand and apply its concept, the information which they would gain might not, in most cases, be as valuable to them as would be the same information presented according to the concept now in almost universal use. When a man says that he was worth $1,000 a year ago,

virtually all people instinctively understand that the man
means that he was worth one thousand of the kind of dollars
existing a year ago. When a man says that he earned
$10,000 during the calendar year 1930, virtually all
people instinctively understand that the man means that
he earned ten thousand of the kind of dollars in existence
when he earned them. That is the concept now in almost
universal use, and it is capable of conveying valuable information that cannot be conveyed by the commodity dollar
concept. It is important to know that, barring capital changes
and dividends, if a business reports net earnings of
$100,000 during a year, its net worth in money at the end
of the year must be exactly $100,000 greater than it was at
the start of the year. Stabilized Accounting might easily
report net earnings of $100,000 for a business and yet
show that it was worth considerably less money after making these earnings than before it earned them. It is important to know that earnings mean an increase in dollar value
and that losses mean a decrease in dollar value, even though
either of these conditions might mean an increase or a decrease in purchasing power.

A man in an airplane traveling toward the setting sun
may conceive that he is traveling westward, or he may conceive that he is traveling backwards eastward at a rate of
speed equal to that of the rotation of the earth less that of
his plane. The latter concept is more accurate than the first
because it conforms to a broader set of facts, but the former
concept is much simpler, more practical, and more valuable
for the vast majority of earth dwellers. Stabilized Accounting, through the use of a complex technique, expresses a
concept which is admittedly capable of withstanding more

tests than the more simple concept now almost universally held. But it is seriously to be doubted that the simpler concept cannot be made the more valuable. The great need of accountancy is to tell economic truths, honestly expressed in terms of the concept now in universal use. Until this has been done, it seems futile to ask the accounting profession not only to tell the truth, but to express it in terms of a difficult and unfamiliar concept which at the present time would be incomprehensible to vast numbers of people.

VII

MARKET PRICES

It has been stated that the economic value of a thing is its market price or is evidenced by its imputed market price. But what is meant by market price? A shopper may buy a reproduction of a painting at one store and then walk across the street to a less expensive store and buy an exactly similar reproduction for one-half as much. Do such prices constitute market prices and, if so, which price represents the value of such a picture? In other words, what sort of market must exist in order to make its prices acceptable as economic values?

Markets. In a sense any place where goods are bought and sold is a market and the prices there established do constitute values *within that market*. Hence, if a picture is sold for ten dollars in a store, the value of such a picture at the time of the sale is ten dollars *within the market established by the store*. If such a picture is sold for five dollars in a less expensive store across the street, the value of the picture at the time of the sale is five dollars *within the market established by the less expensive store*. If the two sales take place simultaneously, then the picture has two different simultaneous values, each obtaining in a different market. In an economic sense each market is a world in itself. It is a place where buyers and sellers meet and make prices. These prices are conclusive within that market. *But that market may be far from representative of the world at large or of the community within which it functions.* Its prices may be not at all representative of the prices that might be established in a freer, broader, more competitive market which embraced all of the effective supply and demand within that community. Not every market turns out prices that may be used by an accountant as economic values. As a matter of fact, very few of them do. The decision of an accountant as to whether a market is acceptable or unacceptable for the determination of economic values is perhaps the most important decision that will confront him in connection with the whole subject of the valuation of assets.

In order to produce market prices that may be taken as economic values in a community or world sense, a market must give free rein to the law of supply and demand because, as has been seen, economic values are created by the counteraction of supply and demand and a market is merely a place where these two forces meet and equalize at a price. If either supply or demand is prevented from functioning freely, the existing market price will not truthfully reflect the result of the counteraction of these two forces and consequently cannot be accepted as economic value. The market may faithfully reflect the result of the counteraction of a part of these forces, but that is not enough. Only prices which are the result of the counteraction of substantially all the effective supply and demand within a community can be said truly to determine the economic values of that community. A market suitable for the constant reflection of economic values must possess the absolute characteristics of being free and competitive, and must possess to a satisfactory degree the relative characteristics of being broad and active.

FREE MARKETS. A free market is one in which no constituted authority interferes with the free functioning of supply and demand. A market where sellers are prohibited by law from asking more than a certain price for their wares is not a free market. Thus, if the Government decrees $1.00 a bushel to be the maximum price at which wheat may sell on the Chicago Board of Trade, this wheat market is no longer free, its wheat prices no longer faithfully reflect the counteraction of all the effective supply and demand within the community, and are no longer acceptable as economic values. There is some question as to whether a price of less than $1.00 a bushel in such a market would not fully reflect the counteraction of supply and demand and thus constitute a true economic value, but it is probable that the governmental limit of $1.00 would be used by sellers as a backlog and would thus tend to restrict the free operation of supply and demand regardless of the price. In general it may be said that no market where constituted authority arbitrarily limits supply or demand, or fixes or restricts prices, is a free market or one whose prices may be accepted as economic values.

COMPETITIVE MARKETS. A competitive market is one where buyers and sellers compete not only with each other but among themselves. A threefold competition of buyers with sellers, buyers with buyers, and sellers with sellers must be present if the complete market process is to prevail. This threefold competition is the very essence of the market process. It alone creates prices which may be used blindly and automatically as economic values.

If competition between buyers and sellers is lacking, the result may be merely a private price, determined in pursuance of some ulterior motive. A holding company may purchase some of the assets of its subsidiary at a price far below that which would prevail were the assets to be purchased under competitive conditions. The motive may be to defraud minority stockholders. A president may sell his corporation some land at a price vastly exceeding the price that could be obtained by its sale under competitive conditions. The motive may be to enrich the president at the expense of the corporation.

If competition between sellers or between buyers is lacking, the result will be a monopoly price, not a competitive market price. A group of men may corner the wheat market and temporarily raise the price of wheat to unprecedented levels. A water company supplying a desert town with artesian well water might, if unrestricted by law, temporarily raise its rates a hundredfold until new wells could be dug. A large canning company, controlling the demand over a large area, may for a time depress the price of farm produce and impoverish farmers within the area. These things might not happen, for a monopoly might earnestly desire to fix its price at a true economic level, but the fact remains that the monopoly can hardly know what the true economic value would be under competitive conditions. Therefore monopoly prices cannot be accepted as economic values.

A specialty company may manufacture a patented article and maintain a fixed sales price for it. This sales price should not be used as economic value because the market is noncompetitive save in the sense that possible substitutes may exist for the article in question. The specialty company should not therefore value its unsold articles at this sales price for balance sheet purposes. On the other hand, a copper company may produce refined copper and sell it in the open market in competition with other copper producers. The sales price of this copper does represent economic value and the copper company may properly value its unsold copper at that sales price. A department store does not constitute a competitive market, because the store itself is only the potential seller. When a holding company sells property to its wholly owned subsidiary, the price does not establish economic value because competition between buyer and seller is lacking.

Whenever an examination of a market reveals the fact that the threefold competition of buyers with themselves, sellers with themselves, and buyers with sellers, is lacking, then that market must be designated as noncompetitive and hence unsuitable for the creation of prices which may be taken as economic values.

BROAD MARKETS. A market is broad to the extent that its prices represent the counteraction of world supply and demand. Many organized commodity markets exist in the United States which may truly be said to be world-wide in their scope. Except during transitory periods of governmental interference, the price of wheat in Chicago is in actual fact determined by the potential supply of, and demand for, wheat the world over. The market price of copper depends as much upon supply and demand in foreign countries as in the United States. Several organized stock exchanges in American cities reflect world forces of supply and demand. These markets may therefore be said to possess broadness in the maximum degree because the attention of the potential buyers or sellers of the world is directly or indirectly focused upon them.

But suppose that the wheat buyers of a small local community meet the wheat sellers of that community and, without knowledge of world supply and demand, proceed to buy and sell wheat at $5.00 a bushel. The prices they establish do constitute values within the market that has been set up, but that market is far from broad. If one of the buyers or sellers should learn about Chicago prices for wheat, the prices obtaining in the small community might undergo instant revision because any buyer or seller might buy in Chicago and sell in the community and thus bring the community prices into line with Chicago prices. Since the Chicago market is infinitely broader than the community market, the effect on Chicago prices would be infinitesimal, whereas the effect on the community prices would be very great indeed. It may therefore be said that the broader the market, the more reliable are its market prices, and consequently the more readily may these prices be accepted as economic values.

The question of how broad a market must be before an accountant is justified in accepting its prices as economic values is peculiarly a question of judgment in the light of the existing facts. From an economist's viewpoint, economic values within a community are conclusively evidenced only by market prices established in free and competitive markets which are sufficiently broad to reflect substantially all of the supply and demand within that community. The question facing an accountant is whether a market is sufficiently broad to include the forces of supply and demand with which a business deals. In general it may be said that no market should be considered satisfactorily broad which does not include both buyers and sellers of a type that may reasonably be presumed to be well informed regarding the greater part of the entire effective world supply and demand of the things being marketed. Thus a local small-town real estate market might be considered amply broad for the recording of economic values because all of the supply of, and probably most of the demand for, real estate in that town comes from that immediate vicinity, and local real estate men undoubtedly would be familiar with local conditions. But semi-private transactions in ivory tusks between well-informed buyers, on one hand, and African natives who are ignorant of the world value of ivory, on the other hand, do not constitute a market broad enough to make prices acceptable as economic values for a company engaged in the ivory trade on a world-wide basis.

ACTIVE MARKETS. The activity of a market is measured by the frequency with which sales are made. If bid and offered quotations are available, activity is not essential, because the fluctuation of the bid and offered figures will supply a dependable clue to economic values. If bid and offered quotations are not available, then, in the absence of actual sales, an accountant will have no means of determining the probable rise or fall in value since the date of the last sale. If the elapsed time has been considerable, the probability of unknown changes in value may be very great.

The degree of activity necessary to constitute an acceptable market depends largely upon the commodity in question and its susceptibility to sudden changes in value. The question is one involving the judgment of an accountant as to the probable facts. Where conditions are such as to make it unlikely that the last market price would approximate a present market price, it cannot be accepted as representing present economic value.

ACCEPTABLE MARKETS. Although it may seem that the requirements necessary to qualify a market for the constant reflection of economic values are stringent, yet it should not be inferred that few markets suitable for the reflection of economic values exist. In the United States free, competitive, broad, and active markets normally exist for trading in most of the important raw materials and in not a few finished articles. These include: stocks, bonds, cotton, wool, rubber, tin, copper, lead, zinc, tobacco, wheat, corn, rye, oats, barley, silk, cocoa, hides, pepper, gasoline, crude oil, ribs, lard, bellies, coffee, sugar, molasses, flax seed, cotton seed, cotton seed oil, cotton seed meal, bran, middlings, soya beans, clover seed, timothy seed, butter, eggs, potatoes, naval stores, fish, and poultry.

Once the magnitude of the field covered by the above items is comprehended, the importance to accountants of a knowledge of markets and market prices becomes evident. The existence of market prices which enable accountants to determine truthful economic values accurately and effortlessly has become a commonplace part of our present civilization.

DETERMINATION OF MARKET PRICES. A man may own an ordinary scale for weighing people. He steps on the scale and immediately the indicator rises from zero to 150 pounds, which is his weight. The downward gravitational force exerted by his body is equaled by the upward thrust of the scale at 150 pounds. If it be assumed that the downward force of his body represents demand, that the upward thrust of the machine represents supply, and that the weight indicated represents price, a fair illustration is presented of how market prices are determined. A market price is the price at which the forces of supply and demand are equal in the sense that supply is greater than demand at any higher figure, and demand is greater than supply at any lower figure. If supply or demand should change and be no longer equal at the old price, a new point of equalization would result which would be a new market price. A market is a very sensitive indicator of value, and if the relation of supply to demand changes, the market price will change, just as a weighing scale will indicate different weights if a person gains or loses weight. In each case, however, the existing market price will accurately reflect present economic value, just as in each case the weighing machine will reflect present weight.

Few markets are so active that sales of a given commodity or thing are made constantly. The period between sales may be hours, days, weeks, or months. In the absence of actual sales the relative position of supply and demand may be made known by bid and offered prices. A bid price is the highest price bid by any potential buyer in the market in question, and an offered price is the lowest price at which any potential seller is willing to sell. Thus if the highest bid price for wheat is 80¢ per bushel and the lowest offered price is 81¢ per bushel, a request for a quotation on the price of wheat will elicit the reply that wheat is 80¢ @ 81¢. The next sale of wheat may be at 80¢ if the supply is more urgent than the demand, or the next sale may be at 81¢ if the demand is more urgent than the supply. On the other hand, the bid and offered prices may be changed as potential buyers or sellers withdraw old bids or offers and make new ones, without any sales at all having been consummated in the meantime.

Suppose that the last sale of wheat in a given market on a given day takes place at 82¢ and that after this sale the market closes with wheat bid at 80¢ and offered at 81¢. Which of these three prices constitutes the market price of wheat, and upon which of them should an accountant base his valuation of wheat at the close of the day in question? Before attempting to answer this question an inquiry into the nature and source of published bid and offered prices must be made. Unfortunately published bid and offered prices often do not tell the whole story about supply and demand due to the limitations of the different market mechanisms for recording bids and offers. In unorganized markets such as local real estate markets no provision at all is made for a public record of bids and offers, whereas in organized markets such as the various stock and commodity exchanges the mechanism provided may at times prove faulty.

For example, a member on the floor of the New York Stock Exchange may buy or sell for his own account or for the accounts of his clients. Buying or selling for the accounts of clients usually originates by means of bids or offers, called orders. These orders may be limited orders, market orders, or discretionary orders. A limited order may be a bid for a certain quantity of a certain stock at not more than a certain price per share, or it may be an offer to sell this stock at not less than a certain price per share. A market order is an order to buy or sell stock at the most favorable price immediately obtainable, whatever that price may be. A discretionary order allows the broker to use his own judgment in one or more particulars, and may range from a simple instruction covering 100 shares of stock to commitments charging a broker with the accumulation or liquidation of hundreds of thousands of shares over weeks or months of time.

Of the different types of orders that may be on the floor of the stock exchange, only the limited orders usually have much part in determining the bid and offered prices published at the close of the market, and at times even some of these may not be taken into consideration. Suppose for instance that a customer in a broker's office gives an order to buy 100 shares of Auburn at 80. This order is telephoned to the broker on the floor of the exchange who takes it to the Auburn post where he finds that Auburn is currently selling at 85. This broker may be busy with other orders and, not wishing to wait at the Auburn post on the chance that Auburn may sell down to 80, he places his order with the Auburn specialist who will execute it for a small commission provided the opportunity arises. This specialist has written in his book a number of limited orders both to buy and to sell Auburn at different prices, all of which have been placed with him by other brokers who did not wish to wait at the Auburn post. Now assume that another broker who is not busy receives an order to buy 1,000 Auburn at 84. This is an important order, so the broker decides not to give it to the specialist but to wait at the Auburn post himself in the hope that Auburn may sell down to 84 and that he may be able to execute the order himself without paying the specialist a commission. Auburn does not sell at 84 that day, however, and closes at 84½. After the close, the Auburn specialist finds from his book that his highest bid for Auburn is 80 and the lowest offer is 85. He therefore turns in the bid and offered prices on Auburn as 80 @ 85. Specialists for other stocks also turn in their bid and offered prices, and these are printed on the tape and published in the newspapers as the bid and offered prices existing at the close of the stock exchange on that day. But, in the case of Auburn, the published bid and offered prices were not accurate because there was an unannounced bid on the floor for 1,000 Auburn at 84. Also there may have been brokers on the floor at the close willing to sell Auburn at 84⅝ or to buy it at 84⅜ if they had the opportunity. But the public is not informed about these bids and offers unless they are announced by the brokers in question and are proclaimed to be still good at the close of the market.

Hence it can be seen that bid and offered prices, even where obtainable, may not always accurately reflect the true status of supply and demand for the good in question, although they do fix the maximum spread that may exist. If the published bid and offered prices for a thing are 80 @ 85, it is obvious that any correction of these two figures must be in the direction of moving them closer together, not farther apart. If a bid actually exists at 80 and an offer actually exists at 85, a lower bid or a higher offer would not affect the validity of the 80 @ 85 quotation in the least because bid and offered prices consist by definition of the highest bid and the lowest offer. Also it is certain that no bid could exist at a price equal to or higher than the published offer because in this case a sale would have resulted and the respective bid and offer would have been taken out of existence. Similarly, it is sure that no offer could exist at a price equal to or lower than the published bid, otherwise a sale would have resulted and this bid and offer would have been eliminated. If the bid and offer were not for equal quantities, then all of the smaller and an equal quantity of the larger would have been eliminated.

When this is understood it becomes evident that published bid and offered prices, when available, constitute extremely important indices of market prices. They may not tell the whole truth but they do tell the truth and nothing but the truth, as far as they go. Market price has been defined as the price at which the forces of supply and demand are equal in the sense that supply is greater than demand at any higher figure and demand is greater than supply at any lower figure. This being the case, it is clear that market price must necessarily fall somewhere between the published bid and offered prices. It also necessarily follows that the only situation in which a last sales price could be taken as the closing market price, without reference to bid and offered prices, would be where the closing gong actually sounded at the precise moment that such a sale was made. Such a sales price would necessarily fall within the limits of the highest surviving bid and the lowest surviving offer. At this point, therefore, at least part of the question which initiated this discussion can be answered. If the last sale of wheat is at 82¢ per bushel, whereas the closing quotation is 80¢ @ 81¢, it is certain that the closing market price cannot be higher than 81¢ or lower than 80¢ and that therefore the last sales price of 82¢ must be disregarded.

But the question at once arises as to what point, between the bid and offered prices, shall be taken as the market price. This is a difficult question because, as is usually true of difficult questions, all of the facts upon which to base a decision are not known. If one could be sure that the published bid price was really the highest bid, and that the published offered price was really the lowest offer, one would have a solid basis of fact upon which to rear a sound conclusion. Unfortunately, however, one cannot be sure of these things, due, as has been explained above, to the faulty mechanism that usually exists for recording bids and offers and making them known. Under the circumstances the most logical thing that can be done is to accept the published bid and offered prices as being the highest bid and the lowest offer existing. There is no way in which to determine on which side the error exists, if any does exist, and in any event it is probable that, in the vast majority of cases, either no error will exist or that it will be insignificant. Usually bids and offers on active stocks and commodities are very close together, and it is precisely on the less active stocks and commodities that there is the least chance of unrecorded bids or offers existing.

If published bid and offered prices are accepted, the rest is pure reasoning. In the problem cited, the highest bid is 80¢ and the lowest offer is 81¢. But both of these figures cannot be used as a market price. One figure only may be used. Demand exists up to 80¢ and supply exists down to 81¢. At 80¢ demand exceeds supply and at 81¢ supply exceeds demand. But what about the vacuum in between? Here there is no supply and no demand. Clearly 80½¢ represents the point that is equidistant from both supply and demand and constitutes the only price at which they may be said to be equal. The market price therefore is 80½¢, and 80½¢ is the economic value of wheat as long as 80¢ remains the high bid and 81¢ remains the low offer.

Here the objection may be entered that the bids at 80¢ and below may represent a much greater quantity of wheat than the offers at 81¢ and above. For example, there may be 1,000,000 bushels of wheat wanted at 80¢ whereas only 10,000 bushels may be offered at 81¢. In this case a wheat speculator would be certain to describe the wheat market as very strong and to conclude that the price of wheat was more likely to advance than to decline. The accountant, however, is not concerned with forecasting the probable future price of wheat. He is concerned only with a determination of its market price under existing conditions. The market price of wheat could not possibly advance or decline unless a change took place in its demand or supply. Such changes cannot be foretold with accuracy. It is possible that the bid for 1,000,000 bushels at 80¢ might be withdrawn and an offer of 1,000,000 bushels at 81¢ be entered in a few seconds' time. Under the circumstances, an accountant is not justified in prophecy. He must, under all conditions, stay as close to the facts as he can. Wheat is in supply down to 81¢. It is in demand up to 80¢. Not one bushel is wanted above 80¢, nor is one bushel offered at less than 81¢. The price of wheat is therefore 80¢ @ 81¢ under

conditions as they actually exist. The accountant may logically reduce this price to one figure, equidistant from the
bid and offer, but he has no justification for assuming conditions to be different than they actually are, however
probable he may think such a change to be, or however
soon in the future he may think it likely to occur.

From the foregoing, it can be seen that market price is in
reality a price equidistant from the high bid and the low
offer, and that this market price can be in error only to the
extent that not all the facts may be known regarding the
high bid and the low offer. Allowing for such errors as may
occasionally occur, there is good reason to believe that market prices so determined will on the average be considerably more accurate than the use of last sales prices. This is
because last sales prices need not necessarily bear any fixed
relation to the position of supply and demand existing after
the sale takes place. The use of last high bid prices is entirely unjustifiable, because such bids cannot possibly represent market prices. The greater the disparity between the
high bid and the low offer, the greater the injustice to potential sellers. If a corporation owns a large block of inactive bonds, quoted at 40 bid, 80 asked, stockholders who
wish to sell their stock in the corporation should not be led
to believe that the bonds are worth only 40, to the enormous
advantage of those who wish to buy the stock. The fair price
of the bonds, based on the existing situation, is 60.

Economic values should be determined from both bid
and offered prices whenever these are available. Bid prices
alone should never be used for this purpose. Last sales
prices should be taken to indicate economic values only
when bids and offers are unavailable, on the ground that

they probably come closer to indicating the state of supply and demand than would imputed market prices.

Use of Market Prices. All this is quite contrary to present accounting practice. When a modern accountant desires to value something at market he uses either the last sales price or the published bid price. He is wrong on both counts because market price is neither the last sales price nor is it the bid price, as has been explained above. The use by an accountant of sales prices, when bid and offered prices are available, is probably caused by a lack of understanding of the mechanics of price making through the counteraction of supply and demand. The use of bid prices as values probably occurs partly because of an accountant's tendency to understate values to please creditors and partly because he assumes that what he is attempting to do is to record liquidating values. But the value of a thing is not what it *could* be sold for *if* it were offered for sale. Its value is what it *is being bought and sold for* or, if it is not being bought and sold, its logical price under the ratio of supply and demand that *actually exists*. Assuming a high bid of 80¢ and a low offer of 81¢, no accountant should arbitrarily lower the offer to 80¢. He should understand that just as many people may be harmed by an understatement of assets and earnings as by their overstatement, and that just as many people may be interested in the purchase price as in the sales price. He should realize that both buyers and sellers look to him to give them an impartial statement of present fact on which they can base their own estimates of the future. It would be no worse arbitrarily to raise the bid to 81¢ and to use that figure as value. It is an accountant's duty to deal with the facts as he finds them, not to alter them to conform to some imaginary action on the part of his client. Economic values are determined by the counteraction of supply and demand as it actually occurs, not by what *would* occur under different conditions.

For illustration, an accountant may be preparing the balance sheet and profit and loss statement as of December 31, of an investment trust which owns 100,000 shares of General Motors stock. The accountant may have read "The Fable of the Two Investment Trusts" in the first chapter, and may have resolved to value this stock at its economic value and to treat unrealized profits or losses as earnings. No sooner will he have made this resolution, however, than a number of perplexing doubts and fears will assail him. It will occur to him that he is committing himself to the valuation of this stock on a liquidating basis, i.e., on the basis of what it could be sold for. He may know that the closing market price of General Motors stock on December 31 was $40 a share, but he also knows that if the investment trust had attempted to sell 100,000 shares of General Motors stock on December 31, this additional supply of stock would have depressed the market price so that much less than $40 per share would probably have been realized. He also knows that, if this 100,000 shares had been sold, a large broker's commission would have had to be paid and, assuming a profit on the sale, a large liability for income tax would have been incurred. He will therefore argue to himself that $40 a share is far more than the stock would have brought, that the broker's commission should be deducted from any value set up, and that the liability for income tax should be reflected in the accounts before preparing either balance sheet or profit and loss statement. Thus he will have reasoned himself into a predicament where he must guess what the stock could have been sold for, and then must calculate a broker's commission and an income tax on the basis of this first guess. At this point he will be apt to give up in despair and to revert to his old practice of using original cost as value.

The flaw in the accountant's reasoning is that he has forgotten that it is his duty to record present values under conditions as they are, and that it is decidedly not his duty to record values as they might be under an entirely different set of conditions. The accountant knows that the value of General Motors stock at the close of the market on December 31 *was $40 a share under conditions that then existed.* Why should he arbitrarily assume an increase of urgent supply on that date to the extent of 100,000 shares? It would be as reasonable to assume an increase of urgent demand to the extent of 100,000 shares. The stock was not sold and it may not be sold for fifty years. When it is sold the sale may be a private one with no broker's commission involved and the income tax may have been repealed many years before. Many things may happen in the future to prevent a sale, a broker's commission, or an income tax. An accountant should not act as a prophet. Creditors and stockholders can do that as well as he can. His duty is to tell the present facts, not to indulge in private prophecies. In his report, or as a footnote, he can state what might happen if the stock were sold, he can call attention to his own opinion of what would be realized, what the broker's commission would be, and how much income tax would have to be paid if the income tax law were not changed. He can also, if he desires, state his own opinion of what would happen if civil war broke out, or if all General Motors executives were assassinated. But he has no right to prepare financial statements on the basis of such prophecies as these, no matter how firmly he may be convinced of their probability. When financial statements purport to tell facts as of December 31, they should tell those facts as truthfully as possible, unmodified by future improbabilities, probabilities, or even certainties. To do otherwise only deceives stockholders and creditors, and deprives them of a truthful basis of present fact upon which to base their own estimates of the future.

A company may carry in its inventory a million pounds of refined copper having an economic value of 7¢ a pound. This means that 7¢ is the price at which it is equally easy either to sell or to buy copper, without more effort than is occasioned in offering it or in bidding for it. The company may be a purchaser of copper or it may be a producer and seller of copper. Perhaps a million pounds could neither be purchased nor sold at 7¢ a pound, or perhaps much more than a million pounds could be either purchased or sold at 7¢ a pound. This would depend upon how the ratio of demand and supply changed at the time the copper was bid for or was offered. In other words, it would depend upon future conditions. The accountant cannot presume to know future conditions but he does know, within practical limits, what the economic value of copper is under conditions that actually exist. He is therefore justified in showing the million pounds of copper in the company's balance sheet at its present economic value under the conditions that existed as of the date of the balance sheet. Whether more or less than this would ultimately be paid or realized by the company is a matter for the future to decide. The accountant has done his duty in supplying to interested persons a truthful statement of present fact upon which they can base their own calculations of the future.

Brokers' Commissions and other Expenses. An explanation may here be in order relative to the treatment of transportation charges, brokers' commissions, and similar items normally incurred in connection with purchases or sales. If a Chicago flour mill possesses wheat purchased on the Chicago Board of Trade, it will have paid not only the market price of the wheat, but also the cost of transporting the wheat to its mill, and the commission charged by its brokers for executing its buying order. Should it desire to resell the wheat on the Chicago Board of Trade, it will have to transport it to a designated Chicago grain elevator and pay a broker's commission to have its selling order executed. The question at issue is at what price the flour mill should value its wheat after it has purchased and transported it to its mill. Present accounting procedure sanctions the grouping of the charges for transportation and brokers' commissions with the actual cost of the wheat, and treats the combined total as the original cost of the wheat and hence as its value.

A moment's consideration will suffice to reveal how wrong is this method of valuing assets. In order to present an impartial statement of fact which will be of value equally to potential buyers and to potential sellers, a balance sheet should exhibit assets at their economic value. Economic value is the amount for which an asset is, or logically could be, either bought or sold with *equal* facility at a given moment. If the wheat is valued at its market price plus brokers' commissions and transportation charges, the value exhibited will not be impartial as between potential buyers and sellers of the flour mill's securities, but will be weighted in favor of potential sellers and to the disadvantage of potential buyers. The truth of the matter is that the wheat could be replaced only at its market price plus transportation and commission, and it could be sold only at its market price less transportation and commission. Why, then, should it be valued at its market price plus transportation and commission when it could be sold only for this amount less duplicate transportation and duplicate commissions?

Obviously the value for which the wheat could be either bought or sold with equal facility is its market price unmodified by any additions or deductions whatsoever. The market price which would most nearly represent *both* the highest net amount realizable from its sale and the lowest total cost of buying and transporting it to its present location, is its price in the nearest acceptable market. Since brokers' commissions must be substantially the same in any two competing markets, it is clear that when transportation charges are at a minimum the discrepancy between market price and net realization, or total cost, must be at a minimum. Under all ordinary conditions, marketable assets should be valued at their prices in the acceptable market nearest to the actual location of the assets. Transportation charges, brokers' commissions, and similar items should be treated as expenses, not as assets. To do otherwise deprives present and prospective security holders of an impartial basis of present fact by which to appraise the worth and earnings of a business.

In certain instances, when two or more acceptable markets exist for a given asset, inaccuracies may result if market prices in the nearest acceptable market are used as the sole index of economic values. Such instances are rare, but, when they exist, it may be necessary to give consideration to the prices prevailing in a second acceptable market, as well as to consider the prices prevailing in the nearest acceptable market alone. For example, acceptable markets for wheat exist both in Chicago and in New York. In New York, cash wheat consistently sells for approximately 6¢ more per bushel than in Chicago, due largely to the greater expense of transporting it from the Middle West where most of it is grown. Let us assume, therefore, that on a certain date cash wheat is selling in Chicago for $1.00 per bushel and in New York for $1.06 per bushel, the difference of 6¢ per bushel representing the freight rate between Chicago and New York. A Chicagoan may correctly value his wheat at $1.00 per bushel and a New Yorker may correctly value his wheat at $1.06 per bushel because in each of these instances the values used will most nearly represent *both* the highest net amount realizable and the lowest total cost, when all expense factors are considered. But assume wheat to be owned by an Ohioan, located one-third of the distance from Chicago to New York. Theoretically this Ohioan could buy wheat in Chicago for $1.00 per bushel plus 2¢ freight and could sell it in New York for $1.06 per bushel less 4¢ freight. His wheat should therefore be valued at $1.02 per bushel, which is the true market price at which it could be either bought or sold with equal facility. In other words, the differential of 6¢ between the two market prices should be allocated in accordance with the location of the asset between the two markets. The asset is located one-third of the distance from Chicago to New York, hence the Chicago price of $1.00 per bushel should be increased by one-third of the differential, or 2¢ per bushel. This will result in a figure of $1.02 per bushel, which is the true market price of the wheat in question. Situations such as this can arise only when several simultaneous circumstances prevail, namely: When the source of supply is localized, when the asset is expensive to transport, when two acceptable markets exist at considerably different distances from the localized source of supply, and when the asset is located between these markets and at a material distance from each.

CONCLUSION. The subject of acceptable market prices may be left with the reassertion that they, not original costs, are present economic values and that they should be used in financial statements in all cases where they are available, unmodified, save by way of comment, by any subsequent event, or supposition of an event. When two or more acceptable markets exist for the same asset, accountants should normally use the prices obtaining in the acceptable market nearest to the actual location of the asset. When a difference in distance, from a localized source of supply, causes two acceptable markets to register different market prices for the same asset, and when the asset is located between these markets, the difference in price should be prorated according to the location of the asset. Brokers' commissions, transportation charges, storage, insurance, and similar items are expenses, not assets. They merely cause a present sacrifice of cash for the expected benefit of a future gain. They are not balance sheet assets, any more than are other types of expenses. This reasoning is discussed more fully in Chapter XIII under "The Balance Sheet Function."

It may also be reasserted that market prices are the point at which supply and demand are equal, at the moment. If a sale is being made, that is momentarily the market price. After the sale has been made, the market price is midway between the highest surviving bid and the lowest surviving offer. Since sales are instantaneous affairs, whereas bids and offers are enduring until canceled by their makers or eliminated by sales, it follows that assets should be stated at prices determined by bids and offers, unless these are not available, in which case last sales prices should be used.

All this is predicated upon the market in question being free, competitive, and satisfactorily broad and active, as previously discussed. When market prices are not available, or when the existing market is not free and competitive, or is not sufficiently broad and active, then a new problem arises which will be discussed immediately, namely: that of imputing market prices which will evidence economic values in the absence of acceptable market prices.

VIII

IMPUTED MARKET PRICES

THE PREVIOUS chapter discussed the valuation of marketable assets, i.e., those assets which are traded in markets which are free, competitive, and satisfactorily broad and active. Such assets should invariably be valued at market price. Some assets, however, are traded only in markets which lack one or more of the required characteristics, and others are not traded in any market at all. Such assets are described as nonmarketable, and their economic values can be determined only by estimating or imputing the market prices that would prevail were acceptable markets to exist.

The imputed market price of a thing is an estimate of what its market price would be if existing supply were put in touch with existing demand through the medium of a free and competitive market. If all the facts were known regarding existing supply and demand the imputing of an exact market price would be a simple matter. Unfortunately such information is rarely, if ever, available. An imputed market price must therefore be determined by a less direct method. In other words, the factors influencing supply and demand must be analyzed in a search for a factor or a combination of factors that will lead to an approximation of market price, i.e., an index of economic value. Four important theories along this line of thought have been advanced by economists.

KARL MARX THEORY. Among these theories is the labor theory of value, commonly called the socialistic, or the Karl Marx theory. It holds that the economic values of different things tend to be proportionate to the respective quantities of labor required to produce them. Capital is regarded as stored-up labor. Rent of land and interest on capital are disregarded. Quite apart from its other defects, this theory offers little help in the imputation of market price. A calculation of the quantity of labor involved in the making of any fabricated article, from the time when its component elements were taken from the earth, would be extremely difficult because there are different types of labor of widely varying efficiency and difficulty which could be combined into one stated "quantity" only by a system of weighting which would of necessity be arbitrary. Also the facts on which to base such a calculation would probably be, to a large extent, quite as unknown as the market price which the calculation would be supposed to reveal.

MARGINAL UTILITY THEORY. Secondly, there is the marginal utility theory of value. It has been stated that market price is merely a price at which supply and demand are equal in the sense that sellers will not sell for less, nor will buyers pay more, at the moment. It has also been shown that it is the marginal utility of anything that measures its economic importance to each individual owner. Inasmuch as each buyer will tend to adjust his purchases on the basis of his own marginal utilities, it follows that the aggregate marginal utility of any one thing for buyers as a whole will determine the degree of preference given by buyers to that thing over other things. Therefore, argues the theory, the market price of things must be proportionate to the values of their aggregate marginal utilities. Whatever the merits or defects of this theory, it also fails to help in the attempt to impute market price because the aggregate marginal utility of a thing must be quite as unknown, in the absence of a market price, as is the market price itself.

DISPLACEMENT COST THEORY. Thirdly, there is the displacement cost theory of value. The purchase of any one thing displaces the purchase of something else. The production of any one thing displaces the production of something else. Some things can be produced in progressively larger quantities at decreasing cost, other things only at increasing cost. As changes take place in the amounts of any given thing that have to be sacrificed in order to purchase other things, each consumer will alter his budget in accordance with the relative importance to him of the things he purchases and the things that he must forego purchasing. Thus, between the preferences of buyers on one hand and the technical conditions determining the displacement costs of production on the other hand, there arises a tendency toward values which tends to bring production and consumption into full equilibrium. This theory attempts to explain the whole mechanism of value creation by showing the effect of varying supply cost tendencies on demand and by showing the simultaneous effect of demand on supply. It is merely a restatement of the simple concept of value as a product of supply and demand except that, instead of taking supply and demand at a given instant as static forces, it attempts to show how their varying involutions affect each other over the course of time. It is of no service in an effort to impute market price because it supplies no known factor upon which to base a calculation. Displacement cost is, under ordinary circumstances, just as unknown, in the absence of a market price, as is the market price itself.

REPLACEMENT COST THEORY. Finally, there is the replacement cost theory of value. This theory holds that the market price of a reproducible thing tends to be just high enough to pay its replacement cost. Replacement cost is defined as the cost of reproducing a thing plus a profit sufficient to provide a motive for so doing. In its simplest aspect, replacement cost is merely original cost brought up to date. Evidently this theory, if true, helps a great deal in the attempt to find an index of value upon which to impute market prices. Replacement costs are, on the whole, fairly definite and fairly easy of determination. Accountants and the general public are acquainted with them. Almost every business must calculate them, virtually as a matter of daily routine, before it can quote prices on its own goods or before it can prepare its own budget. Appraisal companies have been calculating replacement costs for many years and, in almost every community, professional appraisers exist who are well qualified to calculate them speedily and accurately.

It is probable that the replacement cost theory of value, as an economic theory, justifies its criticism of being one-sided and of failing to explain completely the entire play of forces making for the creation of economic values. The displacement cost theory doubtless fulfills this function in a more satisfactory manner. It is perhaps no more true

that costs of production exert a profound influence upon
demand, than that the state of demand exerts a profound
influence upon how much of a given thing shall be produced and upon what production costs shall be incurred.
The present discussion, however, is not concerned with
framing an all-inclusive theory to account for the interplay
of supply upon demand, but is merely concerned with determining the state of supply and demand at certain specific
times. The problem is to impute market price, not to explain the interworkings of the forces that give rise to it.
And regardless of whether one looks at the supply side of
the equation as with the labor theory, or at the demand
side as with the marginal utility theory, or at both sides as
with the displacement cost theory, it becomes increasingly
apparent that supply and demand constantly tend to
equalize, and that if one is known the other is pretty close
to being known. All theories agree that supply tends to
come into equilibrium with demand, that cost of production
tends to conform with aggregate marginal utilities, and it
matters not whether the forces of supply or those of demand
are the more important inasmuch as the tendency is always
for them to equalize, at a market price. If supply can be
accurately estimated, then demand can be approximately
estimated, and the error, if one exists, will be measured only
by the extent to which full equilibrium does not prevail
at the moment.

If the market price of a commodity should fall below its
replacement cost, production would tend to cease because
the commodity could be produced and sold only at a loss, or
at an insufficient profit. With production stopped, the ratio
of supply and demand would change to the advantage of

sellers, due to the lessening of supply through the consumption of the existing supply of the commodity. This would raise the market price until it became high enough to encourage production again. Similarly, if the market price of a commodity should rise above its replacement cost, increased production would be stimulated because the commodity could be sold at an unusually large profit. With production increased, the ratio of supply and demand would change to the advantage of the buyers, due to the larger supply from increased production. This would lower the market price until it became low enough to discourage production. In this manner market prices tend to hover about replacement costs, with the further tendency to become stabilized exactly at replacement costs. Replacement cost, despite its defects which will be discussed immediately, constitutes the best index of economic value so far discovered, in the absence of an acceptable market price.

DEFECTS OF REPLACEMENT COST. But replacement cost is not the sensitive, accurate, all-sufficient index of value that market price is. It is merely the next best index that has been discovered. It possesses two important limitations. First, it applies only to things that are freely reproducible, and second, during periods of great economic disequilibrium, it may be quite inaccurate.

Replacement cost applies only to reproducible things because, unless an asset can be reproduced, it can have no replacement cost. Also unless the production of an asset can be accelerated or discontinued at will in response to the profit motive, the play of forces described in the preceding paragraphs will not operate to bring economic value into line with replacement cost. Thus replacement cost cannot serve as a value index for assets such as land, mines, patents, trademarks, and copyrights. Replacement cost also cannot serve as a value index for nonmarketable corporate securities because such assets are, strictly speaking, not reproducible. A corporation may issue additional securities, but if these attempt to duplicate those already outstanding they will merely change in some respect the entire outstanding issue. A new corporation may be formed to acquire assets exactly similar to an existing corporation, but it cannot reproduce the securities of the existing corporation. Its personnel will be different, its name, its experience, its location, all will be different. In short, it will be a different corporation issuing different securities.

Replacement cost may be inaccurate during the extreme stages of great economic booms and depressions. Such booms and depressions ordinarily give rise to rapid variations in demand which cause economic values to change with extreme speed. Changes in production ordinarily require time, whereas changes in demand may be instantaneous. Consequently it sometimes happens that variations in demand succeed in altering economic values to a marked degree before the forces of supply have had sufficient time to interpose an effective check. During a great boom period the demand for automobiles may rise to a point where it causes a brief shortage. This may create a temporary economic value for automobiles which is substantially in excess of their replacement cost. Conversely, in times of depression, the economic value of automobiles may fall so low that automobile companies may be forced to shut down or to operate at a loss. Fortunately, however, those goods which are freely reproducible and which are not traded in free and competitive markets—i.e., those goods for a determination of whose economic value the accountant must rely upon replacement costs—are precisely the goods in which great and rapid changes in value are the least to be expected. Booms and depressions are ordinarily caused by the growth and collapse of speculation, and speculation, to serve its purpose of creating large, rapid, and realizable profits, must of necessity concentrate upon goods which are not only not reproducible upon short notice but which are readily marketable as well.

Under such conditions the accountant should keep constantly in mind the play of economic forces described heretofore. He should continually remind himself that what he is really trying to do is to impute economic value, not merely to determine replacement cost. Replacement cost is not economic value. In boom times it may be substantially below economic value, whereas in times of depression it may actually be above economic value. It is, in the absence of an acceptable market price, merely the best indicator or index of economic value available because it tends to fluctuate around market price.

ORIGINAL COST. Present accounting authority uniformly prescribes the use of original cost as an index of value in cases where neither face value nor market value is used, although enlightened accountants tend to describe such cost as "historical data" or as "accounting convention" rather than to maintain that it represents economic value. A moment's reflection will suffice to indicate that original cost can only accidentally approximate present economic value. If an original cost arose from a transaction in a broad, free, and competitive market, it did represent true economic value at the time of its incurrence because it represented a free and competitive market price. This, however, gives no assurance that such an original cost will represent economic value at a later date when market prices may have changed considerably. On the other hand, if the original cost did not arise from a transaction in a broad, free, and competitive market, it may merely have represented a private price paid either in cash or by barter. Such a private price may or may not have borne any recognizable similarity to economic value at the date of its incurrence, and only an accidental set of circumstances could cause it to approximate economic value at a later date when conditions of supply and demand may have changed.

Moreover, if the transaction was by barter, the original cost may have represented neither an economic value nor a private price, but merely an accounting convention obtained through the exchange of one going value for another. The American Institute of Accountants in a recent bulletin relative to financial statements says, "They reflect the combination of personal judgments, accounting conventions and recorded facts, and the judgments and conventions applied affect them materially." If a business exchanges one asset for another through a process of barter, accounting convention ordinarily prescribes that the asset acquired shall be valued at the figure at which the asset exchanged was formerly carried on the books. This may be done even though a great difference exists between the values of the two assets. If capital stock is given in exchange for other assets, accounting convention ordinarily prescribes that the values acquired shall be shown as equal to the par value of the stock given for them, although this par value may in no sense approximate the true economic values actually acquired.

Under the circumstances, it will be readily realized that original costs can present few claims to being acceptable indices of present economic values. Originally they may have represented economic values, private prices, or accounting conventions. At a later date, however, they must necessarily be reduced to the status of representing either historical data or accounting conventions, and only by accident could either of these approximate present economic value.

DETERMINATION OF REPLACEMENT COSTS. Replacement cost has been defined as the cost of reproducing a thing plus a profit sufficient to provide a motive for so doing. In this definition any two things are assumed to be alike if their utilities or serviceableness are identical, regardless of differences in their structural form. The cost of matching the precise physical structure of a given asset is known as its reproduction cost. The cost of matching the utility or serviceableness of a given asset is known as its replacement cost. Care should be used in employing these terms because they may at times have widely different meanings. A factory may possess a ponderous machine for the manufacture of certain parts. This machine may have cost $10,000 and the cost of duplicating it may be $10,000. However, due to technological progress, it may be possible to build or purchase for $5,000 a smaller machine which will perform the same services, will last as long, and will duplicate in every way the utility of the ponderous machine. Under these circumstances, the reproduction cost of the ponderous machine will be $10,000 but its replacement cost will be $5,000.

Wide use has been made by appraisal companies of the term "sound value." For practical purposes this term is usually synonymous with replacement cost, allowance being of course made for depreciation and obsolescence in both instances.

The determination of replacement costs deals roughly with two classes of assets. The first of these consists of standard articles which are produced and sold on a basis of exact duplication, either by the business under review, or by others. The second class consists of special assets which must be built to order. The first of these classifications is unquestionably the larger. For most businesses it constitutes the greater part of all of the assets owned. The second classification consists largely of buildings and special equipment built to order. The appraisal of standard assets requires little technical knowledge not already possessed by accountants. The appraisal of special, or built-to-order, assets may require considerable engineering skill.

The determination of replacement costs for standard assets, as performed by appraisal companies, consists of four relatively simple operations. The first of these is to list each asset, describing it fully. The second step is to determine the cost to the business under review of currently producing or purchasing each asset, as the case may be. No profit is added to this cost. The third step is to calculate the depreciation or obsolescence suffered by each asset in the light of its age, general condition, and relative effectiveness from the standpoint of newer developments. This is the same calculation that accountants make during the course of an ordinary audit. The final operation is to deduct the amount of each asset's depreciation and obsolescence from its present production or purchase cost new, and to record the remainder as its present value. This practice is not ideal, but it does undoubtedly serve to bring original costs up to date and to eliminate errors that may have existed in the original costs through collusion of the parties at the time of purchase, or through the recording of accounting conventions. It unquestionably succeeds in determining present economic values more accurately than does the present accounting method of using original costs. From a practical point of view the method must be approved, because no better technique seems to be possible. Theoretically, however, the procedure may be subject to two objections.

In the first place, the above procedure may tend to treat monopoly costs and prices exactly as though they were prices established in broad, free, competitive markets. The product of each manufacturer is apt to be different from the products of other manufacturers. To a certain degree, therefore, each manufacturer may enjoy a monopoly in the supply of his own product. If the degree of this monopoly is large, he may deliberately incur costs far greater than necessary and yet enjoy a profit sufficient to encourage him to continue producing. Under such circumstances these costs will tend to be an index of monopoly price, rather than an index of a free and competitive market price that may be used as economic value.

When a manufacturer sets a sales price on one of his

products, he may, to an extent, be establishing a monopoly price. This price may be above or below the price that would exist were there more than one producer, and were producers and buyers brought together in a competitive market. Yet the manufacturer may maintain his price, even though during depression periods he sells no goods and during boom periods he cannot meet the demand. To the extent that sales prices are monopolistic they may fail to reflect competitive market prices, and to that extent their use in the calculation of replacement costs by the method outlined above may prevent a true determination of economic values.

In practice the degree of monopoly enjoyed by producers of standard assets is apt to be small because substitutes almost always exist and exert a distinct competitive pressure. Also, instances of philanthropic monopolists are undoubtedly rare, and doubtless the costs incurred by most monopolists are as low as competitive conditions will allow. However, should an accountant encounter an effective monopoly, he should not use as values the costs or prices incurred or fixed by the monopolist, but should make his own appraisal of the replacement costs that would obtain under competitive conditions, as outlined below for special assets. Otherwise the procedure outlined above may be followed on the ground that no better practical method is available. At least it can be said with assurance that the replacement costs so determined will reflect economic values more accurately than does the present use of original costs and accounting conventions.

A second objection to the appraisal company method of valuing standard assets may be that under certain circumstances it will value identical assets differently in the hands of different owners. An automobile manufacturer may produce a number of identical cars, each costing $700.00. His price to a distributor may be $750.00 per car. The distributor's price to a dealer may be $800.00 per car. The dealer's price to a consumer may be $1,000.00 per car. None of these purchasers could buy these cars for less than the prices named. An appraiser would value the cars at $700.00 each in the hands of the automobile manufacturer. In addition he would value these cars at three different figures in the hands of the three different purchasers, even though the cars were identical. The reason for this is that three different restricted markets exist, each with a different price. These markets are noncompetitive and cannot possibly reflect economic value in a world sense. Each reflects values only within its own restricted sphere. From the standpoint of an accountant endeavoring to impute the market price that would prevail were all potential buyers and all potential sellers brought together in a free market, it must be admitted that the discovery of four different values is absurd. Yet each of the three purchasers must actually buy only within his own market. For him that market is just as binding as though it were a free and competitive world market. He cannot possibly get out of it. Stockholders in his business will profit or lose according to the dictates of that market. It would be obviously unfair and wrong to set up values based on demand and supply in a market in which the business cannot possibly operate. Hence, in the case of restricted markets, values must be calculated on the basis of conditions as they exist in the markets in which a business must operate. In the case cited, the situation is the same as though each business was in a different world and as though each had to compute its own values in its own world, irrespective of conditions in other worlds. The situation is identical with that sanctioned by present accounting principles in connection with the use of original costs, except that present accounting principles do not cause original costs to be brought up to date as is the case when replacement costs are used.

Although the use of different replacement costs for identical assets in the hands of different owners is admittedly not ideal, it must not be thought that it prevents the ready comparison of the worth and earnings of different businesses, as does the use of original costs. The replacement costs used will in each instance represent the present value of each owner's assets *in the market within which he operates*. These values will be calculated as of the same date and will include any price changes that may have occurred in the respective markets between the dates of acquisition and the date of the financial statements. All identical assets will be exhibited at identical values in the financial statements of each individual owner. These values will approximate the prices at which each owner could just as easily sell as buy. They will approximate the present money value of his assets in the market open to him. They will approximate the present capital outlay required of any newcomer who might desire to compete with him. In short they will exhibit the present value of each owner's assets stated in terms of present dollars, and such dollar values will be strictly comparable as between the different owners. They will represent the present capital in use in each instance. Earnings calculated on this capital will accurately indicate the percentage earned on each dollar of net worth. The fact that a given money value will represent in each case a different quantity of physical assets is of little importance as long as the money values are shown correctly. Money is the common denominator of business. It is the universal standard by which all businesses may be compared.

Now consider the situation when original costs instead of replacement costs are used as values. The exhibition of original costs in a balance sheet gives little enlightenment regarding the value of the assets in question at the date of the balance sheet. It frequently results in identical assets being shown at different values in the hands of the same owner, a situation that is impossible when replacement costs are used. When original costs are used as values, present net worth must be a matter of conjecture because original costs need bear no resemblance to present values. If present net worth is incorrectly stated it must follow that earnings have been incorrectly stated. The use of original costs as values thus results in a misstatement of the asset values, net worth, and earnings of a business. The amount and degree of this misstatement must vary with the changing circumstances under which each business incurred its original costs. Accurate comparisons between different businesses are therefore not only impossible but, even within a given business, no accurate relation of earnings to present capital can be computed.

The determination of replacement costs for special or made-to-order assets is more difficult than their determination for standard assets, and calls for more technical training on the part of the appraisers. Such assets usually consist of buildings, special machines, dies, jigs, gauges, patterns,

and other assets adapted to specific purposes. If an accountant does not have sufficient skill to determine what they
could be built for under competitive conditions as of the
date of the audit, he can readily find experts in almost
every locality who can make the necessary calculations
with promptness and accuracy. For example, general building contractors and architects must constantly estimate the
cost of proposed structures as an ordinary routine part of
their occupations. Mechanical engineers and others familiar
with shop practice can readily estimate the present cost of
reproducing special machines and tools, or their equivalent
in serviceability. After the appraisal of replacement cost,
new, has been made, the problem of calculating depreciation and obsolescence is a familiar one to the accountant,
who encounters it regularly in the course of different audits.
The resulting figure is used as present value.

USE OF INDEX NUMBERS TO DETERMINE REPLACE-
MENT COSTS. In some instances commodity indices showing
changes in purchasing power may be used to good advantage
in determining present replacement costs for certain types
of assets, particularly industrial buildings. Such indices are
published regularly by a number of public and private
sources. They range from a general commodity index, intended to show fluctuations in the cost of living, to special
indices showing fluctuations in the cost of reproducing many
different kinds of assets in many different localities. By
applying the fluctuation shown by a given index to the
original cost of the related asset, a surprisingly accurate
present reproduction cost may usually be obtained. The
merits of this method rest in its simplicity, inexpensiveness,

and rapidity. Care must always be taken, however, to see that the original cost used really represents a bona fide purchase and not a private price or an accounting convention. Extreme care should also be taken to see that the index used actually refers to the asset being appraised. Much havoc may be wrought by using an index which is not applicable to the business under review.

As a general rule, the use of index numbers in the determination of replacement costs is apt to result in less accuracy than is usually secured by appraisal company methods. This is so because an index must of necessity be general in its scope and thereby fail to take into due consideration the special circumstances that may surround individual assets. Another drawback is that enough accurate indices for short enough periods are not yet promptly available. Many indices are calculated for periods longer than one month, and many others are not available until several months after the date of their calculation. The index method of determining replacement costs will therefore only occasionally be available to accountants, although it may be extremely useful and convenient when it is available.

TRANSPORTATION AND INSTALLATION COSTS. Present accounting practice sanctions the inclusion of transportation and installation charges in its original cost values. Present appraisal practice likewise sanctions the inclusions of these items in its replacement cost values. This treatment is theoretically wrong, and the reasoning involved is the same as that reviewed in the previous chapter in the discussion relating to brokers' commissions and other expenses. Market price is a money measurement of the "power in exchange" of a good. Once the market price of a good has been accurately determined, this market price represents the economic value of that good without any additions or deductions whatsoever.

From a practical standpoint, however, an accountant will seldom be in a position to defend the absolute accuracy of an imputed economic value. Replacement cost is not economic value. It is, in the absence of an acceptable market price, merely the best available index of economic value. As previously discussed, it may, during boom times, be substantially below economic value and, during depression times, it may be above economic value. Normally it will be approximately the equivalent of economic value. As a general rule, an accountant should use unmodified replacement costs as economic values. Transportation and installation charges *as such* should never be added to replacement costs. However, situations may arise where replacement costs are clearly inadequate to express current economic values. In such cases an accurate appraisal would necessarily involve an adjustment of replacement costs in order to reflect economic values in the light of the current situation.

At times a question may arise as to whether certain charges are installation costs, or are an inherent part of the replacement cost of an asset. A steam boiler may be installed in a new building. The cost of installation may equal, or even exceed, the purchase price of the boiler. It may be debated whether the boiler should be valued separately, excluding its installation cost, or whether both the boiler and its installation cost should be considered an integral part of the replacement cost of the building. If one reasons too strictly from the first premise, he may eventually conclude that the bricks and mortar in a building should be valued at their replacement costs, and that the cost of transporting them to the site and of erecting them into walls should be treated as expense. On the other hand, if one reasons too strictly from the second premise, he may eventually conclude that an entire business should be valued as a whole and not as a combination of separate assets and liabilities.

The writer knows of no infallible test that may be applied in connection with the grouping of assets for valuation purposes. A functional test cannot be used because there seldom exists anything but an arbitrary division between functions. A bolt, a machine, a building, a plant, a whole business; each has a function which merges into the function of the others. The test of "greatest value" can hardly be used, for this would result in all sorts of complexities. Frequently a business as a whole is worth more than the combined values of its individual assets. The greatest value method might appraise such a business at one figure representing the value of its securities in the stock market. Obviously, this would supply little information to anybody. Under these circumstances the safest guide to follow is custom. Buildings are customarily valued as a whole, equipped with essential equipment such as electric wiring, boilers, and elevators. The cost of installing this equipment is considered to be an integral part of the cost of the building. Machinery for manufacturing purposes is usually valued separately, as are furniture and office equipment, and inventories. This treatment, which is more or less uniform for all businesses, affords a means of comparison between different businesses, and although it is based on ex-

pediency rather than on a fully developed theory, it probably serves most practical purposes better than any available
alternative.

Summary. In the previous chapter, it was shown that
acceptable markets exist for trading in a large number of
different types of assets. These assets were described as
marketable assets. It was stated that marketable assets
should invariably be valued at their market prices, as of the
balance sheet date. This discussion dealt with the subject of
the valuation of marketable assets but did not cover the
subject of nonmarketable assets.

In the present chapter, replacement cost was recommended as an index of value for those nonmarketable assets
that are freely reproducible. Doubtless the great majority
of nonmarketable assets are included in this category. However, the category does not include a small group of assets
which are both nonmarketable and not freely reproducible.
These will be discussed in the following chapter.

Replacement cost, despite its defects, constitutes the best
available index of economic value, in the absence of an
acceptable market price. The replacement costs of standard
competitive assets produced by a business under review may
be easily determined by ascertaining their current costs
of production. The replacement costs of standard competitive assets purchased by a business under review may be determined by ascertaining their current purchase prices. The
replacement costs of special made-to-order assets, or assets
not produced and sold under competitive conditions, may
be ascertained by calculating the cost of reproducing them

or their equivalent in serviceability, under current competitive conditions.

Transportation and installation costs should not be included in replacement costs save where they are actually part of the cost of the physical reproduction of the asset concerned. Hence, the cost of transporting and installing the wood floors of a building would be part of the replacement cost of that building. But the cost of transporting a piano to that building, and of installing it in a top-floor studio, is not part of the replacement cost of the piano.

IX

TRUTHFUL FINANCIAL STATEMENTS

So FAR this work has reviewed some of the evils caused by present accounting principles and has described, and commented upon, the arguments used by accounting authorities to defend these principles. The origin and development of accounting principles have been surveyed, and it has been noted that these principles are, in the main, a natural outgrowth of primitive conditions which have now largely ceased to exist. It has been indicated how accounting principles may justifiably be said to have "just growed" like Topsy, rather than to have been consciously formulated by men of intelligence. Also, the nature of economic value and of money has been studied, and a review has been made of market prices and of methods of imputing or estimating market prices when these are not immediately available. However, no comprehensive plan has been offered to remedy the evils caused by present accounting principles, nor has it been explained how the difficulties in the way of changing the present principles are to be met and surmounted. These are the purposes of the present chapter.

APPROACH TO PROBLEM. It seems to the writer that it is feasible to approach these problems by reconstructing the most perfect conditions under which accounting could be practiced, and by determining what the ideal aim of accounting should be under such conditions. After this has been done, it can be determined how far present conditions vary from perfect conditions and what compromises this variance necessitates in the practical accomplishment of the ideal aim. In this manner one may, by not losing sight of the ideal aim, make as few concessions to expediency as practicable, and thus stay as close to the ideal aim as present conditions will permit.

In other words, if the problem is approached by assuming an ideal situation and by adapting this ideal to present conditions, it seems reasonable that less deviation from the ideal will occur than would be the case were one to start from a basis of expediency and to work toward the ideal only as expediency might dictate. This latter method is the historical course which accountancy has followed, and its practical effect is to put a premium on expediency and not on ideals. If expediency seems to lead away from ideals, the tendency is to change the ideals themselves by inventing theories which justify the practices necessitated by expediency. The results from this tendency are particularly bad when conditions are changing. A given course of action may be very necessary under a certain set of conditions, even though this course of action may far from conform to an ideal course of action. If a theory is invented to justify this faulty course of action, then later on, after conditions have changed to permit of a more ideal course of action, the tendency will be to cling to the theory rather than to change the course of action. This tendency will exist because the ideal course, being temporarily impossible of attainment, will have been obscured, or even denied, by the theory which was invented during the prior period.

If accountants would determine their ideal, and hold it always before them as their ideal, meanwhile frankly admitting the practical imperfections of accounting methods under conditions which do not allow a realization of the ideal, they would thereby place themselves in a position where their tendency would be to change their methods as changing conditions allow a closer approach to the ideal. This accomplished, accountancy would have come very close to a scientific attitude with reference to its own conduct, and would tend to become a progressive, forward-looking profession, instead of a static one relying upon sophistry and specious reasoning to defend its ancient dogmas.

IDEAL ACCOUNTING CONDITIONS. From one point of view the growth of civilization is merely the growth of coöperation between human beings. Trade, even by barter, is a relatively high form of coöperation. There is little or no barter among wild animals in the jungle, and in primitive human society trade tends to be very limited. Under these conditions each individual tends to produce the sum total of his physical needs and to be independent of other individuals. With the growth of intelligence, human beings discovered little by little that they could produce more, and thus have more, if labor were specialized and if one man were allowed to become an expert at one occupation which he practiced for the benefit of an integrated group, other members of the group meanwhile specializing along other lines. Obviously trade was necessary when this development occurred.

In primitive times integrated groups were very small,

but with the advancement of civilization they have tended to grow larger and larger until it seems, from one point of view at least, that the progress of man has consisted largely in his learning how to coöperate in larger and larger groups. The setbacks that history records were occasioned largely by the injection of disorganized groups into highly integrated ones, thus necessitating readjustments until the combined group could be made sufficiently homogeneous to permit again of extensive coöperation between the individuals comprising it. The Dark Ages were a period during which the barbarians of northern Europe were attempting to fit themselves into the highly civilized group comprising the Roman Empire. These ages were dark only in comparison with the high degree of coöperation formerly existing between individuals of the Roman Empire. From the standpoint of barbarians of the North, the Dark Ages were a long progression toward greater coöperation in larger groups and hence toward greater civilization.

If trade, even on a barter basis, implies a high degree of intelligence and coöperation, then trade by means of money implies a still higher degree of coöperation and intelligence. The form of trade which requires the highest degree of intelligence and coöperation, however, is trade through the medium of a free and competitive market. Such a market is possible only after society has reached a very high degree of organization and integration. It is clearly evident from a study of economic history that the growth of free and competitive markets roughly parallels the growth of trade and the growth of the integration of human society. If it is true that human society is in the process of becoming more and more closely integrated, and more and more highly organized, then it is probably also true that, as a concomitant of this development, there will be formed more and more great free competitive markets where economic values will be made and changed by buyers and sellers merely through the process of announcing bids and offers.

Under ideal conditions, all trade would be through the medium of free and competitive markets. The establishment of private prices and the use of vast sales organizations and vast advertising effort implies waste in an economic sense. Such sales and advertising effort are largely for the purpose of influencing buyers, and of subjecting them to psychological pressure, instead of providing them with goods which they need. A buyer paying a private sales price is in reality very apt to be buying two different goods. He is buying the goods which he thinks he is paying for, but all of his money may not go to pay for that good. Some of this money may go to pay for an entirely different type of good, consisting of advertising, interviews with salesmen, and all the elaborate and subtle psychological influences to which he may be subjected. It may, of course, be argued, and perhaps justly argued, that all of this advertising and sales expense is a splendid economic investment for society in that it permits business to develop on a scale which would otherwise be impossible, and thereby permits low costs to be obtained which more than offset the cost of the advertising and sales expense. However, it cannot be effectively argued that such advertising and sales expense would be justified in a more intelligent community which kept itself informed regarding goods capable of satisfying its wants, and had the ability to provide for the purchase and sale of these goods through the medium of free and competitive markets.

Civilization seems to be trending inexorably toward the creation of more and more free and competitive markets where true economic values obtain and where a prospective buyer or seller may procure or dispose of goods with a minimum of economic waste. It may be assumed, therefore, that this is a trend toward an ideal condition, and that accounting principles should be reconstructed so that advantage may be taken of it to improve the service for which accountancy exists.

IDEAL ACCOUNTING AIM. In a former chapter it was stated that the technique of modern accounting was first described in 1494 by Lucas Pacioli of Venice. It was noted that the values prescribed by Pacioli, and used for centuries by subsequent accountants, were based on original costs because these were the only figures available. Later, when free and competitive markets did come into existence, the practice of exhibiting assets at original cost was so ancient and so completely embedded in the accounting mind that theories were invented to justify this practice, rather than to justify a change in procedure which would permit the exhibition of economic values. This was the more natural in that there did not, at the time, seem to be any compelling reason for stating economic values in preference to original costs, because of the nonexistence of uninformed stockholders or creditors. Also, since the economic values of the vast majority of assets were either unknown or difficult of attainment without the employment of men who possessed specialized knowledge, it was only natural that accountants should not tend to change their principles merely because economic values had become available in a few instances.

But suppose that free and competitive markets had existed for all assets from the beginning. In other words, suppose that economic values had been readily available to every accountant for every asset at any time. No one can doubt that, if this had been the case, accounting principles would automatically have been predicated upon the exhibition of economic values. The course followed by accounting practice was the course of least resistance. If the course of least resistance had been to exhibit economic values, these economic values would have been exhibited, not only because they were easy of attainment, but because it would then have been immediately apparent that the earnings and balance sheet information supplied by them was vastly more important and useful than that supplied by deceptive, and frequently quite meaningless, figures representing a variety of original costs incurred at a variety of different dates.

Managers, creditors, and stockholders most desire to know certain important facts about a business. The nature of these facts is obvious to every accountant. With regard to balance sheet information, these persons want to know the present net worth of the business, i.e., the present value of its net possessions. The capital account, combined with the surplus account, should give them this information truthfully. They desire to know the present value of each of the different classes of assets. They wish to know how much the company owes and, within practical limits, to whom.

Managers want this information so that they can know

the present financial condition of a business, and so that they can intelligently consider possible changes in assets, liabilities, or capital. It is evident that figures representing present values are of more service in these respects than figures based upon the historic original cost of assets. Creditors want this information so that they can calculate the probability of their being repaid. It is obvious that the original cost of assets has only an indirect bearing upon this. Stockholders want this information partly for the reason that managers want it, and partly so that they can make intelligent comparisons between the possessions of their company and those of other companies whose stock they may be preparing to buy. It seems clear that balance sheets, prepared on the basis of present economic values, would supply to the three groups at interest information of more value than does the present mixture of original costs, accounting conventions, and market values, with which they are now supplied.

With reference to profit and loss statements, it seems clear that all three groups would be interested in truthful information relative to *all* of the profits and losses made by a business. They would not be interested in learning about certain of these profits and losses, and in having other profits and losses concealed from them. They would certainly not be interested in learning only of realized profits, and in being kept in ignorance of unrealized profits, only to have the following year's statement inform them of the realized profits for that year plus such unrealized profits of former years as may have been realized in that year. Yet this is the type of information with which they are now supplied.

It seems evident that, if present economic values were easily and readily obtainable, accountants would supply these values in their financial statements. It also seems evident that these values would give managers, creditors, and stockholders information of an importance, usefulness, completeness, and truthfulness far beyond that of the information with which they are supplied today.

How Actual Conditions Vary from Ideal Conditions. It has been asserted above that an ideal condition for the practice of accountancy would be one under which the economic value of any asset was easily ascertainable at any time. It has also been asserted that, under this condition, the ideal aim of accountancy should be to exhibit present economic values in a balance sheet and to exhibit *all* profits and losses in a profit and loss statement. But the circumstance remains that the ideal condition above mentioned does not in fact prevail. To the extent that it fails to prevail, it may prevent a realization of the ideal aim outlined. Let us see how actual, existing conditions differ from the ideal condition.

Few people realize the extent to which active, broad, free, and competitive markets exist in the world today. With the increasing organization and integration of society, these markets have been established from time to time, until at present economic values are easily and quickly ascertainable for a large number of raw materials and for a fair number of fabricated products. In the United States alone, acceptable markets normally exist for trading in at least forty different classes of commodities, and many of these classes are subdivisible into different individual commodities. These markets were named in the chapter on market prices. Whenever an accountant is faced with the problem of valuing assets traded in the above markets, he may determine present economic values quickly and easily by reference to daily newspapers or trade journals, or by direct reference to brokers or to the markets themselves. To this extent existing conditions do conform to the requirements of the ideal condition mentioned previously. In valuing marketable assets, an accountant needs no more training than he now has, except that he must understand the economic principles underlying the nature and determination of value. The exhibition of marketable assets at their present economic values will occasion no additional effort or expense in connection with an audit, and thus the argument of "impracticable" cannot be brought to bear here.

Nonmarketable assets are, for the overwhelmingly greater part, freely reproducible, and although their economic value cannot be ascertained merely by reference to a newspaper, either because they are not traded in a market or because they are not traded in a sufficiently broad, active, free, and competitive market, yet their economic value may be estimated or imputed by a calculation of their present replacement costs. Such assets may have been produced by the business under audit or they may have been purchased by that business. If the assets have been produced by the business under review, an accountant is in a much more favorable position to determine their present replacement costs than an appraiser would be. If the assets have been purchased, an accountant is at least as favorably placed as an appraiser would be. Yet, in both cases, an accountant would be very apt to be unable to determine present replacement costs unless he employed an appraiser, or himself undertook to study and master the appraiser's technique.

In view of the great benefits to be gained by the exhibition of these assets at figures approximating their present economic values, it seems inescapable either that appraisers should be called upon to help in the preparation of financial statements, or that the functions of accountant and appraiser should be combined in a single man or in a single firm. Either of these courses would cause inconvenience and annoyance to existing accounting firms, and it would be only natural that their advent should be sternly resisted by the accounting profession as a whole. No one likes to be told that he does not know enough properly to perform his job, and history records no unwillingness quite so persistent as the unwillingness of mankind to abandon time-honored principles. To most accountants it must seem ironical to be told that they are no longer qualified to prepare the financial statements which they and their forebears have been preparing for centuries past, and in addition to be told that they must either employ the services, or learn the technique, of their occasional competitor, the appraiser. Yet there seems to be no other solution if financial statements are to supply present facts in the place of incomprehensible mixtures of present facts, historical data, and accounting conventions.

There remain a few assets which may not be traded in any acceptable market and which may, by their nature, not be freely reproducible. These comprise assets such as patents, copyrights, trademarks, mines, and oil wells. Since these assets tend to constitute natural monopolies, it is scarcely likely that they would be traded in broad, free, and competitive markets. Hence, no market prices will be available to be used as economic values. On the other hand, since these assets cannot be reproduced, it will usually be impossible to compute their present replacement costs. Even were this possible such computations would not indicate economic values because the assets in question are not freely reproducible, and consequently their supply could not be increased or decreased in accordance with the economic laws that alone make replacement cost an index of value. Patently, in the case of nonmarketable, nonreproducible assets, present conditions do not conform at all to the ideal condition outlined in the preceding section. To this extent at least, it seems impossible fully to realize the ideal accounting aim predicated upon this ideal condition.

CONCESSIONS TO EXPEDIENCY. The question here arises as to what accounting principles can be adopted that will be practicable in the light of existing conditions, and yet will vary as little as possible from the ideal aim previously outlined. Although it be maintained that this ideal aim is completely desirable, it must be conceded that the aim is not susceptible to full realization under conditions as they now exist. The problem consists in adapting the ideal aim to existing conditions with as few concessions to expediency as possible.

It has been noted that, in the case of assets which are traded in acceptable markets, market prices, and hence economic values, are readily and easily obtainable. When dealing with these assets no concessions at all need be made to expediency. The existing condition conforms completely to the ideal condition, and accounting principles may therefore be made to conform completely to the ideal accounting aim. An accountant has merely to use economic values when dealing with marketable assets, in place of the mixture of original costs, accounting conventions, and market values that are now used. By so doing he will be presenting the simple truth as of the date of his financial statements.

With reference to reproducible nonmarketable assets, it must be admitted that existing conditions do not fully conform to the ideal condition. However, in the case of these assets, reasonably reliable estimates of economic values are obtainable by an appraiser or by an accountant. Although conditions are not completely ideal, a close approximation of these conditions does exist and, with the exercise of some effort, no serious deviation from the ideal accounting aim need be made. The question here is whether or not the good to be gained by approximating the ideal aim is worth the amount of effort occasioned by doing so. When one stops to realize the amount of harm occasioned by not doing so, it seems reasonable to suppose that this effort could easily be justified.

As a matter of fact, either the accounting profession must make this effort, and must prepare financial statements which are in fact what they purport to be, or it must eventually tell the public what financial statements really are, namely: a conglomeration of historical data, accounting conventions, and present facts, wherein no one can discern truth from fiction, and which are fully as likely to deceive the enlightened as the ignorant, to the advantage of individuals who have inside knowledge of the facts misleadingly exhibited. Such a confession, once it were fully comprehended by the public, would lead either to public contempt for the accountant's work or to a public demand for financial statements which exhibited facts as truthfully as they could be ascertained. Surely the avoidance of the first outcome is worthy of effort and study on the part of accountants, and the second outcome would necessitate that effort and study in any event. Under the circumstances, it seems inescapable that the good to be accomplished is worthy of the effort, and that nonmarketable reproducible assets should be valued at their imputed economic values.

This leaves, finally, a third class of assets which are nonmarketable and nonreproducible as well. Patents, copyrights, trademarks, mines, and oil wells comprise the bulk of this group. The determination of economic values for these assets on any accurate basis seems impossible. Fortunately such assets are few in number and are not often encountered under conditions where their importance would have a predominating effect upon financial statements. However, such assets do exist and in some cases they do exert a predominating influence as, for instance, in the case of mines. In theory, present accounting principles direct that such assets be valued at original cost less amortization or depletion, but in actual practice they are apt to be written off as rapidly as earnings permit. Inasmuch as an accountant has no means by which to determine a present economic value for these assets, the question arises as to how he is to value them. Only two methods seem to be available, and each of these methods may result in figures which are very far from true. An accountant may follow present accounting theory and base the value of these assets on original cost, or he may, in the absence of any known economic value, refuse to value them at all, and may exhibit them in the balance sheet without a value, supplemented by a separate schedule containing factual and descriptive data relating to them.

The fact of the matter is that no known present economic value is likely to exist for the assets in question. Therefore any value shown is apt to be extremely misleading. If an accountant values these assets at nothing, he can no more defend this valuation than he can defend a valuation at original cost. Yet he would be called upon to defend it much more certainly than he is called upon to defend original cost, because large numbers of the public accept his original cost figures as present economic value, whereas few people would be prepared to believe that such assets had no value at all. This might mean that the valuation of these assets at nothing would result in less deception than their valuation at original cost, because interested persons would have their attention called to the uncertainty of the values in question. But the valuation of these assets at nothing is open to several grave charges. In the first place, the omission of all value would probably be farther from the truth than the use of original cost as value. This would be true with reference both to the balance sheet and to the profit and loss statement. In the second place, the omission of all value in cases where this was predominating, as with mines, would be so far from the truth as to make the financial statements appear absurd. In the third place, it is probable that, if these assets were valued at nothing, most laymen would fail to appreciate the need of provision for amortization or depletion. Even if a separate schedule, containing complete factual data and including original cost, were supplied concerning the assets in question, it is probable that most laymen would be unable to make intelligent use of it.

Under the circumstances a big concession to expediency must be made with reference to these assets. At the present time they are sometimes valued at one dollar, as in the case of the patents held by the General Electric Company, or their value is based on original cost. The writer believes that, if the public could be educated to understand the true nature of these assets, their uniform valuation at original cost less amortization or depletion would, in the long run, be preferable both to their valuation at nothing and to the present nonuniform practice, even though it would fall far short of the ideal accounting aim. Such an education might be afforded by describing the original costs of the assets in such a manner that one reading them would have called to his attention the fact that the assets could not be valued with accuracy. The words "Valued at original cost, not susceptible to accurate valuation" might be made invariably to precede the exhibition of these original costs. In this way the public would be put on notice that this part of the balance sheet, and that that part of the profit and loss statement relating to the depreciation or depletion of these assets, was not to be trusted and was merely a concession to expediency. If this were done over a period of years, many people might come to understand that the important thing about these assets was the uncertainty of their value, and to realize that conclusions drawn from factual data might frequently be more accurate than the conclusions supplied by the financial statements.

THE TRUTHFUL BALANCE SHEET. It is now appropriate to consider a balance sheet prepared along the lines suggested above, namely, with marketable assets valued at market price, nonmarketable reproducible assets valued at replacement cost, and occasional nonmarketable, nonreproducible assets valued at original cost. With the exception of occasional nonmarketable and nonreproducible assets, this procedure would produce a balance sheet whose fluctuations of net worth, between the beginning and the end of any period, would describe accurately the net total of all profits and losses during that period from whatever sources. This fluctuation in net worth would instantly reveal how the business as a whole had fared during the period in question. It is true that this fluctuation would comprise all profits and losses whether capital, current, unrealized, or realized, and that the reader would have to refer to the profit and loss statement for details, but nevertheless, from a series of balance sheets alone, he would be able to obtain an accurate account of what the business as a whole had accomplished.

By referring to the values of the fixed assets in such a balance sheet, a reader would have the information that a prospective mortgagee would demand were he to lend money on these assets. If a mortgage already exists, the reader of the balance sheet would be able to determine at a glance the status of this mortgage as regards its security. If the mortgage were about to mature, the reader of the balance sheet could at once see whether it could be refunded upon favorable terms, upon unfavorable terms, or not at all. This information is not available from balance sheets as now drawn, and such balance sheets usually do not give the slightest inkling as to whether the security behind a funded debt is ample or insufficient, or whether an expiring mortgage can be refunded with ease or will plunge a business into bankruptcy. Mortgagees have long realized that valuations placed by accountants on fixed assets are entirely undependable, and it is almost the invariable rule that an independent appraisal of the replacement cost of these assets must be made before a mortgage loan can be consummated. The information given by balance sheets as now drawn is virtually worthless as regards the status of present or prospective mortgages. It leaves creditors, stockholders, and sometimes even managers in doubt as to whether the value of the assets is sufficient to support a new mortgage, or to refund an old one.

A comparison of the current assets and current liabilities shown by a balance sheet drawn upon the lines suggested above would supply a correct current asset ratio and liquid asset ratio. Readers of balance sheets, as now drawn, are fairly sure that current asset ratios are at least as favorable as indicated, but they have no means of knowing how much more favorable they may be. Occasionally a business will exhibit a low current asset ratio which may effectually prevent it from obtaining a short-term bank loan to finance additional inventory, or to serve some other legitimate purpose. The loan may be highly proper and profitable to the business in question. Yet, because of the current asset ratio disclosed, the loan may be refused, or may be granted at higher interest rates than would otherwise be the case had the current assets been exhibited at their present value. The valuation of current assets at "cost or market whichever is lower" is occasionally productive of grave harm when the economic value of the assets is greatly in excess of their original cost.

If balance sheets were prepared as suggested above, no "melon" could be earned by a business without stockholders being currently advised. In the past many a business has had certain of its assets increase in value to a tremendous extent throughout many years and yet, because these assets were carried at original cost, has failed to inform its stockholders. As a result insiders, who have been cognizant of the facts misrepresented upon the balance sheet, have been enabled to accumulate the company's stock up to the date when such assets were sold and an enormous dividend was declared. This state of affairs actually defrauds stockholders of their share in the earnings of a business by keeping them in ignorance of its real earnings. If balance sheets were made to exhibit economic values, rather than original costs, such situations would be avoided.

A balance sheet drawn upon the lines indicated above would make large secret reserves, or watered stock, impossible. If assets are valued at their economic values, it is obvious that neither secret reserves nor watered stock can exist because secret reserves depend entirely upon an undervaluation of assets, whereas watered stock depends entirely upon their overvaluation. In both cases stockholders and creditors are deprived of accurate knowledge relating to their company's affairs and, even though they do suspect the existence of one or the other of the conditions named, they have no means of determining how large a secret reserve exists or how much water exists. The effect of water in a balance sheet is, of course, the reverse of the effect occasioned by secret reserves. Many stockholders may be informed year after year that a company is doing nicely, only to have it end in bankruptcy despite the prosperous condition still shown by its balance sheet. Under conditions that now exist, no stockholder can see the approaching maturity of a bond issue with anything but misgivings as to whether his company will be able to refund or not. This must necessarily be so as long as asset values are unreliable.

A balance sheet drawn upon the lines suggested above would state truthfully the amount of present capital which a business is using. This amount, taken in conjunction with the current earnings, would supply an accurate index to the efficiency of the management when compared with other businesses. Two businesses may each be earning one million dollars a year, but if it is discovered that one business is employing ten million dollars' worth of assets whereas the other business is employing twenty million dollars' worth of assets, it is obvious that the former company is in reality earning money at twice the rate of the latter. Balance sheets that exhibit present values would reveal this condition at once, whereas balance sheets drawn in accordance with current accounting practice would be very apt to obscure it. Failure to exhibit present values makes the comparison of one company with another extremely difficult and enables managements to possess varying degrees of efficiency without stockholders being the wiser.

A balance sheet drawn upon the lines indicated above would reveal fully the capital profits and losses of a business, and the terrific variations in asset values caused by booms and depressions. At the present time most stockholders seem to be completely unaware of the magnitude of these variations, and they are kept in ignorance largely because balance sheets exhibit the same values for most assets whether the industry be in a boom or in a depression. The social good which might be accomplished through educating the public to the actual state of affairs is incalculable. The stabilization of money is to most individuals a meaningless phrase, but if these individuals could once be brought to realize what stormy oceans most businesses now ride, they would quickly realize that it probably describes the chief need of our present economy. Booms and depressions probably engender more financial catastrophies than all other causes put together, and yet their influence on assets and on the financial standings of companies is largely concealed in the financial statements now published. Values may decline to a point where a mortgage cannot be refunded, or they may rise to a point where it is obviously common sense to convert them into cash. Yet in each of these cases stockholders and creditors are kept in ignorance of the true situation.

Balance sheets drawn upon the lines indicated above would keep stockholders and creditors apprised of material changes in the values of assets. It is the belief of the writer that, if stockholders were informed of these changes, they would be astounded at the instability of our economic structure. Such information might cause laboring men and politicians to realize that business under present conditions is of necessity a gamble. It might cause the public to relinquish its impression that invested capital is entirely safe, and that the wish for reserves is fostered largely by greed.

THE TRUTHFUL PROFIT AND LOSS STATEMENT. A profit and loss statement prepared along the lines suggested above may now be considered. This profit and loss statement would be similar to the ones heretofore prepared, with a few important exceptions. The statement would include an exhibition of all capital profits and losses whether realized or not. These capital profits and losses would be placed in a separate section of the statement devoted entirely to them. Unrealized gain or loss due to changes in the market prices of inventory on hand would be included in the conventional operating section of the statement. Depreciation would be calculated on the present economic value of assets, rather than on their original cost, as is now done. The calculation of depreciation in this manner is fully covered in a later chapter. With these and a few other minor differences, the profit and loss statement would be constructed in the customary manner.

Profit and loss statements prepared along these lines would supply the information now given by profit and loss statements and, in addition, would furnish a complete statement of all other losses and profits so that the reader might be informed regarding every profit or loss sustained by a business during the period in question. The profit and loss statement of a manufacturing business would exhibit the gross sales, the gross profit from operations, and the net profit from business activities exactly as do most present profit and loss statements. Following the net profit from business activities, however, the statement would relate in detail the capital appreciation and depreciation of fixed and non-operating assets whether realized or not. The final net profit or loss shown would equal the change in net worth shown by the business between the beginning and ending dates of the period reviewed, exclusive of dividends and changes in the capital structure.

Accounting authorities have argued that the magnitude of the capital profits and losses shown by a profit and loss statement prepared in this fashion might completely dwarf the operating results of a business. It seems to be the opinion of these authorities that it is better to conceal capital profits and losses from stockholders and creditors than to risk placing emphasis on capital profits and losses instead of on profits and losses resulting from the operation of the business. The evils involved in accepting this point of view have been reviewed elsewhere in this work. Those who have a right to receive financial statements relating to a business have a right to be informed of all of the profits and losses of that business, and it should not be the function of an accountant to determine what information should be given and what should be withheld. Surely it must be evident that, if stockholders are denied information which they have a right to know, they are placed in a position to be exploited by individuals who do have this information.

It seems to the writer that the tremendous importance of capital profits and losses is the best argument that could be advanced against withholding knowledge of them from stockholders. As Dickinson has said, many cases are on record where a business has been operated for years with poor results but where the capital profits on fixed assets have, in the end, been so large as to dwarf the losses from operation. A profit and loss statement drawn along the lines suggested above would give stockholders and creditors periodic information relative to the progress of capital profits or losses, and would make it impossible for insiders to benefit by accumulating or distributing stock to take advantage of increments or decrements of which stockholders were not advised. As a matter of fact, business men are coming to realize more and more that the external forces influencing a business are fully as important, if not more important, than the skill or lack of skill with which a business is operated. During depressional times, when the values of all assets are declining, it is the exception rather than the rule for a business to earn an operating profit, even though it may have the most skillful management obtainable. On the other hand, during periods of prosperity when the values of all assets are increasing, it is the exception rather than the rule for a business to lose money from its operations, even though the caliber of its management may be quite indifferent.

From a strictly analytical point of view, it seems very doubtful whether profits from business operations can ever be entirely separated from purely external profits and losses. Every sale by a company of its own product involves a non-operating profit or loss, if any change has taken place in price levels between the start of production and the date of the sale. This will be so, regardless of the skill or lack of skill of the management. During good times profit margins will be large, and during bad times profit margins will be small or nonexistent, and this tendency will exist regardless of skill or lack of skill on the part of the management. How then can it be claimed that present profit and loss statements reflect only results from business activities, as distinct from purely external profits and losses arising from extraneous influences? It should be evident that profits and losses bearing no relation to business activities may inextricably pervade an entire operating statement and may color it to such an extent as to be decisive in determining its character.

Despite the foregoing it must be recognized that accountants and laymen have for many years made a distinction between profits resulting from ordinary business activities and those not resulting therefrom. This practice serves, on the whole, a useful purpose and probably little could be gained by disturbing it. Profits of the first type usually arise in connection with the purchase or manufacture and sale of current assets, and hence the term "current profits" is frequently used to describe them. Profits of the second type usually arise in connection with fixed assets, sometimes called capital assets, or in connection with capital stock sold at a premium, and hence are frequently called "capital profits." Perhaps the terms "operating profits" and "non-operating profits" would be more suitable, except that "operating profit" has come to have a meaning which is much too restricted to designate all profits arising from ordinary business activities. For lack of a more satisfactory terminology the terms "current profits" and "capital profits" will be used henceforth in this work.

It is true that the line between profits arising from business activities and those not so arising cannot be drawn too closely. If a sufficiently broad interpretation is adopted, even realized appreciation of land and buildings might be construed to be related to business activities and thus to be a current profit. On the other hand, if a sufficiently narrow interpretation is adopted, gross profit from sales might be construed to be a mixture of current and capital profits arising both from business activities and from external economic forces bearing no relation to business activities. In the writer's opinion the best practicable treatment is to consider the matter from the viewpoint of the ordinary and usual functions and purposes of the business in question. Changes in the economic value of fixed assets, exclusive of depreciation, amortization, or depletion, definitely constitute capital profits or losses. Changes in the value of marketable securities, even though current assets, constitute capital profits or losses unless their owner is in the business of trading in securities. On the other hand, changes in the value of inventories constitute current profits because the acquiring and selling of inventories is presumably an ordinary function of the business in question and an important part of its purpose. The chief objective of the classification is to separate extraneous, accidental, and non-recurrent profits from those produced as a result of activities constituting the main function of the business under review. This objective is not new to accountants.

The preparation of a profit and loss statement upon the lines suggested above is an extremely simple matter after the balance sheet has been properly drawn. Ascertained capital profits and losses, whether realized or not, should be credited or debited to capital profit and loss account to be closed into capital surplus and exhibited as the second section of the profit and loss statement. Unrealized profits on inventories should be included in the calculation of cost of sales in the same manner that accepted accounting practice usually adopts with reference to unrealized losses on inventories. For the rest, the statement should be constructed in the conventional manner, and the resulting current profit figure should be closed into earned surplus. A detailed discussion of the preparation of balance sheets and profit and loss statements, along the lines suggested in this chapter, is contained in the following pages. The relation of inventories to profits, and the proper treatment of profits on inventories, are examined in Chapter XIV.

X

BALANCE SHEET ASSETS

It has been shown that the best indication of the economic value of an asset is its price in an acceptable market, that the next best indication is its replacement cost, and that the third and least accurate indication is its original cost. It follows that a balance sheet which aims to present economic values must exhibit acceptable market prices when these exist, replacement costs when no acceptable market prices are available, and original costs only when, due to the nature of the asset, neither an acceptable market price nor a replacement cost is obtainable. The preparation of a balance sheet along these lines will involve changes from customary accounting methods, and it has been thought best to discuss separately the different classes of items ordinarily found in a balance sheet in order that the variation in treatment may be contrasted with methods existing heretofore.

Land (For Surface Use). Present accounting authority directs that land held for the permanent use of a business be valued at original cost despite a decline or rise in its market value. Legal sanction for this view has been given in the courts, which have held that not only need a company not reflect on its books an increase or decrease in the value of its land but that, in so far as this may affect the showing of profit, it is not right to do so.[1] The argument

[1] *Bolton* v. *Natal Land and Colonization Co. Ltd.* (1892) 2 Ch. 124 (Eng.)

is that of "going values." It is reasoned that the land will not be sold, that its value to the company was, in the first instance, represented by its original cost, that its service to the company cannot change, and hence that its value to the company must remain the same.

It is surprising that such a theory should have been able to withstand the scrutiny of writers, accountants, jurists, and business men for half a century. In the first place, the land is permanently held only in the misleading sense that a corporation, as a fictitious legal person, may perhaps not part with it for a long period of years. But the real people who own the corporation, the stockholders, may be constantly selling their individual stock ownerships in the corporation, and thus the equitable ownership of the land may be constantly changing. Each share of stock represents the ownership of a part of the land and, when one share is sold, a part of the land acquires a new owner. If the land is not correctly valued, a seller may have no way of determining the value of his equity at the time of the sale, and may be left at the mercy of insiders who do know its value and who may deprive him of his share of any market appreciation that may have occurred.

In the second place, it is incorrect to assume that the original cost of the land now represents, or ever did represent, the value of the service of the land to the company. The subjective value, or value in use, of a good is not measured by its cost. Cost is an economic fact. Subjective value is a psychological concept. Subjective value must always exceed cost at the time of a purchase, otherwise no consumer's surplus would exist to provide a motive for the purchase. Under most conditions, the amount of consumer's

surplus involved in a transaction must remain both unknown and unascertainable. This has been discussed in detail, in Chapter V.

In the third place, it is wrong to assume that, because
the service rendered by the land remains the same, the
value of this service remains the same. Value is expressed
in terms of dollars representing a given weight of gold, and
gold itself is one of the most volatile of commodities. If the
value of gold declines, the value of this service, expressed
in terms of gold, must rise. It would be as reasonable to
assume that each ton of steel used by the business was of
equal value, as to assume that the service rendered by
the land for the tenth year of operation was of the same
value as its service during the first year of operation.

The writer has in mind a corporation which for years
owned and occupied its own plant covering a number of
acres situated in a large city. As time went by, the city
grew and the value of the plant increased enormously.
No cognizance of this increase was taken in the accounts
of the corporation, and the stockholders either remained
in ignorance of the value of their company's holdings or
were deluded by the prevalent accounting theory into believing that the "going value" of the plant could never be
greater than its original cost. Speculators accumulated a
large portion of the company's stock in the open market
and, as the price rose, many small stockholders sold their
holdings because the certified published statements of the
corporation showed that neither from the standpoint of
assets nor earnings was the stock worth so much. However, the stock continued to rise and eventually the corporation moved into the country, selling its old plant at a

profit of several million dollars. This was sufficient to pay the large funded debt and to place the corporation in a different financial category altogether. The point is that stockholders of the corporation were in effect deprived of the capital profits that their company had been accumulating over many years, because they were kept in ignorance of these profits and were not supplied with the facts necessary for the formation of a rational estimate of the value of their stock.

Present accounting and legal authority to the contrary, financial statements which do not display the whole truth as nearly as it is possible to do so are apt to be worse than no financial statements at all. Stockholders should not be kept in ignorance of the value of their assets, or of the profits and losses accruing from changes in this value, under the demoralizing theory that a change in value does not constitute a profit or a loss until it has been realized. Stockholders should be informed of changes in the value of their assets and should be told that such profits or losses have not been realized. They should be taught that a rise in land values does not immediately give their company more cash with which to pay dividends, although it may increase the value of their stock. In this way stockholders may be placed on some degree of parity with informed insiders, and may be protected from the forces which now make them likely victims of every rumor because they cannot rely for truth upon the certified reports supplied to them.

Some authorities hold that land held for resale should be valued at "cost or market whichever is lower," but should in no case be carried at its market price if this is higher than its original cost. The reasoning responsible for this dictum conforms to that pernicious accounting rule for "conservatism": "Never anticipate a profit but provide for (i.e., anticipate) all losses." This rule was discussed in Chapters II and III.

Simple honesty requires that all land, whether held for permanent use or for resale, be exhibited at a figure as near to its economic value at the date of the balance sheet as is possible. The best index of economic value is market price, provided that a free, competitive, broad, and active market exists. Such markets for land commonly exist in populated communities. It is mere quibbling to contend that each piece of land is unique in the world and that, therefore, the sale of one piece does not determine the value of another. In every community there are men in close touch with real estate values, having knowledge of each sale that takes place. Such men, for a small fee, can come very close to determining the buying and selling prices of any land in the light of the current condition of the market and the peculiarities of the land. A reasonably accurate market price is therefore easily obtainable. This market price should be used to exhibit the value of the land.

BUILDINGS. Present accounting authority prescribes that buildings be carried at original cost, less depreciation and obsolescence. The assumption of facts and the reasoning supporting this rule are based on substantially the same theory as in the case of land, namely, that the buildings will not be sold and that their service, and consequently their value to their owner, will remain unchanged. This is the theory of "going values." Clearly the same objections apply to the theory here, as apply to it in the case of land.

In the first place the equitable ownership of the buildings may be continually changing with the sale of each share of stock. In the second place there is no basis for the assumption that the cost of the buildings originally represented their subjective value, or value in use, to their owner. In the third place the value of the service rendered by the buildings changes with each variation in the purchasing power of money. Fourthly, through depreciation, the buildings are constantly being sold and, through maintenance, are being constantly repurchased at prices which may be higher or lower than original cost.

For example, consider the application of the theory to a company owning a factory building with a life of twenty years and an original cost of $100,000. Each year one-twentieth of the original building would theoretically enter into the cost of the company's operations and, in a sense, would be sold as a component part of the company's product. To completely offset depreciation, $5,000 would theoretically have to be spent each year on maintenance, provided the purchasing power of money remained the same. But if the purchasing power of money declined, i.e., if wages and commodity prices rose, perhaps $6,000 or $7,000 would have to be spent in one year to maintain the building in its former state. Theoretically, if adequate maintenance expenditures were made, the building would be as good as new at the end of twenty years and it would still be carried on the books at $100,000. But the truth of the matter would be that the company would in effect have sold all of the original building and would in effect have purchased a different building for the sum total of its twenty years of maintenance expenditures. This sum total might have been $150,000, or even $200,000, but the "going value" theory would require the building to be still shown at a value of $100,000. Yet, if an exactly similar building were purchased for $150,000, the theory would direct that this second building be shown at a value of $150,000.

An accountant, in exhibiting the first building at a value of $100,000, is not exhibiting value at all, for after twenty years there is little possibility that values will have remained unchanged. He is not even exhibiting the cost of the building, although he thinks he is, for the actual cost is made up of twenty years of maintenance expenditures during which time the building was constantly being worn out and rebuilt. Actually the accountant is exhibiting a meaningless figure and in so doing is conforming to the dogma of "going value" with which accounting theory is handicapped.

Accountants are hampered by two erroneous ideas concerning fixed assets, such as land and buildings. First, they maintain that, if a fixed asset does not physically change, its value to its owner cannot change. Yet they are quick to reduce the value of a current asset, such as inventory, in case its market price declines. The truth is that the value of all assets is very apt to be changing constantly, both from the standpoint of owners and from the standpoint of others. If the purchasing power of gold falls by one-half, commodities will double in price and a plant which could formerly turn out $1,000,000 of product will be able to turn out $2,000,000 of the same product. At the same percentage of profit, it will be able to earn twice as much money. Why has not the value of the plant doubled in terms of gold? It has, and its former value will now buy only one-half of a similar plant, as every business man knows. To refuse to exhibit the plant at double its former value is simply to undervalue it by one-half in terms of all other commodities.

Secondly, accountants maintain that changes in the value of fixed assets are properly to be ignored because they are due to forces without a business which have little effect upon its operating results. They describe these changes in value as "fluctuations." It is the writer's belief that the year-to-year profits or losses of a normal business, as well as its ultimate showing, are more dependent upon so-called outside forces than they are upon any skill or lack of skill shown in the operation of the business itself. Consider the long decline of the coal mining, textile, sugar, coffee, rubber, and oil industries. Consider the rise and fall of the aviation and radio manufacturing industries. The varying fortunes of the individual companies comprising these industries were not due to manufacturing economies or uneconomies, nor to wise or unwise administration. Their good or bad fortunes were due primarily to world situations influencing the market prices of their products, or the market prices of the commodities and labor they consumed. Such situations are apt to be as entirely without the scope of control of the management of one individual business as is the orbit of the moon.

Furthermore, what importance can be attached to so-called results from operations when non-operating results are unknown? Present accounting principles make it possible for stockholders to receive certified financial statements showing excellent results from operations, and simultaneously to receive notices that their business has failed because a mortgage could not be renewed on fixed assets whose value has "fluctuated" downward. Would a stockholder sacrifice his stock in despair because of operating losses, if he knew that the appreciation in his company's fixed assets offset these ten to one? Many a business has shown dismal operating losses over a period of years and has finally liquidated at a figure sufficient to make its owners rich, all because of appreciation in fixed assets which accountants would scorn to put upon the books.

So-called fluctuations in the value of fixed assets are frequently not fluctuations at all but are long-term trends which may take many years to spend their force and to turn in the opposite direction. By refusing to recognize them no one can make certain that they will shortly return to where they started. Rather it is likely that they may become more and more pronounced as time goes on, until they produce values that bear no resemblance to book values. Clearly, original cost is a very poor index of the value of a building and is open to objections from every side simply because it does not necessarily bear any relation at all to present economic value. The more remote the date of the original purchase, the greater is apt to be the discrepancy between original cost and present value. Present replacement cost is a much better index of the value of a building than is original cost, because present replacement cost approximates what the original cost would be were the building to be purchased or constructed at the present time under competitive conditions. Present replacement cost undertakes to eliminate changes in price levels that may have taken place since the purchase of a building, and that may be largely responsible for changes in its value.

It has been said that the best index of value is market price in an acceptable market, that the next best index of value is replacement cost, and that the third and least accurate index of value is original cost. It often happens that no acceptable market may exist for particular types of buildings, primarily because buildings are apt to be built for specific purposes and consequently often have a limited number of potential buyers and sellers. If such a market does exist, as may be the case with standard office or residential buildings in a city, its prices should be used as present values. In all probability the real estate men consulted to determine the market price of land will also be consulted to determine the market price of a building. Frequently, however, an accountant will find no suitable market from which to determine the value of a building. Especially is this true in the case of buildings for specialized purposes. Values must then be determined from appraisals of present replacement costs and, if an accountant is not qualified to prepare such figures, he must ask an appraiser to prepare them for him. The determination of the replacement cost of a building is not a particularly long or difficult procedure, although one must be sufficiently familiar with building construction to know the types, quantities, and cost of the material and labor required. The process is a matter of frequent routine to contractors, who must estimate building costs before they can submit bids covering proposed construction. After the initial appraisal has once been made, its revision during subsequent audits will occasion little time and effort. The time may come when an accounting firm that does not have at least one man able to perform such work will be considered hardly qualified to undertake the preparation of financial statements.

MACHINERY, TOOLS, AND EQUIPMENT. Present accounting authority directs that these assets be valued at original cost less adequate depreciation and obsolescence. This practice is open to the same objections that apply in the case of land or of buildings. Machinery, tools, and equipment, in common with other assets of a depreciatory nature, usually have no satisfactory market and should be valued at present replacement cost less adequate depreciation, care being taken that obsolescence is considered as carefully as depreciation from wear and tear. This is especially necessary when valuing small tools, patterns, and dies, which are apt to become obsolete very rapidly. The problem of obsolescence is not a new one, and an accountant is faced with it regardless of whether he uses original cost or replacement cost as his basis of value.

The task of determining the present replacement cost of machinery, tools, and equipment falls roughly into two divisions. One of these deals with the appraisal of special or made-to-order items, and the other deals with the appraisal of standard mass-production items. In the case of special items that have been produced by the business under review, the accountant may usually determine present replacement costs merely by calculating the present cost of material, labor, and burden comprising the original costs. This is not apt to be a difficult matter after the variation in price and wage levels has been determined.

Frequently, however, one or more of three complications

will arise to prevent such an easy appraisal of special or made-to-order items. Original costs may not be available, they may be inextricably combined with experimental expenses, or the items may have been produced outside of the business under review. These conditions will usually necessitate an outright appraisal. If the accountant is not sufficiently familiar with shop practice to determine what the items, or their equivalent in serviceability, could be built for under competitive conditions as of the date of the audit, he must employ the services of a qualified appraiser. After the initial appraisal has been made, the following year's audit will be considerably simplified, due to the fact that only new items built during the year will have to be completely appraised. The reappraisement of the old items will consist merely of translating the cost composing them into terms of current commodity price and wage levels.

A calculation of the present replacement costs of standard items will ordinarily involve no difficulty for an accountant. If the items compose the product of the business under review, the accountant need merely ascertain the current costs of production. For this task he is much better qualified than the usual appraiser would be. A determination of the present replacement cost of standard purchased items will consist, as a practical matter, merely in ascertaining the prices for which the items could be purchased new as of the date of the balance sheet, and of determining whether these prices should be adjusted, in view of existing economic conditions, to bring them into line with probable economic values. If the industry producing these items is operating normally, no adjustment will be necessary. On the other hand, if the industry is profoundly affected by a great boom or depression, an adjustment may be necessary to bring prices into conformance with obvious economic values. The judgment of the accountant will be called into play here, but he should never allow himself to lose sight of the economic principles relating to replacement cost as an index of economic value, explained in Chapter VIII.

INVESTMENTS. Present accounting authority generally directs that securities held as temporary investments be exhibited at original cost or at market price, whichever is lower. Rarely do authorities sanction the exhibition of temporary investments at a figure higher than original cost, except in the case of mortgages and bonds to be held until maturity. Here the amortization principle is generally adopted. This principle will be discussed in the following section.

If securities are held as permanent investments, accounting authority prescribes several different rules, each applying to a different situation. In case the permanent investment comprises all or virtually all of the voting stock of another company, modern practice requires the preparation of a consolidated balance sheet in which the balance sheet items of the two companies are combined and the item of investment consequently disappears. If the permanent investment comprises control, but substantially less than all, of the voting stock of another company, modern practice either consolidates the balance sheets or carries the investment at original cost plus or minus the proper proportion of the current earnings or losses of the junior company after payment of dividends. In case the permanent investment comprises less than control, modern practice exhibits it at original cost regardless of its present market price.

The practice of consolidating the balance sheets of a holding company and its wholly owned subsidiaries is sound, provided that the income accounts are also consolidated. There can be no misrepresentation if the companies are treated as one and if all of the facts relative to their assets and earnings are made public. The procedure adopted by some holding companies of carrying their investments in wholly owned subsidiaries at cost, and of treating dividends received as the income therefrom, is maliciously misleading and is apt to be fraudulent in the worst sense. Dividends of subsidiaries, being controlled by the parent company, can be declared in any legal amount regardless of earnings and, if the investment is carried at cost, its value will not change to reflect conditions within the subsidiary and to counterbalance a profligate or a stingy dividend policy. By this method, a holding company may show virtually any earnings desired, whether earned or not. The practice is indefensible and yet unbelievably prevalent, especially among public utility holding companies.

When a company owns control, but substantially less than all, of the voting stock of another company, the equities of the situation will usually require the preparation of both individual and consolidated balance sheets and profit and loss statements. Individual statements will frequently be necessary to inform minority stockholders of the status of their holdings. Consolidated statements are necessary to inform majority stockholders of the status of the entire undertaking as a whole. Consolidated statements unaccompanied by individual statements, however, may at times be seriously misleading. In a recent widely publicized case a large holding company issued its consolidated balance sheet just prior to filing a petition under Section 77B of the Bankruptcy Act. Subsequent events revealed that the parent company was in a very frozen condition but that one of its subsidiaries was in an extremely liquid condition. By consolidating the statements and by not showing separate statements for each company as well, the consolidated group was made to appear reasonably liquid. However, there was a sizable minority interest in the subsidiary above mentioned which prevented the liquid assets of that company from being transferred to the parent company and used for its current needs. The result was that the security holders of the parent company were very much deceived by the apparent ability of the consolidation to pay interest on its outstanding bonds. Whenever there is a possibility that such a situation might arise, no accountant should authorize the issuance of consolidated statements unless these are accompanied by individual statements as well.

When control is not held, all marketable investments should be valued at market whether this be above or below cost. This should be done whether the securities are considered temporary or permanent, for, in a true sense, permanent investment is impossible. At some time in the future there will be a merger, a consolidation, a dissolution, or even a sale of the investment. When this time comes it will be unjust to give stockholders, then existing, the benefit of values that have been forming over many years by virtue of the use of former stockholders' equities. If an investment is held fifty years and appreciates in value each year, it is clearly unfair to wait fifty years before informing stockholders of the value of their holdings. In the meantime many stockholders may have died, or may have sold their interest for a fraction of its value because they were kept in ignorance of the melon to be cut in the fiftieth year. When an accountant labels an asset "permanent," he is acting as a prophet and not as an accountant. He may be well within the bounds of temporary probability in his prophecy, but nothing is more certain than that eventually he will be proved wrong. Permanence is not of this world, and change is a law of nature. When an accountant refuses to exhibit an asset at its present value because he regards it as permanent, he is merely favoring present stockholders at the expense of later ones, or vice versa, and in either case he may be actively promoting the cause of injustice.

A glance at "The Fable of the Two Investment Trusts" in the first chapter will suffice to show the evils of carrying securities at cost when their market price is higher. Reasons for this mistaken practice have been discussed elsewhere in this work. Suffice it to say that the procedure has no justification, either in theory or in practice, when all of its aspects are considered. If a balance sheet is to be impartial, it must reflect economic values as of its date, as nearly as such values can be determined. To the extent that it fails to do this it may become a tool of knaves.

FALLACY OF THE AMORTIZATION PRINCIPLE. The custom of carrying bond investments at cost, plus or minus

amortization of discount or premium, had its origin in a
curious manner. State laws prescribe that the assets of life
insurance companies, computed at market prices, be sufficient to equal the present value of policies in force plus
certain other liabilities, if the company is to be considered
solvent. In 1905 sixty bonds, comprising a representative
index, were selling at prices which made their average yield
slightly more than 4%. From this point bond prices declined until on December 31, 1907, the sixty bonds in this
index were selling to yield an average of 4.9%. Almost all
life insurance companies showed an alarming decrease in
surplus at December 31, 1907, as compared with the previous year, due largely to the decline in market value of the
bonds held in their portfolios. Inasmuch as these bonds
were to be held until maturity, and inasmuch as there was
little question of the safety of most of them, much attention was attracted to the question of whether market price
was not an erroneous basis of valuation, and much emphasis
was placed on the "advantages" offered by the principle of
amortization. Subsequently many financial institutions
adopted and followed the amortization principle in their
accounting methods, with the full consent and encourage-
ment of accounting authorities. The mathematics of different methods of computing amortization has been reduced to formula and presented to students in textbooks
and lectures in a very comprehensive way. This branch of
accounting is so extensive and formidable that it is regarded
as a separate field in itself under the appellation "Accountancy of Investment."

On its face the principle of amortization, applied to
bonds to be held for income until maturity, looks decep-

tively reasonable and sound. Suppose a high-grade bond to have been purchased at 80, payable in twenty years at 100. Roughly speaking, why should not that bond be valued at one point more each year, and such yearly increase in value be added to the nominal interest and treated as income? At the end of twenty years the bond will be valued at 100, this will be received in cash, and everything will balance. Or suppose a high-grade bond to have been purchased at 110, payable in ten years at 100. Roughly speaking, why should not that bond be valued at one point less each year, and such yearly decrease be deducted from the nominal interest to determine the real income? At the end of ten years the bond will be valued at 100, this will be received in cash, and everything will balance.

Investment amortization is based on an ingenious theory which, barring accidents, will work out splendidly in the end as far as the books are concerned. From the standpoint of a permanent owner it is apt to save many a headache and to carry a business smoothly into the harbor of its destination, meanwhile keeping the management sublimely unconscious of the discomforts of the voyage. Yet it should be evident that the theory does not conform to the facts and is therefore untrue, that it serves only the purposes of an assumed permanent owner who probably does not exist, that it does not protect the interests of creditors, depositors, or policy holders who do exist, and that it is extremely likely to work great injustice on stockholders.

The theory is untrue because the value of a bond is its market price, and this fact is deliberately misrepresented. The theory seems to assume that, aside from original cost and maturity date, the only factor affecting the value of a bond is the safety of its principal and interest, provided that it is to be held until maturity by a permanent owner. But the permanent owner exists only in legal fiction and really represents a multitude of more or less temporary stockholders. These stockholders are from time to time increasing their holdings or selling them. If a stockholder's transactions are based in part upon the asset values shown by his company's balance sheet he is being deceived, for these values would be equivalent to a different quantity of the same assets in the open market. To the extent of this difference, the stockholder is getting the better or the worse of the bargain, depending upon whether he is buyer or seller.

Assume, for instance, an investment trust of the fixed type, investing only in bonds and keeping its books on the amortization principle. A depression ensues and the bonds in its portfolio decline far below their book value. An investor, who may have waited years for the opportunity, buys some investment trust stock on the basis of its certified net worth. This investor has been cheated, for less money would have purchased in the open market exactly the same bonds as are represented by his investment trust stock. If he sells his stock after prices have risen above book values, he will again be cheated, this time because the bonds will be worth more than their certified value. It is begging the question to say that fixed investment trusts do not invest in bonds and that, if they did, they might exhibit market values. To the extent that any company carries its bonds on the amortization principle, it is deliberately misinforming its stockholders regarding the present value of its assets, and is catering to injustice or worse.

Returning to the discussion of bond values, it has been stated that the amortization theory seems to assume that, aside from original cost and maturity date, the only factor affecting the value of a bond to be held to maturity is the safety of its principal and interest. Accountants know that many factors may temporarily affect the value of a safe bond, but they are apt to think that, *from the standpoint of an assumed permanent owner,* safety of principal and interest is, after all, the only contingent factor that matters. Even this contention must be denied. Every close student of economics is aware that the value of a dollar, measured in terms of commodities other than gold, i.e., its purchasing power, varies enormously. Compared with the average 1913 dollar, the value of a dollar at the beginning of 1865 was about 48¢. From this date its value rose until in 1896 it was about $1.50. Then its value started falling until in 1920 it was about 44¢. In 1932 its value was about $1.05. The causes of variation in the value of money are fairly well known and under certain circumstances future variations can be predicted with a fair degree of accuracy.

For an admittedly extreme illustration let one assume the existence of an issue of perfectly safe 5% bonds which will mature in ten years. Excluding consideration of its other qualities, this issue will normally sell at a premium or discount, depending upon whether its interest rate is more or less than the market price of the time utility of money, *provided that bond buyers and sellers expect the value of money to remain unchanged until maturity.* But suppose certain forces to be at work such as greatly increasing gold production, or progressive inflation by governmental agencies, which give rise to a conviction among bond

buyers and sellers that the purchasing power of money will
be only one-half as great at the maturity of the bond as it
is now. If this conviction is well founded, a man who now
purchases a bond for $1,000 will receive $1,000 ten years
later, but the $1,000 repaid will be worth only one-half
of the $1,000 invested, so in reality the man will have lost
one-half of his property. Under these circumstances the
bond will sell now for about $500 in present dollars and at
maturity it will not be worth more than this number of
present dollars, although, in the accepted sense, it is perfectly safe in every way.

Let one suppose a company to be holding some of these
bonds for maturity. They were purchased at their face
value of $1,000 each, before the forces above mentioned
caused their market value to decline to $500 each, and are
carried on the books at original cost, no amortization being
necessary because there is neither discount nor premium.
Each bond is now worth five hundred present dollars, or
one thousand dollars of ten years hence. Obviously, by
being carried at $1,000 each, the bonds are not being valued
in dollars of the date of the balance sheet, but are being
valued in dollars of the date of maturity. Yet other assets
in the balance sheet, including the cash, are valued in pres-
ent-day dollars. Is not the misrepresentation obvious? No
amount of contention that the decline of the bonds to 50,
and their future rise over ten years to par, will constitute
a mere fluctuation, can alter the fact that the decline in
value to 50 is real and permanent, and that the loss will
never be made up, even to a supposed permanent owner.
The real change in value occurred ten years before maturity
when certain world conditions or national policies changed.

Although this change in value was expressed in the market price it was not indicated on the books. But the $1,000 redemption value of each bond at maturity will not be worth more than the $500 market value of each bond now. In the light of these facts the refusal of a permanent owner to write his bonds down to market value, on the ground that no loss will result at maturity, assumes the proportions of grotesque humor, and this assumption of the amortization theory falls down even if one subscribes to the possibility of a permanent owner.

Of the fact that the amortization theory does not protect the interests of creditors, depositors, or policy holders, little need be said. Creditors have the same right to know the true status of a company as do stockholders. If the facts are misrepresented, creditors are deprived of a sound basis for deciding whether to extend or to withhold credit. The same reasoning applies with even more force to depositors and policy holders. It has been argued that because of the valuation of bonds at market prices, the policy holder, whose policy expired in the depression year of 1907, received no dividend for his final year; whereas policy holders, whose policies expired in 1908 after bond prices had recovered, received a double dividend; and that this was obviously unfair. But the 1907 policy holder was paid off in 1907 dollars and could purchase more with them, even without his dividend, than could the 1908 policy holder who was paid in 1908 dollars.

One can deplore changes in economic values all he likes and can argue that such changes should not occur, but the fact remains that they do occur and that anyone who ignores them is exceedingly apt to find himself in the same predicament as the mythical ostrich who buries his head in the sand when pursued by danger. The investment amortization theory is false, both in its premises and in its conclusions. It is unjust and pernicious in its results, and the high favor in which it is held by the accounting profession reflects no credit upon the members of that profession.

XI

BALANCE SHEET ASSETS
Continued

INVENTORIES. Present accounting authority directs that inventories be valued at "cost or market, whichever is lower." The argument used is that of "conservatism," supported by the rule: "Never anticipate a profit but provide for all losses." Thus Hatfield says:

> General usage prescribes that merchandise on hand shall be inventoried at cost rather than at selling price. Prudence further demands that merchandise which evidently cannot be sold except at a loss, be marked down even below the cost price. If one could count not only on good faith but as well on unbiased judgment in making inventories, the taking of the present market value, instead of the cost price would not be objectionable, but rather to be commended. . . . Logic perhaps demands that the quoted price should be taken as well when over as when below cost price, but this is not permitted by German law, although the Austrian law allows it to be done.
> American practice agrees with the German law. . . . The conservative rule, generally adopted, is that merchandise is to be inventoried at cost except where there is a decline in value, in which case the lower value is to be used.[1]

Dickinson says:

> On the other hand a balance sheet is required to show the true financial position as a going concern. The inventory at actual cost

[1] Hatfield, *op. cit.*, pp. 101, 102.

may represent more or less than the market value, and, therefore, overstate or understate the assets; but to change the valuation would be to take up a profit or provide for a loss which might never be realized owing to subsequent changes in market value. Sound commercial principles require that no credit be taken for profits until they are realized; but further, that if there is any possibility that what remains unsold may not realize its cost, a proportion of the realized profits on sales which have been made, should be carried forward to cover these possible losses. It is accordingly generally recognized as a correct accounting principle that if the cost value of the inventory exceeds the market value, a reserve should be created to bring it down to the latter value, while, on the other hand, if the market value exceeds the cost, no credit should be taken for the profits until they are realized by an actual sale.[2]

And Montgomery says:

If purchases have been made on a falling market, it is not conservative to place a higher value on an inventory item than the price at which the same thing can be duplicated in the open market. It deceives the banker, creditor, and stockholder, who have a right to believe that the values stated are real values as of the date of the balance sheet.

It may seem inconsistent to advocate a somewhat different principle when purchases have been made on a rising market and where the goods cannot be duplicated, except at a higher price. In this case, however, the conservative course is to carry the items at cost and thus do away with the objectionable practice of anticipating a profit.

The safest rule is the better one to follow, and this is unquestionably cost or market, whichever is the lower . . . bankers are never pleased to learn that an inventory has been marked up and a profit taken which is not yet realized.[3]

[2] Dickinson, *op. cit.*, p. 94.
[3] Montgomery, *op. cit.*, p. 104.

Except for the statement about pleasing the banker, the above quotations can be boiled down to two principles which may be worded as follows: "It is better to understate values in the balance sheet than to include an unrealized profit in the income account," and "It is better to include an unrealized loss in the income account than to overstate values in the balance sheet." Accounting authorities seem to have assumed that either the balance sheet or the income account must of necessity be wrong and to have decided to make the error an understatement in each case, either of assets or earnings. Apparently it has never been thought possible to state correctly both the balance sheet and the income account at the same time.

It seems to be conceded by the accounting authorities cited that, strictly from the point of view of the balance sheet, and ruling out all questions of income, it is better to exhibit inventories at market value than at cost. This is sound reasoning, for the banker, creditor, and stockholder do have a right to believe that the values stated are real values as of the date of the balance sheet. Any other course results in opening the door, with relation to inventories, to the injustices and absurdities that have been shown to result when any asset is stated at other than its economic value. Inventories should always be valued at market whenever an acceptable market exists. The question of bookkeeping entries and the treatment of profits or losses resulting therefrom will be covered in later chapters.

An acceptable market will be found to exist for almost all inventories consisting of basic commodities such as wheat, provisions, coffee, rubber, cotton, copper, and many others. These items should all be exhibited at market prices. But many inventories will be found to contain items such as goods in process, or finished goods, which have no acceptable market and which must therefore be valued at the best remaining index of value, namely, present replacement cost. Here an accountant is confronted with the problems that have always existed with relation to this class of assets. Suitable allowances must be made for obsolete, damaged, or unsaleable merchandise, and values must be scaled down accordingly. The use of replacement cost as an index of value does not affect such matters in the least. It merely seeks to bring the basis of original cost up to date by determining what such a cost basis would be as of the date of the balance sheet. Thereafter, the valuation process should be performed as heretofore except that present replacement cost, instead of original cost, should be used as a base.

In the determination of present replacement costs for inventories, an accountant can usually very well act as his own appraiser. He can easily determine the original cost of work in process, or of finished goods, because this has long been a familiar part of his work. After he has determined original cost according to his usual methods, his only new problem will be to translate this original cost into present replacement cost. If the inventory is of recent origin and if no appreciable change has meanwhile occurred in elements of cost, such as wages, cost of material, or methods of manufacture, an accountant may safely assume that original cost is identical with present replacement cost. If, however, the inventory was manufactured from raw material costing more than its cost at the audit date, the calculation of present replacement cost would involve a reduction of original cost by the amount of the decline in the cost of such raw material. Or, if the raw material had increased in cost, the original cost should be correspondingly raised to arrive at present replacement cost. Similarly, if the wage scale had changed, original cost should be increased or decreased by the amount of this change. In case improvements in manufacturing methods had been made, the resulting decline in production costs should be applied to the whole inventory to calculate present replacement value. The theory is simple, although the application may at times present difficulties. Where intelligence is applied, however, the results can hardly fail to be more indicative of present economic values than the results to be obtained from a blind reliance upon original costs.

There will occasionally be situations where judgment must be used in accepting replacement costs, within a plant under audit, as being indicative of economic values. An accountant should never forget that he is trying to determine economic values, not replacement costs. Replacement cost is not value but is, under normal conditions, merely a reliable index of value. Under abnormal conditions replacement cost possesses grave defects as an index of value, discussed in the chapter relating to imputed market prices. Yet it is, in the absence of an acceptable market, the best index of value available. In the long run, granted the absence of monopoly and a potential supply equal to demand, the value of any useful asset will normally fluctuate around its replacement cost. This will occur because, if value remains below replacement cost, production will tend to cease and demand will raise value until production is resumed. Or, if value remains greatly above replacement cost, the profit motive will encourage production until the competition of sellers causes value to decline. It is obvious that, to serve as an index of value, replacement cost must be looked at in the light of potential production. An isolated case of high or low replacement cost no more establishes economic value than one swallow makes a summer. In abnormal situations due regard must be given to the probability that value may be either above or below replacement cost.

Hence, in case of a decrease in the cost of raw materials, labor, or manufacturing processes, it is right to adjust replacement costs accordingly. These factors are broad in their influence and affect costs, not only in one plant, but in other existing or potential plants as well and, by increasing the competition of sellers, weaken price structures and reduce values. But it may happen that a plant, through lack of sales, may gradually reduce its operations throughout a year with the result that its last production order may show an enormous factory overhead percentage and, consequently, a very high replacement cost. If this high replacement cost is adopted as an index of value, the accountant will be flying in the face of the facts. In the first place, supply is greater than demand and thus it can logically be assumed that economic value will, at the time, be below replacement cost. Secondly, the replacement cost that functions best as an index of value is not that of an isolated production order, but that typical of an industry as a whole. An isolated case of high cost has little standing as an index of value. In such a case an accountant would do well to use the prime cost of the last production order, plus a reasonable overhead percentage, as his replacement cost index of value. This procedure, in the hands of an intelligent person, is almost certain to result in a more accurate statement of present value than is the present accounting method of relying blindly on original costs regardless of the circumstances under which they have been incurred.

CASH, ACCOUNTS AND NOTES RECEIVABLE. Present accounting procedure ordinarily exhibits accounts and notes receivable at their face amounts, especially if the notes bear interest and if the accounts are due after short periods, such as thirty or sixty days. If the notes do not bear interest, a reserve is frequently set up to cover interest at a reasonable rate to each maturity. If there is doubt as to the collectibility of either the accounts or the notes, a reserve for bad debts is usually created and, in most cases, the amount of the credit to this reserve is based upon the volume of sales for the period under review. With these exceptions, accounts and notes receivable are customarily valued at their face amounts.

There seems to be no better way of handling accounts and notes receivable than that now used. Such items are not the equivalent of cash because they lack the factor of time utility possessed by cash. Yet they commonly have no market price, and their replacement cost would normally be the exact equivalent of their face value. In the case of short-term accounts, an attempt to determine the value of the missing time utility factor would hardly seem to be worth the trouble. In the case of notes, interest may be assumed to represent the value of the time utility factor, although in exceptional instances this may turn out to be far from the truth. A company manufacturing locomotives may sell these to foreign governments in exchange for interest-bearing notes maturing five years hence. During the five years the purchasing power of money may decline one half and thus the time utility factor, in this one respect alone, may prove to have been worth one-half of the face amount of the notes. If market prices were ascertainable for accounts and notes, the only justifiable course would be to exhibit these market prices as values, for the same reasons that apply to the proper valuation of any asset. But, in the absence of a market price, an accountant can hardly presume to weigh and value the many imponderables that go to make up the value of the time utility factor. Under the circumstances, for sheer lack of a satisfactory alternative, he must continue to exhibit such items at their face amounts, less suitable reserves, and to leave to others the task of estimating the extent to which the future may show this amount to have been incorrect.

Cash should be exhibited at its economic value which, under normal conditions, will be its face value. In countries with a depreciated and unstabilized currency, such as postwar Germany, there would seem to be much merit in presenting balance sheet values on a gold basis, and this would entail the exhibiting of ordinary currency at an amount less than its face value. The consideration of such a situation is, however, without the scope of this work.

GOODWILL. Goodwill, according to current usage, has become a sort of optional asset. Now you see it and now you don't. Companies whose large earnings prove that they possess goodwill in abundant quantities would scorn to display it. Other companies, whose earnings are such as to entitle them to claim no goodwill whatever, display it in profuse amounts, only to write it off if later good fortune grants them a real claim to it. Except in exceptional instances, the appearance of goodwill in a balance sheet has become a badge of badwill, a sign of trouble, an indication of watered stock, or the hallmark of a young company which has not yet created sufficient real goodwill to enable it to dispense with the item in its balance sheet. Recognizing this, many sound companies display goodwill prominently in their balance sheets opposite a valuation of $1.00, to indicate that they possess goodwill and that they therefore do not intend to exhibit it as an asset. Under these circumstances goodwill has become largely meaningless. As a matter of ordinary business it serves merely to excite suspicion or to arouse adverse comment. No intelligent method is used to value or to revalue it from time to time except that accountants insist that it be valued not in excess of what they are pleased to call its cost. Most accountants will sanction its reduction, or its total elimination, at any time.

If goodwill constituted an asset, it should appear in the balance sheet of every company possessing it, and no accountant should sanction its being written off while it still exists. But it is not an asset, in the sense that other assets in the balance sheet are, and this fact is well supported by practice even though it be vigorously combated in theory. In theory goodwill is an attempt to capitalize the future excess earning power of a business, as indicated by the relation of its past earnings to its present net assets. This capitalized amount is called an asset and is placed in the balance sheet to make the net assets conform to the theoretical total value of the going business as a whole. Thus goodwill might more properly be labeled "Expectation of extraordinary profits in the future." If this were done, at least the nature of the item would be explained to the public, and perhaps the accounting profession would be called upon to amplify its rule that it is unwise to anticipate a profit.

The notion of treating goodwill as an asset arose from a misconception of the function of a balance sheet. This subject is discussed in Chapter XIII under the caption "The Balance Sheet Function." In the absence of a market price no one can intelligently attempt to determine the total value of a going business as a whole, save by an inspection both of its balance sheet and of its profit and loss statement. Balance sheets do not exhibit the total value of a going business as a whole. They exhibit its financial strength, which is an important element of its value. A second important element is its earning power, as displayed by its profit and loss statements. By earning power is meant the amount of earnings, the stability of earnings, and the trend of earnings. These two elements, financial strength and earning power, considered together, may give a clue to the third and most important element of the total value of a going business, namely, the outlook for its future.

Goodwill is, theoretically, an attempt to capitalize future excess earnings and thus to enable a creditor or a stockholder to determine the total value of a going business as a whole, from a glance at the net assets in the balance sheet. In other words, it is an attempt to appraise the present value of the outlook for the future. It is an attempt to cause balance sheets alone to reveal values that can, as a rule, be only roughly indicated by both balance sheets and profit and loss statements, taken together in their relation to the probable outlook for the future. In theory, goodwill should be revalued with the preparation of each new balance sheet. For example, a company may have had large earnings for years, when changing conditions cause obsolescence for its product, or a bad outlook for its industry. The goodwill may disappear over night. Yet then, of all times, will it be retained in the balance sheet because the company's lowered earnings will not permit it to be written off.

The total value of a business as a whole is best expressed by the price of its equities in the market place. The difference between this value and the value of the net assets without goodwill constitutes the present market value of theoretical goodwill. Although, in the event of the outright sale of a business, accountants may use the market value of a company's securities to determine the value of the goodwill involved in the transaction, this method is never used by accountants to revalue goodwill from time to time. If goodwill were accurately exhibited, it would equal the precise difference between the book value of a company's stock and its market price. After being introduced into a balance sheet, it would merely have the effect of causing the book value of the stock to be equal to its market price. In many instances this would require the exhibition of badwill, rather than goodwill, because market prices frequently fall below book values. It would certainly necessitate the adjustment of goodwill with the preparation of each new balance sheet.

But if the business is not a corporation, or if its stock is not traded in a market, how is an accountant to ascertain the present value of its goodwill? If the business has just been sold, the price at which it changed hands might be taken as its total value, except for the fact that, more often than not, this price will be neither a competitive price nor a cash price. Obviously, except in rare instances, accountants will have no means of ascertaining the value of the goodwill of a business. Even though the value of goodwill were ascertainable, no purpose would be served by its inclusion in a balance sheet, because no one would look at a balance sheet to find the market value of a company's stock. He would look at the newspapers instead. On the other hand, such inclusion would be very apt to confuse or deceive many stockholders when they attempted to compare such a company with one whose goodwill was not susceptible to valuation.

So much for the theory by which goodwill is ordinarily explained and justified. In actual practice it finds its way into a balance sheet by a number of methods, and some of them bear not even a remote resemblance to the process of capitalizing excess earnings. In most cases goodwill arises through the purchase of a business, although at least one accounting authority suggests that the first few years' operating losses of a new business be charged to goodwill and set up as an asset. Goodwill arising from the purchase of a business may be the result of a calculation or it may not. Such a calculation may follow any one of a dozen highly different formulas. The ordinary procedure is, first, to determine the earnings which may be considered normal for the existing net assets without goodwill. This sum will vary according to the rate used, which may be 7%, or more, or less. Next, these normal earnings are deducted from the actual earnings of the past year, or from the average earnings of the past two years, or from the average earnings of any number of years, to determine the excess earnings that may be considered applicable to goodwill. Next these excess earnings are capitalized, the multiplier being one, two, three, four, five, ten, or any number considered proper for the type of business being considered. The final result is usually assumed to be a scientific determination of the value of the goodwill in question.

Another example of the calculation of goodwill may be illustrated by a typical consolidation of two businesses. A corporation may approach a business with a proposal to buy it outright and to issue capital stock in payment therefor. The price agreed upon may be merely the value of the assets of the business to be purchased, because this business may never have shown large earnings and consequently may not have been credited with the possession of goodwill. But the capital stock of the purchasing corporation may be selling in the open market at $50, whereas its par value may be $100. Thus when payment is made, $200 in par value of stock is issued for each $100 value of the assets acquired. In order to balance the books an item of goodwill is introduced, making it appear that the goodwill of the business purchased is fully as valuable as all of its other assets put together.

What is the solution to such a muddle? Surely any informed person should concede that, as constituted at present, goodwill is a meaningless figure and is of no help to creditors, stockholders, or management. It serves merely to clutter up a balance sheet, or to obscure a profit and loss statement, and partially to conceal truths that would otherwise be at once apparent. It seems to the author that the solution lies in a recognition of the fact that, although goodwill may be an asset in the sense that a proposed future railroad projection would be an asset to the merchants of a western town, or in the sense that any favorable outlook would be an asset to any business, yet it is not an asset of the kind that can be expressed by a balance sheet. The books of a business are intended to record the transactions and the possessions of a business. They are not designed to record the present speculative value of its future expectations or probabilities. Men and corporations may pay money for such expectations and probabilities, but this does not cause them to become balance sheet assets. The simple truth is that such men and corporations undergo a present sacrifice, or a present loss of capital, for the expected benefit of a future gain. A balance sheet, being merely a statement of present condition, can only exhibit things as they stand after such a sacrifice has been made. The profit and loss statement of an acquired business, compared with its balance sheet, formerly indicated to its owners its probable future, and on this they made the terms of their sale. Such statements, consolidated with those of the purchasing company, will do the same thing as well for the purchasers.

Goodwill is an estimate of the future, as indicated by present assets compared with past earnings, and as modified by all the forces within or without a business of which an estimator has knowledge. It can be created by propaganda and destroyed by a rumor. More frequently than not its value will be both unknown and unascertainable. If goodwill is exhibited in some balance sheets, badwill should be exhibited in others, and both should be revalued with the preparation of each new balance sheet. This procedure would be of doubtful usefulness and of still more doubtful practicability. In the writer's opinion goodwill should have no place in any balance sheet.

DEFERRED CHARGES. Items in this category comprise, on the one hand, a number of prepaid expenses whose time element, or period during which their benefits are to be received, is fairly exact, such as insurance, taxes, interest, rent, subscriptions, and dues. Present accounting procedure requires that the unexpired portion of these prepaid expenses be carried forward as an asset applicable to a subsequent period, and it is entirely proper to do so, for this unexpired portion represents a legal claim for services that have been paid for but not yet received, and constitutes an asset just as truly as does an account receivable. Thus insurance prepaid represents a claim for insurance protection for a definite period. Interest discounted represents a claim for the loan of money for a definite time. Even taxes prepaid represent a claim for governmental protection, or at least freedom from one form of government confiscation, for a definite period. Such assets rarely enjoy an acceptable market price which can be used as an index of their value. They should therefore be valued at present replacement cost which, in almost all cases, will be identical with original cost. If present replacement cost varies from original cost it should nevertheless be used as the index of value in accordance with the principles of valuation previously discussed. Hence, if an insurance policy has six months to run and the premium rate is changed, either up or down, the calculation of prepaid insurance should be based upon the new rate and not upon the average rate for the term of the policy. Otherwise the balance sheet will not state the facts and will be unfair to creditors and stockholders exactly as in the case of the improper valuation of other assets.

Items in the category of deferred charges often comprise, on the other hand, a number of expenses whose time element, or period during which their benefits are to be received, is very inexact and vague, if indeed any benefit at all is to be received. Such items are usually combined under the caption of organization expense and consist of incorporation fees, legal fees, engineering fees, cost of engraving bonds and stock certificates, stock salesmen's commissions, advertising expenses, and even the early operating losses of a new business. Present accounting theory maintains that, because such expenses are expected to produce benefits in the future, they constitute assets that may be written off during the period in which they are expected to produce the benefits. In actual practice both accountants and business men are glad to get such doubtful items out of their balance sheets and usually write them off as rapidly as the amount of earnings or surplus will permit.

Practically, therefore, there is no more uniformity in the treatment of these so-called assets than there is in the treatment of goodwill. If they produce benefits, and thereby justify to some extent their appellation of assets, they are apt to be immediately written off. If they do not produce benefits, and thereby forfeit any shadow of right to be called assets, they are very apt to be continued in the balance sheet as assets. No accountant would allow the omission of insurance prepaid from a balance sheet to which he was expected to certify. He would claim that such an omission constituted a deliberate misrepresentation. Yet he will sanction the omission of organization expenses at any time without regard to their probable beneficial period. Such items are not assets in a balance sheet sense any more than is goodwill. They constitute nothing physical that can be used, nor do they represent a legal claim upon anybody for anything. They possess value only in the sense that an estimate of the future possesses value.

Suppose a man should say to himself: "Much money has been spent for my health and education since I was born. I have a reasonable expectation of increased earning power later on because of the expenditure of this money. Presumably I have better prospects than I should have had, had not the money been spent. I shall therefore exhibit the total of these expenditures as an asset in the balance sheet that I am about to submit to my banker for a personal loan." Upon receipt of the balance sheet the banker would be certain to disregard this item. True, he would give much consideration to the man's chances of success in the future, as anyone would. But he would decline to treat this favorable outlook as a balance sheet asset, much less to value it in money in terms of its original cost. And that is exactly what any informed person does when he sees organization expense or goodwill in a balance sheet. Mentally he draws a red line through them. For he knows that such items represent nothing more than estimates of the future, valued in the crudest and most unscientific manner. Furthermore, he knows that few individuals could hope to value a mere outlook with any degree of accuracy, and he will prefer to rely upon his own guess, in the light of other information available, rather than to take an accountant's figure which is here today and gone tomorrow and which no one could consider to be a sincere value based upon a rational attempt at valuation. No good is accomplished by placing fictitious values for goodwill and organization expense in some balance sheets, by omitting them altogether from others, and by placing half-written-off values in others. This procedure merely confounds the ordinary creditor or stockholder and serves to hide the real situation which otherwise might be quite apparent. Organization expense and similar items have no more place in a truthful balance sheet than has their unsavory brother, goodwill.

It seems extraordinary to what extent human nature will go to ignore, or to conceal, unpleasant facts and to deceive itself into believing that such facts do not exist because it does not believe that they should exist. Most of us are a great deal more like the mythical ostrich than we should care to admit, and we bury our heads in the sands of illusion at the first approach of unwonted circumstance. Every experienced business man knows that, normally, the first thing a new business does is to lose money. A manufacturing company will lose 20% of its stockholders' capital in stock-selling expenses, and a new hotel will operate five

years at a loss before it succeeds to a profitable basis or
fails altogether. Most people know that this initial period
of probation, when the new company is losing money, is
an exceedingly dangerous period with failures rising so
high as to make a successful issue almost an exception. Yet
who ever heard of any company boldly facing the facts
and informing its stockholders and creditors truthfully
about the money it had lost during such a period? Instead
it calls a loss an asset. It capitalizes expenses and carries
them as assets. It adopts a dozen different expedients to
conceal the truth and somehow to avoid showing a deficit
in its balance sheet. It is no defense to say that such expedients do not deceive the informed and that every intelligent person knows that such assets are fiction and
should be disregarded. The fact remains that the whole
truth about profits and losses has not been told, that the
surplus shown is a deliberate misrepresentation, and that
the truth can be obtained only, if at all, by processes of
deduction and analysis on the part of one familiar with the
absurdities of present accounting practice.

Why should it be considered a disgrace for a new business, or for any business, to show a deficit? Some of the
most successful businesses have concealed deficits. Suppose
a man started in the chewing gum business. He raised
$1,000,000. He spent $900,000 of this on advertising
before his sales were sufficient to meet current expenses.
Then he made many millions in profits and paid them
out in dividends, operating merely on the remaining
$100,000, which was sufficient. Why should he consider it
a disgrace to tell the truth about what he is doing? He
possesses $100,000 in assets and is making a million a

year. Must he make believe that the original $1,000,000 capital is all intact and that he never spent any of it? The highest valuation an accountant would permit him to place on organization expense, or goodwill, would be its cost of $900,000. Yet this would probably only be one-tenth the value it could command were he to sell the business. After he had set up $900,000 of organization expense and goodwill in his balance sheet, his accountant would, in following years, urge him to write off these items and to replace them with assets he did not need. Thus he would carry the items at nothing in the end anyway. Have they less right to be called assets after the business has earned $900,000 than they had when it was just breaking even? Obviously not.

The simple truth is that organization expense and goodwill are not balance sheet assets. They are estimates of the future, and they are used guiltily and shamefacedly in balance sheets only as temporary stop-gaps to conceal a supposedly disgraceful condition until the business succeeds or fails. Deficits, of themselves, should not be considered disgraceful. They may often be evidence of extraordinary business acumen. The disgraceful thing is to conceal their existence from those who have a right to know about them. If the accounting profession would once and for all renounce its fitful use of organization expense and goodwill, creditors, stockholders, and the public would be given an opportunity to look facts in the face and to learn some of the fundamentals of finance.

NONMARKETABLE, NONREPRODUCIBLE ASSETS. This classification embraces chiefly those assets which, by their nature, can have no counterparts but are, in a commercial sense, unique. Such assets are patents, copyrights, trade-marks, mines, quarries, oil wells, in fact any asset which has no acceptable market and which by its nature cannot readily be duplicated. Stocks and investment securities without satisfactory markets usually fall within this classification because, as shown in Chapter VIII, they are ordinarily not reproducible in an economic sense. Exceptions to the classification occur in cases where inherently unique assets are yet so similar in their economic uses as to constitute practical duplicates for the purposes of ascertaining market prices. Thus land for surface use is usually so similar to adjoining land that a skilled real estate appraiser can make allowances for slight differences in location or other varying characteristics and, by using the prices for which adjoining land is changing hands, can determine market values almost as accurately as though each foot or acre of land were in fact interchangeable. For practical purposes such land, and other assets in a similar position, should not be considered nonmarketable.

Nonmarketable securities, patents, copyrights, trade-marks, mines, quarries and oil wells, however, are usually true examples of nonmarketable, nonreproducible assets. These assets, being alone in the world, will only in the rarest of instances be traded in a free, competitive, broad, and active market. Hence, in most cases no market prices will exist which can be taken as economic values. Inasmuch as these assets are not freely reproducible, but tend to constitute natural monopolies, present replacement cost would be no index of value even were it possible of computation. This leaves only one remaining index of value, namely, original cost.

Present accounting practice uses original cost as the

valuation basis for these assets. But the use of original cost as a measure of value is subject to such flagrant abuse in the case of nonmarketable, nonreproducible assets, that it may well be considered if all concerned would not be better informed were accountants to omit any attempt at valuation and in its place to supply a résumé of the known facts. The abuse of original cost as a measure of value flourishes in the case of these assets because there is no check in the nature of a market price, or a replacement cost, to limit it to some semblance of probability.

A group of men may own a building. They may form a company and may issue some of its capital stock to themselves for the building and may offer some of it to the public in exchange for cash. Obviously it is to their advantage to sell the building for as much capital stock as possible. They may value it for twice, or even three times, its replacement cost. But there is a point beyond which they dare not go, not because of accountants who will as a rule blindly exhibit original cost as value, but because of the ever present possibility that the courts may declare the transaction fraudulent or that the public itself may have enough knowledge of replacement costs to refuse to buy the stock. Thus the very existence of replacement costs, even though ignored by accountants, serves as a check to the abuse of original cost as a measure of value.

In the case of nonmarketable, nonreproducible assets, however, no such checks exist. There are no market prices and there are no present replacement costs. Accordingly any amount of cost may be set up as value and no one can prove its falsity. A man may obtain a patent. No one knows its economic value. He may form a company and may sell the patent to it for any amount of capital stock that comes into his head. The company may then sell additional stock to the public for cash. The patent may prove worthless and the valuation of the patent may be shown to be utterly fictitious. The same thing may be done with a mine or with other nonreproducible assets. Should the accounting profession lend itself to this sort of thing? Is a man really honest if he certifies to a value of which he knows he is utterly ignorant? The General Electric Company carries all of its priceless patents at a valuation of one dollar, and its balance sheet is certified by reputable accountants. Can anybody claim that, under these circumstances, the values currently attached to nonmarketable, nonreproducible assets mean anything? Is it not better to omit them altogether than to run the risk of deceiving people who may place confidence in the values shown? One is tempted almost to answer in the affirmative.

There are, however, several cogent reasons why the omission of all values for nonmarketable, nonreproducible assets might prove to be a greater evil than their valuation at original cost. Quite frequently these assets possess great value and it seems logical that, on the whole, their valuation at nothing would be much farther from the truth than their valuation at original cost. With reference to mines, quarries, and oil wells, such a procedure would, in many cases, remove values from a balance sheet representing the greater portion of the entire assets of a business. It is indisputable that, in many instances, the omission of such values would result in a great overstatement of earnings due to the consequent lack of provision for amortization and depletion. In some states such an omission might prevent the payment of dividends, or might lead to other legal entanglements.

Under the circumstances, it seems best to value nonmarketable, nonreproducible assets at original cost, although this is admittedly far from an ideal procedure. The fact that original cost is not an ideal basis on which to value these assets does not, however, justify their valuation on a still less ideal basis. In no case should an accountant sanction the writing off of such assets on grounds of conservatism, as is now frequently done. This practice is especially prevalent with reference to patents. If such assets are in use and presumably of value, they should be shown at original cost less allowances for amortization or depletion, as the case may be.

The fact remains, nevertheless, that the valuation of an asset at original cost may at times result in an exhibition of value which varies in an extreme manner from the truth. Creditors and stockholders should be put on notice that this may be the case, and should be informed that original cost has been used only because the actual value is unknown and cannot be determined. It is suggested that this be done by causing the words "Valued at original cost, not susceptible to accurate valuation" to precede the exhibition of each original cost figure in the balance sheet. If this is not done, interested persons may assume that the values shown are economic values, and may rely upon them to their great disadvantage. An accountant cannot be expected to divine the unknowable, or to exhibit values which no one can determine, but he should hold himself duty-bound to warn those who may rely upon his figures whenever those figures might mislead and deceive rather than inform.

XII

VALUATION ACCOUNTS

A VALUATION account is an account set up to adjust the value of an asset. Thus an account entitled "Reserve for Depreciation of Buildings" is in reality a part of the buildings account, but is carried separately for purposes of convenience. The credit balance shown in such a reserve account is commonly deducted, on the face of the balance sheet, from the debit balance appearing in the account of its related asset. Similarly, valuation accounts may be used to record increases or decreases in the economic values of assets due to changes in their market prices. The use of various types of valuation accounts will be discussed in this chapter.

DEPRECIATION. Depreciation is the loss in value suffered by an asset because of its physical deterioration through wear and tear, or through the action of the elements. A mere change in the market price of a fixed asset is not depreciation in an accounting sense. Such changes in market values constitute capital losses or capital gains. Depreciation is physical. It is recognition of the inevitable fact that man-made assets are on their way to the junk heap, that destruction is a law of nature. Orthodox accounting opinion places capital losses and gains in a far different category from depreciation. Capital losses and gains are considered to be extrinsic matters, usually not even to be recognized as profits or losses. Depreciation, on the other hand, is regarded as an intimate operating expense of a business. A factory machine may change in value, due to a rise or fall in its market price, and present accounting practice will scarcely take notice. As this machine wears out, or deteriorates with the passage of time, however, present accounting procedure will require that it be depreciated and that the depreciation written off be treated as a manufacturing expense, just as labor, material, and power are treated as expenses.

Present accounting procedure sanctions two widely used methods of calculating depreciation. One of these methods, known as the "flat basis," calculates depreciation at a fixed percentage of the original cost of an asset. The other method, which is known as the "declining value basis," bases its calculation on a fixed percentage of the depreciated original cost of the asset, commonly called its "declining value." The arguments for and against the use of one or the other of these methods are well known, and it is not pertinent to the scope of this work to review them here. However, it is pertinent to call attention to the fact that the ultimate aim of both methods is to charge off, as depreciation, the total original cost of an asset, less its residual value if any. Both methods are based on the assumption that original cost, less residual value, constitutes the measure of the total depreciation of an asset over its life. The first method calculates this depreciation as a series of equal yearly sums. The second method regards depreciation as a series of declining yearly sums. At the end of the asset's life both methods will have set up the same total amount of depreciation, and the total amount of depreciation will in both cases equal the original cost of the asset less its residual value.

A moment's reflection will indicate how incorrect both of these methods may be, not only with reference to the yearly provision for depreciation but with reference to the total provision as well. The original cost of an asset does not necessarily measure the loss caused by its wearing out. The destruction of an asset may occasion a loss either far more or far less than its original cost. Depreciation is loss in value occasioned by the physical deterioration of an asset. If an asset deteriorates by a given percentage of its value in a given year, it is obvious that the amount of the deterioration will depend entirely upon the value of the asset. If the value is large, the amount of the deterioration will be large and, if the value is small, the amount of the deterioration will be small. Clearly, if depreciation is to be arrived at through the use of a given percentage, the amount to which this percentage is applied becomes all-important. If the amount used represents value, the calculation will result in a percentage of value. If, however, the amount used represents original cost, which may or may not bear any recognizable relation to value, then the calculation may or may not result in a figure which bears any similarity to the actual loss in value. Such a figure might be a microscopic portion of the value of the asset, or it might be equivalent to several times its total value.

For example, during September 1929 a business bought a machine for delivery on January 1, 1930. The price paid was $1,000 cash, which may be assumed to have been its

economic value under the conditions existing at the time
of purchase. This type of machine was well known, completely standardized, and had a life of five years with no
residual value. The financial collapse of 1929 greatly
altered the demand for machines of this type and, by the
end of 1929, their market value new had declined to $100,
at which price they were actively bought and sold during
the following five years. The business in question depreciated its machine at the rate of 20% per year on original
cost and hence, during each of the five years in question,
it exhibited in its profit and loss statement an item of $200
representing depreciation. A second business purchased one
of these machines for $100 on January 1, 1930, and de-
preciated it at the same percentage of original cost, thus
showing an item of $20 each year as depreciation. The
machines were identical, their value during the five years
of their life was at all times the same, and their loss in
value, due to wear, was the same in each year. Yet the
first business informed stockholders, creditors, and the
public that not only was its machine worth more than the
machine owned by the second business, but that the loss
caused by its physical deterioration was ten times as great.
The untruths are evident. The machines were of equal
value and they deteriorated in the same amounts over the
same period of time. Nine-tenths of the depreciation exhibited by the first business was a capital loss, caused in
1929 by external market conditions and having nothing to
do with the operating expenses of the business. Stockholders, creditors, and public, who were led to believe that it
cost more to produce the goods of the first business than
it did to produce the goods of the second business, and

that the second business owned a less valuable asset than did the first business, were simply deceived.

Present accounting authority as a whole protests rather vigorously against the practice of revaluing, upward, assets of a depreciating nature, and thus in effect "calculating depreciation on appreciation." It is contended that this practice is futile because the assets must be entirely depreciated in the end, that it complicates the records, and that it violates the principle of valuation at original cost. Those few accountants who do approve the calculation of depreciation on appreciation, justify their approval on the ground that it tends to conserve the physical capital of a business by creating depreciation reserves sufficiently large to cover increased costs of replacement. In the writer's opinion, both of these arguments miss the point. In the first place, it is an accountant's duty to reveal truthfully the present status and the past history of a business. It is not an accountant's duty to misrepresent the past and present condition of a business for any purpose whatsoever. In the second place, it should be quickly apparent to any accountant that it is impossible to calculate depreciation correctly from year to year and at the same time to have any assurance that the total depreciation written off will alone be sufficient to conserve any kind of capital, whether physical or otherwise. Moreover, if entries both for depreciation and for capital loss and gain are considered, the net amount of these can result only in the writing off of original cost.

From the above it should be evident that if depreciation percentages are to fulfill their purpose, they must be based on values and not on original costs. It should also be clear that several important general influences may affect the value of a depreciating asset. Only one of these is physical deterioration. Another is the ratio of supply to demand, which may directly affect the value of an asset, entirely apart from its physical condition or element of utility. A third influence is obsolescence, which decreases value by having a special influence on demand. This much of the theory of depreciation is rather simple. Its application will now be reviewed.

A new asset with a life of ten years is purchased. Its value in new condition at the time of purchase is $1,000, and its value in new condition one year later is assumed to be $1,200. It is desired to charge off depreciation on a flat basis, i.e., at the rate of 10% per year on the value of the asset in new condition. Since the year-old asset is worth $1,200 in new condition and, since it is assumed to have a total life of ten years, its value in present condition must be $1,200 less one-tenth or $1,080. At this point a question arises as to how much of the change in value is due to depreciation expense and how much is due to capital gain. The asset was worth $1,000 when purchased and it is worth $1,080 one year later, a net gain in value of $80. If the 10% depreciation expense rate be applied to the value in new condition at the end of each year, it will give a figure of $120 for the first year's depreciation expense, which will necessarily result in the capital gain being stated at $200 for that year.

At the end of the second year the asset is found to have a value in new condition of $800. Since it is now two years old, its value in present condition will be $800 less two-tenths, or $640. But the asset was worth $1,080 at the end of the first year, so it must have suffered a net decline in value of $440 during the second year. Depreciation expense during the second year amounted to $80, representing 10% of the $800 value in new condition at the end of the second year. The capital loss during the second year must, therefore, have been $440 less $80 or $360. The following table illustrates the application of this method.

DEPRECIATION CALCULATED AT 10% ON VALUE IN NEW CONDITION
AT END OF EACH YEAR

Value in New Condition (Assumed)	Age	Value in Present Condition	Depreciation Expense	Capital Loss	Capital Gain
$1,000	New	$1,000	–o–	–o–	–o–
1,200	1. yr.	1,080	$120		$200
800	2 yrs.	640	80	$360	
1,000	3 yrs.	700	100		160
500	4 yrs.	300	50	350	
500	5 yrs.	250	50	–o–	–o–
500	6 yrs.	200	50	–o–	–o–
1,000	7 yrs.	300	100		200
1,000	8 yrs.	200	100	–o–	–o–
1,500	9 yrs.	150	150		100
1,500	10 yrs.	–o–	150	–o–	–o–
	Totals		$950	$710	$660

If, however, the 10% depreciation expense rate be applied to the value of the asset in new condition at the start of each year, it will give a figure of $100 for the first year's depreciation, which will result in the capital gain being stated at $180 for that year. Similarly, the depreciation expense for the second year will be 10% of the $1,200 value in new condition at the start of the second year, or $120. This will necessarily result in the capital loss for the second year being stated at $320. This method is illustrated by the following table.

DEPRECIATION CALCULATED AT 10% ON VALUE IN NEW CONDITION
AT START OF EACH YEAR

Value in New Condition (Assumed)	Age	Value in Present Condition	Depreciation Expense	Capital Loss	Capital Gain
$1,000	New	$1,000	—o—	—o—	—o—
1,200	1 yr.	1,080	$100		$180
800	2 yrs.	640	120	$320	
1,000	3 yrs.	700	80		140
500	4 yrs.	300	100	300	
500	5 yrs.	250	50	—o—	—o—
500	6 yrs.	200	50	—o—	—o—
1,000	7 yrs.	300	50		150
1,000	8 yrs.	200	100	—o—	—o—
1,500	9 yrs.	150	100		50
1,500	10 yrs.	—o—	150	—o—	—o—
	Totals		$900	$620	$520

On the other hand, if the 10% depreciation expense rate be applied to the arithmetic average value of the asset in new condition during each year, it will give a figure of $110 for the first year's depreciation expense, which will result in the capital gain being stated at $190 for that year. This is illustrated on page 255.

It will be observed that, in each of the three tables given, the value of the asset is the same at the end of any given year, and that the net combined total of depreciation and capital loss or gain is the same in each year. The only variation between the three applications lies in the allocation of the asset value adjustment between depreciation and capital loss or gain. Whichever formula is used, the net result will be the same as regards the value of the

DEPRECIATION CALCULATED AT 10% ON AVERAGE VALUE IN
NEW CONDITION DURING EACH YEAR

Value in New Condition (Assumed)	Age	Value in Present Condition	Depreciation Expense	Capital Loss	Capital Gain
$1,000	New	$1,000	—0—	—0—	
1,200	1 yr.	1,080	$110		$190
800	2 yrs.	640	100	$340	
1,000	3 yrs.	700	90		150
500	4 yrs.	300	75	325	
500	5 yrs.	250	50	—0—	—0—
500	6 yrs.	200	50	—0—	—0—
1,000	7 yrs.	300	75		175
1,000	8 yrs.	200	100	—0—	—0—
1,500	9 yrs.	150	125		75
1,500	10 yrs.	—0—	150	—0—	—0—
	Totals		$925	$665	$590

asset and as regards the total net profit or loss recorded. It will also be observed that, if the first application is adopted, the proper calculation of depreciation for the current period requires merely that the accountant know the age of the asset and its present value in new condition, whereas, if the second or third applications are adopted, the accountant must be informed of the value in new condition at the end of the previous period. In view of the broad generalizations that must be used in the construction of any formula for recording depreciation, it would seem to be the part of wisdom not to attempt to split hairs, but to use the easiest method available, provided that that method seems certain to stay within the broad outlines of probable truth. Whenever depreciation is charged on a flat basis, no criticism can follow if the percentage adopted is applied to the value of the asset in new condition at the end of the period, as illustrated in the first table above.

In case it is desired to charge off depreciation on the declining value basis, a somewhat different calculation must be used. The percentage used should, as with the flat basis, be applied to values rather than to original costs, otherwise there will be no certainty that the result will be even remotely related to present facts. If original costs were used, these might vary so far from present values as to cause the resulting figures to fall far outside a reasonable area of probable truth. In adopting a declining value formula based on values, it is first necessary to adjust the value in new condition, at the end of the period in question, to what it would be in view of the age of the asset, had the percentage used been applied to it all along on a declining value basis. The resulting figure will represent value in present condition and will be the net amount at which the asset will be exhibited in the balance sheet. The difference between this amount and the value in present condition previously carried on the books at the beginning of the period, will be the net adjustment necessary for the period, and may consist partly of depreciation expense and partly of capital loss or gain. The amount of depreciation expense applicable to the period will have been ascertained during the adjustment of the current value in new condition, as outlined above. Thus, on a 20% declining value basis, the depreciation of an asset with a current value in new condition of $1,200 will be $240 for the first year. The depreciation of an asset with a current value in new condition of $800 will be $160 for the first year and $128 for the second year. Similarly, the depreciation of an asset worth $1,000 in new condition will be $200 for the first year, $160 for the second year, and $128 for the third year. The difference between the depreciation for the period in question and the net adjustment for the period will be the capital loss or gain for the period.

The following table exhibits the same fluctuations of value in new condition as the tables used in illustrating the flat basis method. A depreciation percentage of 20% per annum is used, which is approximately correct for calculating depreciation on a declining value basis with relation to an asset worth $1,000 new and having an estimated residual value of approximately $118 at the end of ten years. The table, however, assumes a net appreciation of 50% in the market value of the asset in new condition at the end of the tenth year, so it is reasonable to assume the residual value to have appreciated 50% also.

DEPRECIATION CALCULATED AT 20% ON DECLINING VALUE, I.E., ON ADJUSTED VALUE IN NEW CONDITION AT END OF EACH YEAR

Value in New Condition (Assumed)	Age	Value in Present Condition	Deprecia-tion Expense	Capital Loss	Capital Gain
$1,000	New	$1,000	—0—	—0—	—0—
1,200	1 yr.	960	$240		$200
800	2 yrs.	512	128	$320	
1,000	3 yrs.	512	128		128
500	4 yrs.	204.80	51.20	256	
500	5 yrs.	163.84	40.96	—0—	—0—
500	6 yrs.	131.07	32.77		
1,000	7 yrs.	208.49	52.12		129.54
1,000	8 yrs.	166.79	41.70	—0—	—0—
1,500	9 yrs.	222.26	55.56		111.03
1,500	10 yrs.	177.81	44.45	—0—	—0—
		Totals	$814.76	$576	$568.57

In calculating depreciation as above illustrated, an accountant will have to ascertain only the age of the asset and its present value in new condition. If the percentage be applied to the adjusted value in new condition at the beginning of the period, or to the average value in new condition during the period, it will be necessary to ascertain the adjusted value in new condition at the beginning of the period. The theoretical gain in accuracy that might result from the adoption of one or the other of these procedures is not important in view of the approximation upon which the whole formula must necessarily rest. The important thing is to keep from getting so far away from probable truth that the figures supplied will be essentially misleading. It is unlikely that this could occur through the use of any reasonable formula applied to actual value, corrected yearly. But any formula, applied to original cost rather than to value, may in time lead to figures which are sufficiently out of line with probable truth to be seriously misleading.

Two other methods of calculating depreciation enjoy some use. One of these is the sinking fund method. The other is the production method, which calculates depreciation according to an established rate per unit of output. No serious objection can be brought against either of these methods, provided that the value to be depreciated is actually an ascertained value, and provided that it is revised from time to time in accordance with the facts. If this is done, however, it will usually be found that the values in question will not agree with the original costs used in devising the initial formula, and thus the advantages of both methods will tend to disappear. Deprecia-

tion is not an expense that can be calculated in advance
with any degree of certainty. Depreciation is loss of value
through physical deterioration and, other things being
equal, is wholly dependent upon the current value of
the asset which is depreciating. The calculation of depreciation will tend to be incorrect to the extent that it is not
based upon current economic values.

OBSOLESCENCE. Obsolescence is the loss in value suffered by an asset because it has been displaced in the
public fancy by assets of a newer, more efficient, or different design. Long before a machine has worn out, it
may be supplanted by a more efficient model and may
become virtually worthless. Styles may change and whole
inventories of goods, such as women's wearing apparel,
may suffer great loss in value although they may be entirely new. The calculation of obsolescence, in advance
of its occurrence, is virtually impossible because this would
require the ability to foresee the results of inventive
genius or the vagaries of public preference.

Present accounting practice usually makes little attempt to ascertain the actual amount of obsolescence that
may have taken place with reference to assets, but is apt
to rely instead upon provision for its future occurrence.
This provision may be made, either by the creation of
reserves for contingencies, or by the overstatement of
reserves for depreciation. Present accounting theory apparently assumes that it is not correct to provide for obsolescence when, as, and if it occurs, but that it should either
be provided for in toto in advance, or should be regarded
as a continuing expense of the same nature as deprecia-

tion. The effect of this treatment is to understate the present assets and earnings of a business, in order that the secret reserves thus created may be utilized to overstate the earnings of a possible future period, during which actual losses from obsolescence may occur. The deception is evident, regardless of whether the anticipated losses occur to the amount anticipated, occur to a far greater amount than anticipated, or do not occur at all. Present accounting authority seems characteristically unwilling to be content to tell the simple truth about facts as they occur. The attempt is continually made to forecast the future, in an effort to smooth out the peaks and dips of economic realities, with the result that interested persons are frequently unable to separate prophecies from actualities and are thereby denied a sound basis of fact upon which to base their own estimates of the future.

Obsolescence arises from outside factors which cause a decline in the utility element of the value of a good, thus reducing the demand for it and lowering its economic value. The opposite situation, i.e., a rise in economic value due to extraneous factors, is considered by accountants to be a capital gain when it occurs in connection with fixed assets. Obsolescence of fixed assets must therefore be a capital loss, not an operating expense similar to depreciation. An important reason for dividing profits and losses into two categories, called capital and current, is to distinguish between those caused by outside market conditions having nothing to do with the use of an asset by a business itself, and those caused by the ordinary and recurrent operation of the business. This orthodox distinction, although not wholly practicable, is at times useful, and it would seem that little could be gained by disturbing it. When an accountant attempts to provide for obsolescence on fixed assets before its occurrence, he is in reality attempting to anticipate a capital loss. Carried to an absurd extreme this principle would require him to prophesy the market price of all fixed assets as of the dissolution date of the business. Obviously the thing cannot be done and it would be both foolish and dishonest to attempt it.

If the value in new condition of a fixed asset is determined as accurately as possible, and if depreciation, amortization, or depletion is written off on the basis of this value, the remaining change in value will be capital loss or gain. This capital loss or gain will include the loss from obsolescence, if any, that has actually occurred to the date of the valuation. If an accountant reports this loss or gain he will be doing his duty, fully and honestly. Furthermore he will be supplying stockholders and creditors with facts that may be of great value to them.

AMORTIZATION. Little need be said here about amortization. It applies chiefly to nonmaterial assets whose usefulness has a definite time limit. Patents, copyrights, leaseholds, concessions, and other assets of similar character commonly expire on a specified future date. Such assets are frequently both nonmarketable and nonreproducible. Hence they will often, of necessity, be carried on the books at original cost rather than at economic value. In such cases an accountant will have no choice other than to amortize original cost over the life of the asset, charging current expense and crediting reserve account with the amortization written off. If, however, the asset in question proves susceptible to valuation, i.e., if its actual or imputed economic value can be determined, then the amortization to be written off should be based on value instead of on original cost. The procedure followed should be the same as that previously explained with relation to depreciation, and the changes in value not accounted for by amortization should be treated as capital profit or loss.

DEPLETION. This term is used to describe the loss in value suffered by wasting assets such as mines, oil wells, or quarries, due to the extraction of their wealth giving deposits. Not only are such assets usually nonmarketable and nonreproducible, and thus not susceptible to valuation, but, in all but exceptional cases, the calculation of their depletion can be little more than a guess. Under such circumstances an accountant can only carry the asset at its original cost and write off estimated depletion, based on the original cost of the asset, as a current expense of production. This is the procedure now generally followed. If the asset can be valued, however, as may happen in exceptional instances, honesty requires that depletion calculations be based on value and not on original cost. Changes in the value of these assets, when due to outside economic forces, are just as truly capital profits or losses as are such changes in the value of any other type of asset, and they should be treated as such.

It may sometimes happen that the value of a wasting asset will rise because a demand is created for it for a use different from the one for which it was required. An oil field may be nearly exhausted when the growth of a city nearby gives part of the oil land great value for building purposes. To refuse to write up the land to its new value will merely result in the understatement of assets and the concealment of capital profits. This practice is morally indefensible, even though the land be still used to produce oil. The land should be written up to its economic value for surface use and no further depletion should be charged off due to the production of oil. The land has become susceptible to valuation because it has acquired a market. Its market price is conclusive evidence of its value, and this market relates to the land in its present surface condition. Therefore, the extraction of oil does not affect the value of the land in any way, and no loss, or depletion, is suffered by such extraction. By exhibiting the land at its market value and by showing the change in value as a capital profit, an accountant will be stating the facts as they exist. Not to do so might place uninformed stockholders and creditors at a serious disadvantage, compared with individuals who are cognizant of the actual situation.

BALANCE SHEET TECHNIQUE. Present accounting practice commonly records depreciation, amortization, and depletion by debiting an appropriately described expense account and by crediting an appropriately described reserve account. The expense account appears in the profit and loss statement, and the reserve account appears as a deduction from the original cost of the related asset on the asset side of the balance sheet. This procedure is logical, convenient, informative, and entirely proper, provided that original cost constitutes the only available basis of valuation for the asset in question. This treatment should therefore be adopted in the case of depreciating assets for which no market price or replacement cost is determinable.

A different treatment must be used for those assets which are susceptible to a more accurate valuation than that provided by original cost. In such cases depreciation will have been calculated on value, not on original cost. Furthermore this value will in all probability have changed from time to time and hence the depreciation set up may be either more or less than the amount required to depreciate original cost to value in present condition. For illustration consider the asset described in the first depreciation table in this chapter. At the end of its fifth year this asset had a value in new condition of $500. Since it was assumed to have a life of ten years and to depreciate 10% each year, it had depreciated 50% at the end of its fifth year. Its value in present condition was thus $500 less $250 depreciation, or $250. Upon examining the table, however, it is found that the original cost of the asset was $1,000, that a total of only $400 depreciation had been set up, and that $350 capital loss had been charged off. Thus the accounts on the books would reveal only that the asset had cost $1,000 and that $400 depreciation and $350 capital loss had been written off, leaving a present value of $250.

The book accounts accurately describe the facts because the asset in question had suffered a loss in value through depreciation of only $400, and the remaining $350 of its loss in value was due to capital losses caused by changes in market price. The question is how best to display the facts on a balance sheet. Three methods appear to be available. The first of these is to display the asset at its value in present condition of $250, exactly as would be done were the asset not a depreciating asset, and to omit from the balance sheet both the total amount of its depreciation reserve and the total amount of its capital decrement. This will usually be found the most satisfactory method because of its simplicity. If the method by which the asset was valued is described on the balance sheet, it would seem unnecessary to set out the calculation as well. The exhibition of a depreciation reserve on a balance sheet has little value, other than to assure the reader that at least some provision for depreciation has been made. The reader has no independent way of determining whether the provision is adequate and, since the figure displayed must of necessity be the accumulated total of a number of calculations dating back to the acquisition dates of the assets, he can at best obtain only a general impression from it.

A second method is to display the present value of an asset in new condition and to deduct therefrom the total depreciation which the asset is assumed to have suffered because of its age. This will result in a figure representing its value in present condition. Thus the asset described in the first depreciation table in this chapter would, at the end of its fifth year, be exhibited at $500 representing its value new. Its depreciation at 10% per year for five years would amount to 50% of $500, or $250. This $250 would be shown as depreciation to be deducted from the value new of $500, leaving a value in present condition of $250. This method arrives at a correct result and exhibits a mathematically correct calculation based upon a consideration of the asset alone, without reference to the profits or losses of its possessor. The objection to it is that it exhibits figures appearing only on the auditor's working papers. The books, of course, would contain accounts showing only the $1,000 original cost of the asset, the depreciation actually charged off of $400, and the net capital decrement of $350. These figures result in the same net total as those appearing on the balance sheet but otherwise they are entirely different because they are not based upon a consideration of the asset alone but are based upon a consideration of the profits and losses which it has occasioned its possessor.

A third method is to exhibit value in present condition as the result of a calculation from the exclusive point of view of the possessor of an asset. According to this method, the asset previously mentioned would be exhibited at its original cost of $1,000. From this sum a deduction of $400 would be made for the loss through depreciation actually incurred by its owner, and a further deduction of $350 would be made for the capital loss actually incurred by its owner. The net figure would thus be $250 and would represent the value of the asset in present condition. This method has the advantage of using only the accounts on the books, but it is complicated and might result in causing a balance sheet to become unwieldy. It correctly reflects the facts from one point of view, however, and no criticism can follow its use provided that it is accompanied by sufficient explanation to insure its being understood.

REVALUATION ACCOUNTS. With reference to obsolescence and to other capital profits and losses, present accounting practice follows no uniform method. Sometimes such items are debited directly to current expense, exactly as though they were ordinary and recurrent expenses of operation. This is often the case with reference to provision for obsolescence on fixed assets. Frequently such items are partially concealed by being posted directly to asset account, with the corresponding entries being placed directly in surplus account, or in one of its subdivisions. Most commonly of all, such items, when not realized, are not recorded in any way and no adjustment of any kind is made. It is partly because of this chaotic state of affairs that the deceptive financial statements now generally prepared are possible.

Capital profits and losses, whether realized or not, should be credited, or debited, to appropriately described capital profit and loss accounts. These accounts should be exhibited as capital profits or capital losses in the profit and loss statement, and thence should be closed into capital surplus on the balance sheet. An appropriate name for such an account relating to land and buildings would be "Capital profit and loss on land and buildings." Entries for realized capital profits and losses should be completed in the usual manner by debiting cash, or its equivalent, and by crediting the asset sold. When capital profits and losses are unrealized, the entries should be completed by debits or credits to appropriately named revaluation accounts. These revaluation accounts, combined with the original cost of the assets in question, less depreciation, amortization, or depletion reserves if any, will represent present value. An appropriate name for a revaluation account relating to land and buildings would be "Revaluation account for land and buildings."

Unrealized appreciation or depreciation of inventories, arising from obsolescence or from changes in market values, should similarly be evidenced by debits or credits to revaluation accounts, instead of by entries posted directly to the asset account. This will preserve the original cost of the assets in a separate account which, combined with the related revaluation account, will supply the present value to be exhibited on the balance sheet. Corresponding profits and losses should be included in the current section of the profit and loss statement, as a part of the cost of sales, thence to be closed into earned surplus. A detailed discussion of this subject is contained in Chapter XIV.

The procedure outlined above should effectively prevent the omission from financial statements of known profits and losses, with its consequent deception of stockholders and creditors. Every profit and loss would be reflected both on the balance sheet and on the earnings statement so that inactive stockholders could scarcely be deceived regarding either assets or earnings. These interested persons would be enabled, for almost the first time, to ascertain *all* of the profits or losses of their company. They would be truthfully informed, for almost the first time, of the real wealth of their corporation and its true financial condition. In short they would be put, as nearly as possible, on a par with informed insiders.

Suggested Form for Balance Sheet Assets. The asset side of a balance sheet, drawn in accordance with the principles herein advocated, would not, in its general appearance, differ radically from those now in use. A suggested form is shown below.

Exhibit A

BALANCE SHEET—DECEMBER 31, 1937

ASSETS

Current Assets

Cash			$ 410,457.49
Marketable Securities—at market price			$1,049,685.20
Notes Receivable—at face value	$ 900,864.50		
Accounts Receivable—at face value	1,655,521.00		
	2,556,385.50		
Less Reserve for Bad Debts	145,400.25	2,410,985.25	
Inventories			
Raw Material—at Market Price	865,444.05		
Work in Progress—at replacement cost	1,586,749.23		
Finished Goods—at replacement cost	366,982.31	2,819,175.59	
Total Current Assets			$ 6,690,303.53

Investments—at original cost, not susceptible to accurate valuation

Minority interests in affiliated companies		$ 763,491.85	
Sundry unlisted securities		27,822.19	
Total Investments			$ 791,314.04

Deferred Charges

Insurance Prepaid	$ 4,978.53	
Taxes Prepaid	7,532.08	
Total Deferred Charges		$ 12,510.61

Fixed Assets

Land for surface use—at estimated market price			$ 140,212.34
Buildings—at replacement cost	$1,120,713.64		
Machinery and Equipment—at replacement cost	1,480,220.62		
Tools, patterns, etc.—at replacement cost	371,895.32		
Other Fixed Assets—at original cost, not susceptible to accurate valuation		2,972,829.58	
Mine land, exclusive of buildings, etc.	750,000.00		
Patents, trademarks and copyrights	36,847.16		
	786,847.16		
Less allowance for depletion and amortization	309,342.63	477,504.53	
Total Fixed Assets			$ 3,590,546.45
			$11,084,674.63

XIII

BALANCE SHEET LIABILITIES

THIS CHAPTER will examine the treatment of those balance sheet accounts usually found on the liability side of the balance sheet. As elsewhere in this book the aim will be to contrast present accounting practice with the new treatment suggested, and not to discuss present accounting practice when no deviation therefrom is recommended.

THE BALANCE SHEET FUNCTION. The function of the asset side of a balance sheet should be to exhibit a classified summary of the valuable possessions of a business. The total value of these possessions should equal the total wealth owned by the business as of the date of the balance sheet. The total wealth owned by a business is not necessarily synonymous with the total value of that business as a whole. The value of a business as a whole is only partly dependent upon the wealth possessed by it. The future market outlook for its products may at times have more influence upon its value as a whole than all of its possessions. Its strategic position within an industry may give it a nuisance value in consolidation proceedings that may far exceed the combined value of all its possessions. This subject has been previous discussed in Chapter XI under "Goodwill."

The wealth owned by a business can consist only of material goods, or of legally enforceable claims for goods or services not yet received. The cost of a mere expectation, or of a favorable outlook, does not constitute a balance sheet asset. Accountants cannot undertake to value expectations, outlooks, or strategic positions, because this would imply the ability to determine the value of a business as a whole. Virtually all of the expenses of any business are incurred for the purpose of giving that business a more favorable outlook. But these expenses are not balance sheet assets, unless they enhance the market prices of material goods, or result in legal claims for goods or services.

It may be necessary for a flour mill to transport wheat from a grain elevator to its mill, and the exact cost of this transportation may be easily determinable. After having transported the wheat, the flour mill may presumably have enhanced its outlook for making money, by the exact amount of its transportation costs. Its outlook may be just that much more favorable than the outlook of another flour mill which has not yet transported its wheat. Yet the transportation cost is an expense, not an asset, unless the market price of the wheat has been enhanced. The transportation cost is an expense for exactly the same reason that the cost of the flour mill's telephone service is an expense. Both expenses are necessary, both presumably give the flour mill a more favorable outlook for making money, but neither expense enhances the market price of a material good nor results in a legal claim upon anybody for anything. Both expenses presumably increase the value of the business as a whole, but neither expense enhances the value of the possessions of that business.

Frequently the value of a business as a whole is far less than the combined values of its possessions, often it is far more. Thus, a large buggy whip business, as a business, may be worth little or nothing, and perhaps no one would pay anything for a one-third interest in it, were it to continue in the buggy whip business. Should it continue in this business, its losses would presumably soon consume all of its wealth. Yet the combined value of it possessions, it machinery, its buildings, its land, may be considerable and may be immediately realizable upon liquidation. On the other hand, it is commonplace for a business to face such a favorable future that its value as a whole vastly exceeds the total wealth owned by it. At the start of the World War, many individuals willingly paid sums for stock of the Bethlehem Steel Corporation that were far in excess of values justified either by the wealth possessed by the business, or by its past earnings.

Balance sheets, as constituted heretofore, have made no pretense of exhibiting the total value of a business as a whole. To do this accountants would have to face the necessity of introducing an account, such as goodwill or badwill, into every balance sheet, and of revising these accounts with the preparation of each new balance sheet. Furthermore, accountants would have to face the fact that the credit account for badwill would probably have to be used fully as often as the debit account for goodwill. Furthermore, in the great majority of cases, accountants would probably find themselves totally without the means of determining the value of a business as a whole in the first place. To the best of the writer's knowledge, such a procedure is not followed now, nor has it ever been followed. It would be of doubtful usefulness and still more doubtful practicability. This work does not recommend it.

The function of the liability side of a balance sheet should be to exhibit the equities of different parties in the total wealth of a business, as shown by the asset side of the balance sheet. Employees may have a claim on that wealth for accrued wages. The Government may have a claim on it for taxes. Trade creditors, bankers, and bondholders may have contractual claims for goods or money furnished by them. Finally, stockholders have a claim for everything that is left over. Since the asset side of a balance sheet does not exhibit the total value of a business, but merely exhibits the total wealth owned by that business, neither can the liability side of a balance sheet exhibit the total value of the liabilities of that business, but can merely exhibit the status of these liabilities as legal claims on the undivided wealth of the business.

The bonds of a business may be selling for 90 today and for 95 tomorrow. If the balance sheet of the business is correctly drawn, it will indicate whether or not the wealth of the business was sufficient to meet the bondholders' total legal claim as of the date of the balance sheet. But the bonds may not mature for five years, and the price of the bonds may therefore depend to a large extent upon the future outlook for the business over the next five years. Unless the asset side of a balance sheet is made to exhibit the total market value of a business as a whole, the liability side of the balance sheet cannot be made to exhibit the market values of the liabilities and capital stock of that business. Furthermore, in many cases, the market values of existing liabilities and capital stock may be completely unknown. When such market values are known they are usually as available to stockholders and creditors as they are to accountants, and little additional information would be supplied by using them.

From the above it should be clear that balance sheets are designed to exhibit the value of the possessions of a business, not the value of the business itself as a going concern. Goodwill has no more place in a balance sheet than has badwill, and neither has any place in a balance sheet unless a revolution is to occur in the traditional concept of the balance sheet function. It should also be clear that, until such a revolution takes place, all liabilities should be exhibited at amounts representing their legal claims on the possessions of a business, and that stockholders should be shown as entitled to the difference between these amounts and the total value of the wealth owned by the business.

CAPITAL STOCK. Accounting authorities have for many years dwelt at length upon the legal and accounting questions arising in connection with the issuance of capital stock. Little has been left unsaid on the subject, and it is not within the scope of this work to attempt a detailed discussion of the problems encountered. Part of the difficulty has been engendered by contradictory or hairsplitting legal decisions relative to the liability of holders of capital stock that has been sold for less than the equivalent of its par value. This is a matter which need not directly concern an accountant. Most of the remaining difficulty is caused by the frequent inability of accountants to ascertain, with accuracy, the actual value received in exchange for capital stock.

Entries relating to the issuance of capital stock are extremely simple, provided that the value received in exchange is known. If stock is sold for its par value in cash, the entry comprises merely a debit to cash and a credit to capital stock. If stock is issued for cash at a discount, the accountant should obtain a legal opinion as to whether purchasers are legally liable for the discount. If they are, and if the liability is clearly recognized by stockholders, the discount may be carried as an asset under the heading of uncalled subscriptions. If the liability is not in the nature of uncalled subscriptions, it should be shown on the liability side of the balance sheet as a deduction from the par value of the outstanding stock. If no liability exists, the discount should be shown as a debit to capital surplus. If "no par value" stock is issued, no question of discount will be apt to arise. Premiums received in connection with the sale of stock should be credited to capital surplus. All of this is in line with accepted accounting practice.

The accounting problem with reference to the issuance of capital stock works down almost entirely to the practical matter of ascertaining value. Stock is frequently issued for property or services of an alleged value that seems greatly in excess of its probable economic value. Some accounting authorities urge that such consideration be accepted at its alleged value, while others maintain that it is the duty of an accountant to attempt to determine its true value and to exhibit a discount on the capital stock if one is found to exist. The courts generally refuse to interfere and commonly hold that stock, issued for considerations other than cash, is presumably issued for its full value.

In view of the recognized leniency of the courts, it would seem idle for an accountant to attempt to set himself up as a higher legal authority by exhibiting a discount in cases where the courts would presumably refuse to hold that one existed. In any event, the legal question is the only one that need exist because, regardless of whether capital stock has or has not been sold at a discount, an accountant should invariably value all assets at their present economic values. It is not the duty of an accountant to say whether or not a legal liability was incurred by buyers at the time of the sale of capital stock. It is, however, clearly his duty to exhibit values as he finds them as of the date of his financial statements. The objection of some authorities to the recognition of inflated values, acquired in exchange for capital stock, may well be caused not so much by their zeal for legal theory as by their knowledge that if an inflated value gets into a balance sheet, present accounting principles will probably cause it to remain there indefinitely without modification or revision. These authorities seem able to sanction the exhibition of a bona fide original cost, regardless of its variance from actual value, but they seem unable to stomach the exhibition of an inflated original cost, even though it be no further from present value than other costs of the bona fide variety.

As a matter of fact it is possible for capital stock to be issued for full value and yet be exchanged for balance sheet assets equivalent only to a tithe of that value. The writer has in mind an exclusive and expensive apartment house property. The adjacent land was acquired by a real estate speculator who promptly offered it to the apartment house corporation at an enormously inflated price, stating that if it were not purchased he would erect tenement buildings on it and effectively transform the location into a slum district.

No legal protection was available and the speculator's price was paid. No one can fairly contend that in this instance the action of the apartment house corporation was unsound, nor that the land and the protection from encroachment were not worth the price paid. Yet the land itself was worth only a fraction of its cost, and this worth was all that should have been exhibited in the corporation's balance sheet. The difference between this worth and the price paid should have been treated as a capital loss, to be exhibited in the capital section of the profit and loss statement and thence to be closed into capital surplus.

Frequently an entire business is purchased in exchange for a portion of the purchaser's capital stock. The physical assets acquired may be worth only a fraction of the price paid. Even goodwill may be said to be nonexistent because the business acquired may have had a long series of yearly losses. Yet the strategic advantage accruing to the purchaser may be so great as to make the purchase economically sound, even brilliant. In such cases capital stock is sold for full value, legally and actually. Yet the assets acquired should be exhibited in the balance sheet only at their economic values as individual assets. The difference between these values and the price paid should, in conformance with the reasoning outlined in Chaper XI under "Goodwill," be treated as a capital loss to be exhibited in the capital section of the profit and loss statement and thence to be closed into capital surplus.

A word should be said about the meaning of the words "par value" or "stated value." These phrases do not denote value in an economic sense. They merely denote the minimum consideration per share for which each share of stock must originally be sold if purchasers are to avoid a legal liability for discount. When capital stock is sold for property or services, no accountant is justified in assuming it to have been sold for a legal discount, even though the market price of the property or services may be clearly less than the par value, or stated value, of the capital stock sold. Other intangible, non-balance-sheet considerations may have more than compensated for the discrepancy in value. An accountant should leave such questions to the legal profession and to the courts. He should approve the original entry which proclaimed the property or services to be worth the par value, or stated value, of the stock sold. He should then determine the present economic value of the property and treat as a capital loss the difference between this value and the original valuation. If services received for capital stock were rendered in connection with the usual and recurrent operation of the business, their cost should be treated as a current expense to be exhibited in the operating section of the profit and loss statement and to be closed into earned surplus. If these services were rendered in connection with financing, however, their cost should be treated as a capital loss to be exhibited in the capital profit and loss section of the profit and loss statement, thence to be closed into capital surplus.

A capital stock account is in reality only a portion of the stockholders' account with a business. It records only certain historical and legal facts relative to the origin of that account. The remainder of the account is expressed by surplus, or its several subdivisions. Capital stock account and surplus account, taken together, form the complete proprietorship account denoting net worth belonging to stockholders. The total of the combined capital and surplus accounts will remain the same whether a doubtful discount on capital stock be shown as a debit to capital stock or as a debit to surplus. The book value of the outstanding stock will remain the same, and the total net worth will remain the same. Stockholders can therefore not be deceived, whether a doubtful discount be treated in one way or the other. On the other hand, creditors may be injured by being led to rely on a doubtful item of this nature.

It is unfortunate that custom and legal requirements have combined to encourage the exhibition òf capital stock and surplus as two separate accounts in widely separated places on a balance sheet. This treatment tends to prevent an understanding on the part of laymen of the essential similarity and unity of the two accounts. To overcome this difficulty, both capital stock and surplus should be exhibited under a single caption called "Net worth" or "Capital." In America this caption should logically appear in the lower right-hand corner of the balance sheet.

BONDS. The exhibition of bond liability in a balance sheet gives rise to no difficulty, provided that the bonds are found to have been sold for their face value. In this case, the bonds are exhibited at face value and the actual interest paid on them is treated as an expense. If, however, the bonds are found to have been sold at a discount, present accounting practice reverts to the fallacious principle of investment amortization. Bond discount is treated as an asset, to be written off as interest over the term of the bond issue. Under this procedure, the face value of the bonds appears among the liabilities, the unamortized discount appears as an asset, and interest expense consists of the interest actually paid combined with that portion of the discount amortized during the period in question. If bonds have been sold at a premium, present accounting practice follows the same principle. The bonds are exhibited at face value, the premium appears as a liability, and interest expense is made to consist of the interest actually paid less that portion of the premium amortized during the period in question.

The principle of investment amortization is just as false and just as pernicious when it is applied to bond liabilities as when it is applied to investment assets. The latter subject was discussed in detail in Chapter X. Bond discount is not an asset. It is a capital loss. Bond premium is not a liability. It is a capital gain. A bond discount may be caused by a weak bond market, by unwise financing, or by poor credit. A bond premium may be caused by a strong bond market, by shrewd financing, or by excellent credit. If one is to disregard these factors, it is true that, if interest rates remain unchanged, it may appear in retrospect that such capital losses or gains were created by virtue of low future interest rates, or at the expense of high future interest rates. But it is not the business of an accountant to anticipate the future. It is his business to state present facts, and he fails to do this if he exhibits bond discounts as assets and bond premiums as liabilities.

Bond discounts and premiums are not analogous to interest prepaid, or note discount. When a banker discounts a note he is literally collecting interest in advance. This interest is a definite, contractual charge for the loan of a specified sum of money at a specified rate for a specified number of days. If the loan is repaid before its maturity, the banker will refund the unearned discount. Interest prepaid, or note discount, is a true asset because it represents a definite legal claim for the use of money or for the return of cash. Bond discount, on the other hand, does not represent a legal claim for anything, nor does it represent material wealth. It represents merely a present sacrifice of cash for the expected benefit of future gain, much as would the cost of goodwill. If an issuer defaults in the payment of interest, his bonds may be declared immediately payable at their face amounts, and no attention will be paid to the discounts at which they may originally have been sold. If the issuer retires his bonds before maturity, he must pay their face amounts plus the premium specified in the trust deed, regardless of whether the bonds were originally sold at a discount. At every step in the life of a bond issue, bond discount will be ignored. After its creation it will cease to exist, both legally and practically. It is not a material good, nor does it represent a legal claim on anybody for either goods or services. It cannot, therefore, be considered to be a balance sheet asset.

The amortization principle, applied to bond premium or discount, causes accountants to differentiate between what they are pleased to call the "real" and the "nominal" interest rate of a bond issue. It causes them literally to falsify the balance sheet in order that they may falsify the profit and loss statement by exhibiting this so-called "real" interest. Yet nothing could be more real than the fact that a bond issuer obligates himself to pay a certain sum of hard cash as interest every year. It is by keeping in mind the actual cash amount of this important obligation and by observing the effect of its payment on the balance sheet, and on the profit and loss account, that interested persons may best appraise the outlook for the future. The amortization principle, instead of aiding stockholders and creditors to acquire a clear grasp of fundamentals, tends to accomplish the exact reverse of this by cluttering up balance sheets with incomprehensible assets and liabilities, and by exhibiting theoretical, rather than actual, expense items in profit and loss statements.

Every business man knows that it is more important for a business to have a satisfactory cash position, than to have a satisfactory profit position. An unsatisfactory cash position may, and usually does, result in immediate bankruptcy; whereas an unsatisfactory profit position may persist for years until it finally corrects itself or induces a fatal shortage of cash. The cash requirement for bond interest may easily be the most important single financial obligation of a business, and the ability to pay it may literally mean the difference between life and death for a business. It would seem that, on these grounds alone, nothing should be done to confuse stockholders and creditors with respect to the exact amount of such an important item. Yet when bond discount or premium is amortized, the effect is to substitute a theoretical requirement for an actual requirement and thus to tend to rob these persons of a clear basis of fact upon which to base their own estimates of the future.

When bond discount is exhibited as an asset, or when bond premium is exhibited as a liability, the net worth shown on a balance sheet is misrepresented. When theoretical interest is substituted for actual interest, profits are misrepresented. It is true that, from the viewpoint of a permanent stockholder or creditor, these misrepresentations may be a matter of indifference because they eventually resolve into a truthful statement of condition at the maturity of the bond issue. It is also true that these misrepresentations may tend to equalize the results of intervening years by concealing actual fluctuations in assets and earnings. This will be accomplished by applying the misrepresentation of net worth against the opposite misrepresentation of profits, so that they gradually cancel each other and thus finally result in a mathematical truth. But two wrongs do not make a right, even in accounting. There is a vast difference between a ten-year, interestless bond issue sold at a large discount, and a ten-year 5% bond issue sold at par; even though they may be identical from the standpoint of actuarial mathematics. The former occasions a large initial capital loss, but is thereafter foolproof for ten years. The latter occasions no capital loss, but may plunge the business into bankruptcy at any semi-annual interest date. Accountants should recognize the disparity between the proceeds received from the sale of the two bond issues. Accountants should not assume that there is no disparity, under the theory that the future advantage to be obtained from the first issue should be treated as a present asset and valued at the exact amount of the bond discount. A favorable outlook is not a balance sheet asset, any more than is goodwill.

To the extent that present accounting practice refuses to exhibit plain facts as they occur, it runs the risk of deceiving innocent people to their hurt. If stockholders and creditors could be supplied with clear statements of present fact, they would be placed in a position to make their own forecasts of the future. The general tendency of present accounting practice is to attempt to make its own forecasts of the future and to exhibit averages based on such forecasts, in lieu of the actual facts as they occur. This tendency is confusing and dangerous. It frequently involves financial statements to a point where no one can distinguish between fact and fiction.

Bond premiums and discounts should be treated as capital profits and losses, to be exhibited in the capital profit and loss section of the profit and loss statement and thence to be closed into capital surplus. Outstanding bonds should be exhibited as liabilities at their face values. Interest requirements should be shown in the profit and loss account at their actual, not at their theoretical, amounts. Only in this way can interested persons be given a basis of truthful present fact from which to compute their own estimates of present and future values.

OTHER LIABILITIES. Except in rare instances, most of the ordinary liabilities of a business will be money value liabilities, i.e., they will represent definite claims for definite sums of money. Such items should invariably be exhibited on the liability side of a balance sheet at their face values. Occasionally, however, a real value liability may be encountered, i.e., an obligation to deliver goods or services regardless of what their cost may be. For example, a contractor may be under contract to build a building, or a short seller in the stock market may be obligated to deliver a certain number of shares of stock to replace that borrowed for him by his broker. In each of these instances the money cost to complete the contract may change radically between the date of the contract and the date of its fulfillment.

Real value liabilities should be exhibited on the liability side of a balance sheet at their economic values in money as of the date of the balance sheet. Hence, if a short seller sells stock at $80 per share and its market price declines to $60 per share, he should exhibit his liability at $60 per share. The difference between the current market price and the original sales price represents a profit and should be so treated. Conversely, if the market price of the stock rises to $100 per share, the liability should be exhibited at $100 per share and the difference between this and the sales price should be treated as a loss. Similarly, a liability for the completion of a building should be exhibited at the amount required to complete the building under conditions as of the date of the balance sheet.

The principle governing the valuation of real value liabilities should be exactly the same as that governing the valuation of assets, other than money. The reasoning is the same in both instances. Only by valuing such liabilities in the light of conditions actually existing at the date of a balance sheet can stockholders and creditors be supplied with a truthful statement of present fact.

RESERVES. Balance sheet reserves fall into three categories. They may be liability accounts, valuation accounts, or appropriated surplus accounts. Reserves for accrued taxes and for accrued interest are liability accounts and should be exhibited as such. Reserves for depreciation, for bad debts, or for unrealized losses on inventory, are valuation accounts and should be treated as deductions from the book values of their related assets. Reserves for contingencies, for self-insurance, for bond retirements, or for other purposes for which no unrecorded present liability exists, are appropriated surplus accounts and should be exhibited as a part of the net worth of the business.

The practice of exhibiting appropriated surplus reserves under a separate balance sheet caption, along with other types of reserves, is confusing to laymen and may mislead them into concluding that these reserves are valuation accounts, or liabilities. At least one of the largest American corporations exhibits its reserve for depreciation, its employees' savings funds payable, and its reserve for contingencies, all under the single caption of "Reserves" on the liability side of its balance sheet. In this case, a valuation account, a liability account, and an appropriated surplus account are exhibited as though the function of each was similar. No accountant should sanction the preparation of a balance sheet which does not clearly set forth the equities of the different parties at interest in a business. If a part of the net worth is displayed in such a manner that it may be mistaken for a liability, both creditors and stockholders may be misled. Regardless of how certain an accountant may be that a reserve for contingencies will be needed in the future, he should exhibit the present fact truthfully and display the reserve in its true character of appropriated surplus.

SURPLUS. As previously discussed in this chapter, the comprehensibility of a balance sheet may be improved by exhibiting both the capital and surplus of a business under the same caption. If the business is not incorporated the caption "Net Worth" may be suitable. If the business is a corporation either the heading "Net Worth," or the heading "Capital" may be appropriate. In either case, the total net worth of the business should be exhibited as a single figure at the bottom of a single balance sheet section exhibiting the various subdivisions of capital and surplus. If this is done, it seems reasonable to suppose that there will be less opportunity for misunderstanding the equities of the various parties at interest in a business than is afforded by the current practice of distributing net worth items among several widely separated balance sheet sections.

The surplus account appearing on a balance sheet may be divided into three main sections. Appropriated surplus will be composed of all of the various types of net worth reserves that may have been set up to provide for future contingencies, or for specific future purposes such as the retirement of funded debt. Capital surplus will be composed of the various capital profits and losses that may have occurred from time to time because of changes in values not resulting from the ordinary operation of the business. These capital profits and losses should first be exhibited in the capital section of the profit and loss statement, and only their net total should be carried to capital surplus. Earned surplus will be composed of the remaining conventional current profits and losses carried from the current section of the profit and loss statement in the usual manner.

It is perhaps unfortunate that the caption "Earned Surplus" should have gained such wide use to distinguish current profits from capital profits. Capital profits constitute "earnings" or "income" in just as true a sense as do profits from business activities. After reaching the surplus account, each becomes a part of net worth, and only legal and historical considerations provide a reason for their being separated at all. "Operating Surplus" would probably be a better caption than "Earned Surplus." However, the latter title has gained wide recognition and it is probable that its use could not easily be supplanted.

The liability side of a balance sheet, prepared in accordance with the principles advocated in this chapter, differs from the usual form chiefly because of its greater insistence upon the classification of items in accordance with the equities of the parties at interest. This classification is made with the aim of causing each type of equity to be represented by one figure, in so far as this may be possible. In the past it has not infrequently been necessary for stockholders to select as many as three or four different figures from different places on a balance sheet for the purpose of combining them into one correct figure for net worth. It is reasonable to assume that many stockholders have not possessed the accounting knowledge to do this, and thus have been unable correctly to compute the book value of their shares.

SUGGESTED FORM FOR BALANCE SHEET LIABILITIES. A suggested form for the liability side of a balance sheet is shown below.

Exhibit A

BALANCE SHEET—DECEMBER 31, 1937

LIABILITIES

Current Liabilities

Accounts Payable to trade creditors	$ 190,558.78	
Notes Payable due within one year	50,000.00	
Accrued Wages and Salaries	24,698.70	
Accrued Taxes Payable in 1938	100,800.61	
Accrued Interest	60,402.86	
Total Current Liabilities		$ 426,460.95

Funded Debt

Five year 6% gold notes due May 1, 1941	$1,300,000.00	
First Mortgage 5% Bonds due July 1, 1948	1,400,000.00	
Total Funded Debt		$ 2,700,000.00

Capital

7% cumulative preferred stock, par value $100, authorized		
75,000 shares, issued 38,000 shares	$3,800,000.00	
Common stock, no par value, authorized		
750,000 shares, issued 409,300 shares	1,437,200.00	
Total Capital Stock		$5,237,200.00
Reserve for Self-Insurance	$ 97,800.00	
Reserve for Contingencies	50,000.00	
Total Appropriated Surplus		$ 147,800.00
Capital Surplus January 1, 1937	$1,307,235.69	
Add Net Capital Profit Year 1937 (Exhibit B)	419,941.70	
Total Capital Surplus		$1,727,177.39
Earned Surplus January 1, 1937	$ 570,725.23	
Add Net Profit from Business Operations Year 1937 (Exhibit B)	275,311.06	
Total Earned Surplus		$ 846,036.29

$ 7,958,213.68

$11,084,674.63

XIV
THE PROFIT AND LOSS STATEMENT

THE PURPOSE of this chapter is to discuss the preparation of a profit and loss statement in accordance with the principles outlined heretofore. No effort will be made to review the details of present accounting practice, save where changes therein are recommended.

LEGAL DEFINITION OF PROFITS. Much has been written relative to the legal definition of profits. Over a period of many years, courts and legislatures have propounded conflicting views, until an authority can now be found for almost any viewpoint, no matter how absurd. It has been held that depletion of wasting assets is not a loss,[1] that depletion of wasting assets is a loss,[2] that fixed capital may be sunk and lost without affecting profits,[3] that a decline in the value of fixed assets is a loss,[4] that no profits can be earned until collected in cash,[5] that no profits can exist until all current debts are paid,[6] that stock dividends re-

[1] *Excelsior Water & Mining Co.* v. *Pierce*, 90 Cal. 131. Also *United Verde Copper Co.* v. *Roberts*, 156 N.Y. 585.
[2] 16 Fed. Cas. 506. Also *Balch* v. *Hallet*, 10 Gray, 402.
[3] *Vernier* v. *The General and Commercial Investment Trust, Ltd.* (1894) 2 Ch. 239 (Eng).
[4] *Richardson* v. *Buhl*, 77 Mich. 632. Also *Hubbard* v. *Weare*, 79 Ia. 678.
[5] *Badham* v. *Williams* (1902), 86, L.T.R. 191. (Eng) Also *People* v. *San Francisco Savings Union*, 72 Cal. 199.
[6] *Warren* v. *King*, 108 U.S. 389, 398. Also *Mobile, etc., R.R.* v. *Ten.*, 153 U.S., 486.

ceived constitute income,[7] and that stock dividends received constitute principal.[8] It has been held that when securities owned become worthless they need not be charged against profits,[9] that depreciation is an expense,[10] that depreciation is not an expense,[11] that losses of previous years need not be made good before paying out current profits in dividends,[12] and that losses of previous years must be made good before paying out current profits in dividends.[13]

It is not the purpose of this chapter to review the maze of legal confusion and contradiction relating to profits except to point out that perhaps the accounting profession may itself be partly to blame for the existing state of affairs. In reviewing legal decisions relative to profits it is difficult to escape the presumption that the failure of legal minds to grasp economic realities was encouraged by the illogic and fundamental unsoundness of accounting principles. Apparently judges have experienced the utmost difficulty in trying to reconcile the arguments of accountants with the known laws of economics, and in attempting to pick a middle course have honeycombed their decisions with absurdities. Under the circumstances it may well transpire that before sound accounting law is to emanate from courts and legislatures, sound accounting principles must first be adopted by the accounting profession.

[7] Earp's Appeal, 28 Pa St. 368. Also *Thomas* v. *Gregg,* 78 Md. 545.
[8] *Minot* v. *Paine,* 99 Mass. 101. Also *Gibbons* v. *Mahon,* 136 U.S. 549.
[9] National Bank of Wales (1899), 2 Ch. 629 (Eng)
[10] *Conville* v. *Shook,* 24 N.Y. Supp. 547.
[11] *Eyster* v. *Centennial Board of Finance,* 94 U.S. 503. Also *United States* v. *Kansas Pacific R.R.,* 99 U.S. 459.
[12] See Crichton's Oil Co. Case (1901) 2 Ch. 196. Also Hoare and Co. Case (1904) 2 Ch. 208 (Eng)
[13] *Towers* v. *African Tug Co.* (1904) 1 Ch. 558 (Eng)

PRESENT ACCOUNTING DEFINITION OF PROFITS. The inconsistency of present accounting principles makes it very difficult to give a concise accounting definition of profits. On the one hand, accountants maintain that no profit can be earned until it has been realized. This is exemplified by their refusal to recognize the market value of inventories when it is above original cost. Yet discounts on long-term investments are regularly amortized and treated as current income many years before realization. On the other hand, accountants stress the importance of providing for unrealized losses. This is exemplified by their valuation of inventories at market value when it is below original cost. Yet unrealized losses in connection with fixed assets are commonly ignored. Ridiculous as it seems, the above examples make it appear that present accounting opinion regards unrealized profits on current assets as properly to be ignored, regards unrealized anticipated profits on permanent investments as current income, regards unrealized losses on current assets as ordinary expense, and regards unrealized losses on fixed assets as nonexistent.

If the test of an acountant's recognition of a profit be taken as his willingness to place it in the profit and loss statement, the situation is still further complicated. From this viewpoint, both realized and unrealized profits and losses on fixed assets are apt to be denied recognition, both unrealized and realized losses on current assets are apt to be recognized, unrealized profits on current assets are sure to be denied recognition, and realized profits on current assets are sure to be recognized. At times certain obvious expenses, such as legal fees or stock salesmen's commissions, will be denied recognition and will be treated as assets. At times the cost of enormously valuable assets, such as patents, will be charged immediately to expense.

Under the circumstances, it is next to impossible to frame a definition of profits that will conform to present accounting practice. Such a definition would of necessity contain so many exceptions and inconsistencies as to be of little value. In the light of present conditions, it is small wonder that the legal profession has been unable to accept and abide by accounting principles. To a nonaccounting mind these principles might well appear to have originated in Bedlam.

CORRECT DEFINITION OF PROFITS. There is one correct definition of profits in an accounting sense. A profit is an increase in net wealth. A loss is a decrease in net wealth. This is an economist's definition. It is terse, obvious, and mathematically demonstrable.

Accounting deals exclusively with economic facts. Save in their economic aspects it does not deal with philosophy, religion, law, medicine, physics, or any other subject whatsoever. The function of accounting is to record, collate, and present economic truths. One of the most obvious and important of economic truths is the fact that a profit is an increase in net wealth. If accounting disregards, denies, or controverts this truth, what then can its function be said to be?

The notion that the validity of a profit depends upon its being realized is childish, untrue, and in complete opposition to the realities of modern business procedure. "The Fable of the Two Investment Trusts" recounted in the first chapter serves to illustrate this. As shown in

Chapter IV, the idea originated and was wholly practicable only in an era when business was conducted on a "venture" basis, and when all assets were converted into money as a matter of course at the conclusion of each venture. The notion is hopelessly ill adapted to the continuing forms of business that now exist. No modern business periodically converts all of its assets into cash. Instead, it is constantly reinvesting its cash in other assets and normally retains only a small portion of its total assets in the form of money. To what purpose is a profit designated as "realized" when it is immediately reinvested in other "unrealized" assets? Is such a profit available for dividends? Is it safe? Is it even still "realized"?

The exhibition of large realized yearly profits does not indicate that a business possesses that much cash, or even that it ever possessed that much cash. There is no difference whatever between two businesses with similar assets, one of which has reinvested its realized profits, and the other of which possesses unrealized profits to the same amount. Under modern conditions, the term "realized" applied to profits means literally nothing, for such profits are continually being "de-realized" by reinvestment in other assets. The cash position of a business is evidenced by the asset side of its balance sheet, not by its surplus account, or by its profit and loss statement. The profit position of a business is determined by its increase in net wealth, not by the amount of cash profit that it may have received and retained, or reinvested. Wealth is economic value, and economic value is an element of all assets, not merely of cash alone. From a practical as well as a theoretical point of view, both unrealized and realized profits and losses

enjoy equal status. *The important question is the determination of value, and this question is not answered by
disregarding those changes in value that have not been
translated into cash.* Present accounting authority to the
contrary, the current distinction made by the accounting
profession between realized and unrealized profits is the
sheerest nonsense. It is a relic of medieval conditions that
accounting has not yet outgrown. It is demonstrably absurd,
it is not at all adapted to modern business procedure, and
it serves to conceal and misrepresent economic truths that
an accountant should be duty bound to reveal.

Of the refusal of present accounting authority to require
the exhibition of realized capital profits in the profit and
loss statement, little need be said. This refusal is largely
predicated on the theory that the profit and loss statement
should be reserved for profits and losses resulting from
business activities. The practical effect of this theory is
partially to conceal capital profits and to minimize their
importance. The evils of this practice have been discussed
elsewhere. Capital profits and losses cause changes in net
wealth just as do other types of profits and losses. Their
importance to managements, creditors, and stockholders is
apt to be determined a great deal more by their size than
by their origin. They should be exhibited boldly, in proper
classification, in every profit and loss statement.

THE FUNCTION OF A PROFIT AND LOSS STATEMENT.
Universal custom decrees that the profit and loss statement
of a business be drawn from the standpoint of its owners,
namely, its stockholders, its partners, or its sole proprietor.
Profits and losses are never considered from the standpoint

of a business itself, as a legal entity. If they were, proceeds from the sale of stock would constitute profits and the payment of a dividend would constitute a loss. Hence, when one defines a profit as an increase in net wealth, this definition automatically excludes capital adjustments and the distribution of dividends, because these items occasion no increase or decrease in the net wealth of the owners of a business. No criticism can be made of this custom, because the owners of a business are not primarily interested in increasing its net wealth, but are chiefly interested in it only as a means of increasing their own net wealth.

Present accounting authority generally directs that a profit and loss statement exhibit only net changes in wealth due to the business operations of a stated period. The phrase "business operations" is ordinarily construed to exclude fluctuations in the value of fixed assets. Hence capital profits and losses, due to extraneous influences such as changes in market price, are definitely disavowed. If such capital profits are unrealized, it is usual for them to be completely ignored. Since this procedure is not possible with realized capital profits, they are often credited directly to some subdivision of surplus and are thus wholly or partly concealed. The chief justification for ignoring unrealized capital profits consists in the reasoning employed in the "going value" theory. The fallacy of this theory and the evils for which it is responsible were discussed in Chapter III. No justification is ordinarily cited for the omission of realized capital profits from profit and loss statements, save that this procedure might distort the conventional results shown and thus make comparisons with former periods difficult.

Surely it must be evident that, if a profit and loss statement is to achieve its maximum usefulness, its function should be to inform the owners of a business of all of the profits and losses in which they have an equity. The ordinary business exists for the sole purpose of increasing the net wealth of its owners. Stockholders invest in it for that sole purpose. Anything that will promote that purpose is important to stockholders. When present accounting practice exhibits current profits and conceals capital profits, it tends to ignore the viewpoint of a stockholder and to adopt instead the standpoint of a business itself as a legal entity, or to adopt the viewpoint of a management interested only in perpetuating the business and in increasing its net wealth, as opposed to the net wealth of its stockholders. No business is an end in itself. It is only a means to an end. No stockholder, as such, would hesitate to vote for the liquidation of a business if this would, in the long view, increase his net wealth more than its continuance. Such a stockholder would consider one dollar of capital profit to be the exact equivalent of one dollar of operating profit. Generally speaking, the omission or concealment of capital profits misleads stockholders fully as much as would the omission or concealment of operating profits.

Neither in law, nor in equity, nor in theory, nor in practice, is there any adequate justification of the present accounting procedure with reference to the omission and concealment of capital profits. The function of every profit and loss statement should be to exhibit, from the standpoint of an owner, all of the profits and losses of a business, in proper classification, as accurately as they can be determined. The classification adopted should serve to distinguish, as accurately as possible, between current profits and capital profits. No profit and loss statement, however, should stress a distinction between realized and unrealized profits, because such a distinction is essentially misleading, and because the present existence or nonexistence of realized profits can be indicated only by a balance sheet.

AMORTIZATION OF BOND PREMIUMS AND DISCOUNTS. In the discussion of bond discount and premium in the previous chapter, objections were made to the current practice of substituting theoretical interest expense for actual interest expense. In Chapter X the same position was taken with reference to interest income computed in accordance with the fallacious investment amortization principle. In each of these circumstances the amortization of discount and premium results in a misrepresentation of both assets and profits. These misrepresentations are in opposite directions, and the amortization principle gradually cancels one against the other until finally, at the maturity of the bond issue, the cancellation is complete and a true statement of condition is achieved. This procedure is in line with the general tendency of present accounting practice to ignore large fluctuations in assets and earnings wherever possible, and to attempt to smooth these out by substituting prospective future averages in place of the facts as they occur.

In view of the reasoning adopted with reference to the amortization of bond discount and premium, it is perhaps wise to discuss in some detail the reasoning applicable to the calculation of bad debts, self-insurance premiums, and similar items.

BAD DEBTS. Present accounting practice does not ordinarily wait for an account or note receivable to prove itself uncollectible before setting up a reserve for bad debts and treating the amount set up as a current expense. Instead, it is usual to calculate a certain percentage of current sales and to treat this amount both as a credit to reserve and as a debit to bad debts expense. At first glance, this practice might appear to be a plain case of ignoring present facts and of substituting prospective future averages therefor. This aspect is superficial, however, because there is an important difference between the use of averages as a method of valuation and their use as an end in themselves.

It is obvious that the economic value of a large number of accounts receivable could rarely be as great as their combined face amounts. This would be so because some of the accounts would almost certainly be of doubtful collectibility. An accountant is therefore obliged to devise some method of valuing the accounts. The reserve for bad debts which he sets up is merely a revaluation account for notes and accounts receivable, and it is deducted from the face amount of these to give the present value at which they are exhibited in the balance sheet. Since the value of short-term notes and accounts receivable is determined almost wholly by their collectibility, it is entirely proper to call the revaluation account a reserve for bad debts, and to exhibit the debit side of the entry in the profit and loss statement as a loss under some descriptive heading such as bad debts. Unlike bond discounts, notes and accounts receivable constitute true assets and they should be revalued at each balance sheet date as accurately as circumstances permit. If their present value is less than their face value, this difference represents a decrease in net wealth and, as such, is a loss. Custom decrees that this loss be exhibited in the orthodox profit and loss statement as a current business expense, and this treatment conforms to the facts in the overwhelming majority of businesses.

SELF-INSURANCE. The treatment of reserves for self-insurance gives rise to a somewhat different problem. Present accounting practice ordinarily calculates the premiums on self-insurance exactly as though they were to be paid to outside insurance companies, and exhibits these premiums as current expenses in the profit and loss statement. The credit side of the entry is posted to reserve for self-insurance. Actual losses are not treated as expenses but are charged against this reserve. This treatment constitutes a plain case of substituting theoretical average losses for actual losses. No question of the valuation of assets is involved, for the value of assets is not affected by the fact that they may have been immune to insurable losses for an extended period. A reserve for self-insurance is not a revaluation account. It is a subdivision of surplus.

Present accounting procedure with reference to self-insurance is convenient, but it is not truthful. It may result in a consistent understatement of profits over the entire life of a business. At best, it results in the substitution of average losses for actual losses. At worst, it is wholly fictitious. If the management of a business wishes to set up a reserve for self-insurance and to exhibit this reserve as appropriated surplus, no criticism can be made because no one can be deceived thereby. But the credits to this reserve should be taken directly from surplus, either in lump sums or in small amounts equivalent to insurance premiums. If these amounts are taken from profits and are exhibited in the profit and loss statement as expenses, grave misrepresentation may result. The only treatment consistent with the facts is to report actual losses in the profit and loss statement. The difference between these losses and the normal credit to reserve can then be transferred from surplus to reserve. If these actual losses exceed, in any one year, the amount by which it is desired to increase the reserve, the matter can be adjusted by a debit to reserve and a credit to surplus.

The point may be raised that the exhibition of actual losses, in place of theoretical insurance premiums, will tend to destroy the basis for comparison between a self-insuring business and one that purchases its insurance. Precisely the opposite is true. Present fact is the only dependable basis for comparison. Few accountants would contend that a foundry owning its own unimproved land, used as a storage yard for pig iron, should exhibit a fictitious rent account among its expenses in order that they may be comparable with those of a foundry paying rent for its storage yard. Accountants are in duty bound to reveal known facts. When they conceal known facts and allow averages based on theoretical prophecies to parade as facts, they are not performing their duty.

BOOKKEEPING ENTRIES. The preparation of a profit and loss statement in accordance with the principles advocated in this work will necessitate only the simplest of bookkeeping entries in addition to those required by pres-

ent accounting practice. After an accountant has determined the present economic value of an asset he need
merely debit or credit its revaluation account to make its
book value (i.e., the combined balances of its original cost,
its depreciation, amortization or depletion reserve if any,
and its revaluation account) conform to its present economic value. The entry should be completed by a credit
or debit to an appropriately named profit and loss account.
Current profit and loss accounts resulting from this treatment should be included in the current section of the
profit and loss statement, thence to be closed into earned
surplus. Such profit and loss accounts will usually be
limited to unrealized profits and losses on inventories.
Capital profit and loss accounts resulting from this treatment should be displayed in the capital profit and loss
section of the profit and loss statement, and should then
be closed into capital surplus. As outlined in the previous
chapter, capital profits or losses may occasionally arise in
connection with liabilities, and these should also be debited or credited to appropriate capital profit and loss
accounts.

This is the sum total of the additional entries required
to make the books of any business conform to economic
truth. Moreover, it leaves the orthodox accounts virtually
untouched, so as to facilitate the preparation of federal income tax returns and other governmental reports.

INVENTORIES AND PROFITS. The purpose of this section
is to discuss the effect on profits of three different methods
of valuing inventories. The first of these consists of the
valuation of inventories at original cost. This method causes

the cost of sales account to contain only the original cost of goods sold during a period, regardless of when this cost was incurred and regardless of changes in market prices since the dates of acquisition. The sales account, on the other hand, exhibits figures which are materially influenced by such changes in market prices. Thus the gross profit from sales is made to include, not only the normal profit from sales, but in addition all realized profits and losses from changes in market values regardless of the periods during which these changes took place. An unrealized profit or loss may arise in one accounting period and yet be completely ignored. In a later accounting period, however, this profit or loss may be realized and consequently exhibited as a profit or loss pertaining solely to the later period, when actually all that has occurred is the realization of a previously existing unrealized profit or loss. The evil of this situation was illustrated by the "Fable of the Two Flour Mills" and the "Fable of the Two Investment Trusts" in the first chapter of this book. The harm that may be done thereby is enormous, entirely apart from the harm that may be done by the coincident overstatement or understatement of inventory values on the balance sheet.

A second method of treating inventories is to value them at "cost or market whichever is the lower." This is the practice now in almost universal use. The valuation of inventories at market below original cost results in the introduction of unrealized losses into the cost of sales account and thence into the profit and loss account. This conforms to the facts and is entirely proper. The valuation of inventories at original cost below market, however, is subject to all of the objections outlined above. It misrepresents assets and net worth, and may so manipulate the profit figures as to cause them to be seriously misleading. At best it conceals unrealized profits of which stockholders and creditors should be informed. At worst it permits the distortion of profits for purposes of deliberate fraud.

The valuation of inventories at "cost or market whichever is the lower" conforms to the accounting principle of conservatism as expressed by the rule: "Anticipate no profits but provide for all losses." Its announced purpose is to prevent unrealized profits on inventories from appearing in the profit and loss statement. Ironically, it often accomplishes the very thing it seeks to prevent. Only by consistently valuing inventories at original cost can unrealized profits on inventories be kept out of a profit and loss statement.

For example, assume an inventory of refined copper acquired at an original cost of 17¢ per pound but having a present market price of 7¢ per pound. The copper will be valued at 7¢ per pound, and this value will be used in computing cost of sales, thus causing the profits shown to contain all of the unrealized loss on the copper. So far only unrealized losses will have appeared in the profit and loss statement. But during the ensuing year the market price of copper may again rise to 17¢ per pound. The original copper still held in inventory will this time be valued at 17¢ per pound which is both its original cost and its present market price. This value will be used as part of the ending inventory in computing cost of sales. But the value used for the beginning inventory, in the same calculation, will consist partly of the same copper valued at 7¢ per pound. Thus the profits shown will be made to include a wholly unrealized profit of 10¢ per pound on that portion of the original copper still on hand at the second inventory date. The unrealized loss shown in the first accounting period will have been replaced by an unrealized profit in the second period, thus causing the underlying accounting rule to become a boomerang. Accountants do not like to have this happen and, to prevent it, have decreed that, once an inventory item is valued at market below cost, the lower figure shall thenceforth be considered to be its cost. Despite this, the situation does occur in countless cases and inevitably must occur unless each item of inventory can be identified and its history ascertained.

A third method of treating inventories is to value them at their economic values as of the date of the balance sheet. This is the only method by which the illogic and misrepresentation of other methods can be avoided. Its effect is to cause the stated profits for each accounting period to include all profits and losses actually incurred during that period in connection with inventories, whether realized or not. It enables each balance sheet to exhibit inventories at their economic values as of the date of the balance sheet. Hence it causes both profits and assets to be truthfully and fully revealed. The valuation of inventories in this manner does not anticipate possible future profits, nor does it provide for possible future losses. It is neither conservative nor radical. It is not influenced by fears or hopes, nor does it exhibit prophecies based on these. Instead it supplies an impartial and unbiased statement of actual present fact, upon which each interested person may base his own estimate of the future.

The accounting profession should realize the futility of

attempting to distinguish between realized and unrealized profits and losses. It should realize that only by exhibiting all the facts can it cause both balance sheets and profit and loss statements to portray the truth. Not until the profession has experienced this awakening will it be fitted to prepare an entirely rational form of profit and loss statement. Part of such a statement will be devoted to current profits and losses, germane to business activities, whether realized or unrealized. The remainder of the statement will exhibit all other profits and losses. Inventories will invariably be taken at their present economic values for the purpose of calculating current profits, thus causing such profits to include all profits and losses incurred in connection with inventories, whether realized or not.

SEGREGATION OF SPECULATIVE PROFITS ON INVENTORIES. At the end of Chapter IX and again near the end of Chapter XII, this work recommended that unrealized profits and losses on inventories be included in the cost of sales account. In other words, it was recommended that both beginning inventories and ending inventories be valued at market, or at replacement cost, and that these inventories so valued be used in computing the cost of sales. The practical effect of this procedure is to cause the single figure representing gross profit from sales to include all profits and losses incurred in connection with inventories, whether realized or not. In a manufacturing business such profits would include so-called speculative profits and losses resulting from changes in the market prices of raw material, work in progress, or finished goods, and would also include so-called manufacturing profits and losses resulting from processing operations.

In the recent past, suggestions have been made by practicing accountants that speculative profits or losses on inventories be segregated and shown separately from profits or losses resulting from processing operations. These accountants have felt that some companies make large profits due to their purchasing ability and that other companies make large profits due to their ability in processing operations, and that it would be very desirable if these two different types of profits could be exhibited separately in financial statements. To accomplish this, they have suggested that changes in inventory values, arising from external market influences, be not included in the cost of sales account, but be shown as special items in the profit and loss statement.

The objection to this procedure lies only in the practical difficulty of putting it into effect. In cases where the desired result can be easily and completely obtained no valid criticism can be made, and the procedure is to be recommended for the additional information that it supplies. However, instances where the desired result can be completely obtained, without occasioning prohibitive expense, must necessarily be rare. Moreover, an incomplete result may often be less desirable than none at all, and may result in serious misrepresentation.

For example, if one merely revalues the raw material items as they are charged into goods in progress, and exhibits as speculative profit the difference between these values and the original cost of the items, this procedure may seriously misinform both management and stockholders. In the first place the items may have been acquired prior to the beginning of the current accounting period, and the proper comparison should therefore be with their value on that date, not with their original cost. In the second place, the speculative loss on the material, *after* it was charged into goods in progress but before the end of the current accounting period, may be even greater than the previous profit and hence the speculative profit exhibited may be wholly misleading. This situation is apt to occur and is apt to be very important in industries where large quantities of seasonal goods are placed in production only once or twice a year. It should be evident that, except for purely departmental purposes, any attempt to segregate the speculative profit on inventories should concern itself with each type of inventory and also with all goods sold, if it is to have any certainty of avoiding misrepresentation.

The problem is essentially one of analyzing each item of inventory on hand, and each item of inventory sold during the accounting period, to determine the changes in value resulting from variations in external market conditions and wage levels. The task of ascertaining the speculative profit on raw material inventories on hand is relatively simple, although even here complications may arise if certain items of raw material were acquired prior to the beginning of the accounting period. The problem with respect to work in progress and finished goods is vastly more complicated due to the fact that wages and expense items enter into the calculation on a variety of different dates. The problem with respect to goods sold during the accounting period may be even more formidable. A cost system capable of separating speculative profits from processing profits must of necessity be designed to revalue, on the basis of present market price or present replacement cost, each item of each class of inventory on many different dates during an accounting period. For example, each item of all inventories must be revalued on the first day of the accounting period, raw material items must be revalued when charged into work in progress, work in progress items must be revalued when charged into finished goods, finished goods items must be revalued when sold, and each item of all inventories must be revalued at the end of the accounting period. Obviously few businesses could justify the expense of such a system.

Under the circumstances it seems probable that few accountants will encounter many opportunities to separate speculative profits on inventories from those resulting from processing operations. If such a procedure proves possible in certain instances, advantage should be taken of it to supply the additional information available. Otherwise all profits and losses relating to inventories should be allowed to appear in the gross profit from sales figure, in the manner heretofore recommended.

SUGGESTED FORM OF PROFIT AND LOSS STATEMENT. A profit and loss statement, drawn as recommended, will display a net profit from business activities in the orthodox manner. In its general appearance it will vary from the traditional form only by the addition of a capital profit and loss section. A suggested form is shown below.

PROFIT AND LOSS STATEMENT

FOR YEAR ENDED DECEMBER 31, 1937

Gross Sales			$8,768,445.12
Deduct—Trade Discounts	$1,878,600.85		
Returns and Allowances	8,649.10		1,887,249.95
Net Sales			$6,881,195.17
Deduct—Cost of Sales (Exhibit C)			5,166,092.22
Gross Profit from Sales			$1,715,102.95
Deduct Selling and Administrative Expenses			
Salesmen's Commissions		$ 598,775.60	
Traveling Expense		179,673.90	
Advertising		352,555.86	
Total Selling Expense		$1,131,005.36	
Office Salaries		$ 98,751.50	
Telegraph and Telephone		4,789.12	
Allowance for Bad Debts		68,810.00	
Insurance Administrative		1,245.60	
Amortization of Patents		2,842.36	
General Administrative Expense		14,932.57	
Total Administrative Expense		$ 195,079.81	$1,326,085.17
Net Profit from Sales			$ 389,017.78
Add—Other Income			
Interest Earned		$ 40,768.05	
Dividends Received		65,810.00	106,578.05
			$ 495,595.83

Deduct—Other Expenses

Taxes Paid and Accrued	68,831.22	
Interest Paid and Accrued	151,453.55	220,284.77

Net Profit from Business Operations
(Carried to Earned Surplus Exhibit A) .... $ 275,311.06

Capital Profits

Profit Realized from Sale of Minority Interest in Blank Co.	$ 127,485.00	
Net Increase in market prices of marketable Securities	390,730.11	$ 518,215.11

Capital Losses

Decrease in estimated market price of land for surface use	$ 5,287.66	
Decrease in Replacement Cost of Buildings, exclusive of depreciation	39,856.80	
Decrease in Replacement Cost of Machinery and equipment, exclusive of depreciation	42,622.95	
Decrease in Replacement cost of tools, patterns, etc., exclusive of depreciation	10,506.00	98,273.41

Net Capital Profit (Carried to Capital Surplus Exhibit A) 419,941.70

Total Net Profit from All Sources .... $ 695,252.76

Exhibit C

STATEMENT SHOWING COST OF SALES

FOR YEAR ENDED DECEMBER 31, 1937

Raw Material Used

Inventory January 1, 1937 at market		$ 943,246.35	
Add—Purchases during year		2,482,127.09	
Estimated Mine Depletion		48,638.80	
		$3,474,012.24	
Deduct—Inventory December 31, 1937 at market		865,444.05	$ 2,608,568.19
Productive Labor Used			1,641,009.32

Production Burden Used

Superintendence		$ 41,338.11	
Nonproductive labor		367,124.35	
Heat, light and power		187,466.64	
Depreciation of production assets		420,837.94	
Insurance—Production		28,440.06	
Spoiled parts		15,092.28	
Operating supplies		23,824.14	
Unclassified production expense		38,129.67	1,122,253.19
Total Cost of Production			$ 5,371,830.70

Deduct Net Increase in Stores

Inventories January 1, 1937			
Work in Progress at replacement cost	$ 783,717.66		
Finished Goods at replacement cost	964,275.40	$1,747,993.06	
Inventories December 31, 1937			
Work in Progress at replacement cost	$1,586,749.23		
Finished Goods at replacement cost	366,982.31	1,953,731.54	205,738.48

Cost of Sales (Carried to Exhibit B) .... $ 5,166,092.22

XV

THE FUTURE OF ACCOUNTING

PROBABLY few accountants realize the extent to which recent developments support the hypothesis that their profession is facing a declining future. During the past decade accounting methods have been subject to severe and increasing criticism. This criticism has had the effect of rendering traditional accounting concepts increasingly untenable and has confronted the profession with the choice of improving existing methods so that they justify traditional concepts, or of renouncing these concepts and adopting a more restricted definition of the purpose of accounting.

TWO ALTERNATIVES. On the one hand, accountants may admit that present accounting principles are based on expediency rather than on truth. They may acknowledge that these principles regularly cause balance sheets to exhibit meaningless figures and often cause profit and loss statements to be wholly misleading. They may recognize that neither balance sheets nor profit and loss statements can possibly be of the greatest value to business management and to the public unless accountants discard their use of accounting conventions and historical data, and devote themselves to a presentation of current fact. Having done this, they may frankly revise their principles and their methods to the end that accounting may be enabled to fulfill its traditional concepts and thus to render services of paramount importance.

On the other hand, accountants may refuse to revise present accounting principles and methods. Instead, they may choose slowly to redefine the purpose of accounting itself, as the pressure of criticism makes this necessary. They may alter little by little the traditional concept that accounting should exhibit current facts, and may meet each advance in criticism with a new and more restricted definition of the accounting function. In this manner they may allow accounting gradually to be forced further and further into the category of nonessential endeavor, until it has largely forfeited the public confidence now placed in it.

The first of these alternatives is the more difficult, but it points to a future wherein the accounting profession should occupy a position of the highest public importance. The second alternative may at first seem very easy, but it points to a future wherein accounting will be increasingly recognized as a static, dogmatic calling which has missed its opportunity to be of great public service.

THE COURSE CHOSEN. To those who envisage the future of splendid service that accounting might enjoy, it is disheartening to note that accounting leadership, as apart from the great mass of accounting opinion, seems recently to have embarked on the second course outlined above. It has already renounced the traditional concept of the balance sheet as a statement of present fact and has publicly confessed that balance sheets are largely historical and conventional in character. It appears that sooner or later this confession must logically be followed by a similar admission close more clearly than at present on what basis assets of various kinds are stated (e.g., cost, reproduction cost less depreciation, estimated going-concern value, cost or market whichever is lower, liquidating value, etc.).

3. To emphasize the cardinal importance of the income account, such importance being explained by the fact that the value of a business is dependent mainly on its earning capacity; and to take the position that an annual income account is unsatisfactory unless it is so framed as to constitute the best reflection reasonably obtainable of the earning capacity of the business under the conditions existing during the year to which it relates.

4. To make universal the acceptance by listed corporations of certain broad principles of accounting which have won fairly general acceptance (see Exhibit I attached)....[1]

EXHIBIT I

It is suggested that in the first instance the broad principles to be laid down as contemplated in paragraph 4 of the suggestions should be few in number. It might be desirable to formulate a statement therof only after consultation with a small group of qualified persons, including corporate officials, lawyers, and accountants. Presumably the list would include some if not all of the following:

1. Unrealized profit should not be credited to income account of the corporation either directly or indirectly, through the medium of charging against such unrealized profits amounts which would ordinarily fall to be charged against income account. Profit is deemed to be realized when a sale in the ordinary course of business

[1] The five "broad principles of accounting" named in the letter are reproduced below because they are thought to be indicative of the present situation. A "principle" is an underlying theoretical generalization. Apparently the committee, in its effort to state broad accounting principles, was brought face to face with the illogic and inconsistency of present accounting theory and, rather than attempt to explain the numerous exceptions involved in any statement of present accounting principles, preferred to supply what are, in the main, merely a few secondary accounting rules.

with reference to earnings statements, whose function is necessarily limited to the explaining of fluctuations in net worth exhibited by balance sheets. Once the implications of this situation have been fully comprehended by the public, the scope and importance of professional accounting work will have been definitely limited.

The current situation is evidenced by a letter included in a pamphlet now being distributed by the American Institute of Accountants, and by the New York Stock Exchange, entitled "Audits of Corporate Accounts." The letter was addressed by a committee of the American Institute of Accountants to a committee of the New York Stock Exchange, and was placed in evidence by the latter in a hearing before the United States Senate Committee on Banking and Currency. It is being distributed in accordance with a formal resolution of the executive Committee of the American Institute of Accountants. Portions of the letter pertinent to this discussion are as follows:

The nature of a balance-sheet or an income account is quite generally misunderstood, even by writers on financial and accounting subjects. Professor William Z. Ripley has spoken of a balance-sheet as an instantaneous photograph of the condition of a company on a given date. Such language is apt to prove doubly misleading to the average investor—first, because of the implication that the balance-sheet is wholly photographic in nature, whereas it is largely historical; and, secondly, because of the suggestion that it is possible to achieve something approaching photographic accuracy in a balance-sheet which, in fact, is necessarily the reflection of opinions subject to a (possibly wide) margin of error.

Writers of text-books on accounting speak of the purpose of the balance-sheet as being to reflect the values of the assets and the liabilities on a particular date. They explain the fact that in many balance-sheets certain assets are stated at figures which are obviously far above or far below true values by saying that the amounts at which such assets are stated represent "conventional" valuations. Such statements seem to involve a misconception of the nature of a balance-sheet.

In an earlier age, when capital assets were inconsiderable and business units in general smaller and less complex than they are today, it was possible to value assets with comparative ease and accuracy and to measure the progress made from year to year by annual valuations. With the growing mechanization of industry, and with corporate organizations becoming constantly larger, more completely integrated and more complex, this has become increasingly impracticable. . . .

. . . The task of appraisal would be too vast, and the variations in appraisal from year to year due to changes in price levels or changes in the mental attitude of the appraisers would in many cases be so great as to reduce all other elements in the computations of the results of operations to relative insignificance. . . .

. . . Any consideration of the accounts of a large business enterprise of today must start from the premise that an annual valuation of the assets is neither practical nor desirable.

Some method, however, has to be found by which the proportion of a given expenditure to be charged against the operations in a year, and the proportion to be carried forward, may be determined; otherwise, it would be wholly impossible to present an annual income account. Out of this necessity has grown up a body of conventions, based partly on theoretical and partly on practical considerations, which form the basis for the determination of income and the preparation of balance sheets today. . . .

Within quite wide limits, it is relatively unimportant to the investor what precise rules or conventions are adopted by a corporation in reporting its earnings if he knows what method is being followed and is assured that it is followed consistently from year to year. . . .

It is probably fairly well recognized by intelligent investors today that the earning capacity is the fact of crucial importance in the valuation of an industrial enterprise, and that therefore the income account is usually far more important than the balance sheet. In point of fact, the changes in the balance sheets from year to year are usually more significant than the balance-sheets themselves. . . .

There is no need to revolutionize or even to change materially corporate accounting, but there is room for great improvement in the presentation of the conclusions to which accounts lead. The aim should be to satisfy (so far as is possible and prudent) the investor's need for knowledge, rather than the accountant's sense of form and respect for tradition, and to make very clear the basis on which accounts are prepared. But even when all has been done that can be done, the limitations on the significance of even the best of accounts must be recognized, and the shorter the period covered by them the more pronounced usually are these limitations. Accounts are essentially continuous historical record; and, as is true of history in general, correct interpretations and sound forecasts for the future can not be reached upon a hurried survey of temporary conditions, but only by longer retrospect and a careful distinction between permanent tendencies and transitory influences. If the investor is unable or unwilling to make or secure an adequate survey, it will be best for him not to rely on the results of a superficial one.

To summarize, the principal objects which this Committee thinks the Exchange should keep constantly in mind and do its best gradually to achieve are:

1. To bring about a better recognition by the investing public of the fact that the balance-sheet of a large modern corporation does not and should not be expected to represent an attempt to show present values of the assets and liabilities of the corporation.

2. To emphasize the fact that balance-sheets are necessarily to a large extent historical and conventional in character, and to encourage the adoption of revised forms of balance-sheets which will dis-

is effected, unless the circumstances are such that the collection of the sale price is not reasonably assured. . . .

2. Capital surplus, however created, should not be used to relieve the income account of the current or future years of charges which would otherwise fall to be made thereagainst. . . .

3. Earned surplus of a subsidiary company created prior to acquisition does not form a part of the consolidated earned surplus of the parent company and subsidiaries; nor can any dividend declared out of such surplus properly be credited to the income account of the parent company.

4. While it is perhaps in some circumstances permissible to show stock of a corporation held in its own treasury as an asset, if adequately disclosed, the dividends on stock so held should not be treated as a credit to the income account of the company.

5. Notes or accounts receivable due from officers, employees, or affiliated companies must be shown separately and not included under a general heading such as Notes Receivable or Accounts Receivable.

The Exchange would probably desire to add a rule regarding stock dividends.

PRESENT POSITION UNTENABLE. It will be noticed that this remarkable document starts with a virtually complete renunciation of the traditional concept of the balance sheet function. It then seems to place the responsibility for this shift of position upon industrial growth, by stating that it is now "impracticable" to value the assets of large corporations, although it was formerly possible to value the assets of smaller companies with "comparative ease and accuracy." It further states that variations in value, due to changes in price levels or in the mental attitudes of appraisers, would often dwarf operating profits and losses.

The alleged impracticability of valuing the assets of

large corporations is not borne out by the facts. A building containing five million cubic feet usually presents exactly the same appraisal problem as a similar type of building containing one million cubic feet, the only difference being in the multiplier. A $500,000 turbine requires no more time to appraise than a $50,000 turbine. Furthermore, unlike auditing, annual reappraisals are usually very simple. For the most part they require merely the restating of former appraisal figures on the basis of current price and wage levels, and the listing of newly acquired assets at cost. Most of this work is of a routine nature that can be done by any intelligent clerk.

The fact that changes in price levels would frequently produce variations in value dwarfing operating results, indicates the prime importance of such changes in value. This subject has been discussed in previous chapters. Changes in the mental attitude of appraisers would probably have less opportunity to affect the calculations than would similar changes in the mental attitude of accountants. Appraisers do not look at a plant and guess what it is worth. They are governed by a rigid technical routine which is supported on every side by measurements, quantities, external prices, wage levels, and costs. These considerations probably allow less latitude for individual judgment than is afforded by most audits.

After belittling the importance of balance sheets, the letter in question proceeds to emphasize the importance of profit and loss statements. It seems to assume that, although balance sheets fail to reflect current facts, profit and loss accounts can be made to do so. This assumption is entirely untenable and indicates the next strategic retreat that accounting leadership will be forced to make if it continues in its present course. Balance sheets and profit and loss statements are interdependent. The latter cannot be complete and truthful unless the former are. The sole function of a profit and loss statement is to explain increases or decreases in net worth displayed by its related balance sheet. If the balance sheet does not present a complete and truthful statement of current fact, the profit and loss statement cannot possibly do so.

THE FUTURE. I believe it can safely be said that public respect for the accounting profession is now less high than it was a decade ago. I believe it can also safely be said that this decline in prestige has been caused in large part by a growing realization on the part of the ordinary man that accounting does not talk his language, and that it is quite as apt to deceive as to inform him. The tendency of the accounting profession to ignore the need for changing its methods does nothing to redeem its prestige. On the other hand, its tendency to seek an academic justification of present methods by redefining the accounting function can only end in its eventual admission that all accounting figures, whether for assets or income, are of little value. When this admission has been made, and has been comprehended by the public, accounting prestige will be at low ebb.

The accounting profession should refuse to await such an outcome. Accountants should learn to be valuers or should employ valuers. Only a mastery of the appraiser's comparatively simple technique stands between accountants and a brilliant future of unparalleled service to business and to the public. Accounting is at the crossroads. It can yield to inertia, refuse to recognize its own opportunity, ignore the public need, and continue slowly to dig its own grave. Or it can grasp its opportunity, adopt a progressive, scientific attitude with reference to its methods, and thereby serve both the public and itself to an extent scarcely imagined today.

INDEX

A

Acceptable markets, 125, 134, 225
Accountants, 21-22, 69; alternatives of, 315; certificates of, 20-22; early, 67; prestige of, 323; prophecy by, 102, 141, 145, 215, 285, 300, 303; societies, 21, 68-69, 160
Accounting, accepted practices, 20, 22, 42-43; authority, 18, 25, 28, 32; conventions, 20, 159; criticism of, 315; customs, 20; defense of present practices, 44; eras, 70; function of, 295, 316-317; future of, 315, 323; goal of, 26; history of, 58; ideal aim, 174-176, 179; methods, 20; origin of public, 73; principles, 18, 20, 42-43, 56, 174-176, 320; stabilized, 115-126; standard of, 26; venture basis of, 71-72
Accounts, capital, 180, 279-280, 288; cost of sales, 314; net worth, 280, 288; of London, 60; receivable, 229-230; revaluation, 266; valuation, 247, 286-287
Accuracy, 26
Act, Securities, of 1933, 15-20; Securities and Exchange, of 1934, 15
Active Markets, 133
Actual value, 101-102
Advertising expense, 178, 238
Africa, 69; money in, 104
Aim, ideal accounting, 174-176, 179

Alphabetical index, 61
Alternatives of accountants, 315
American Institute of Accountants, 160, 317
American railways, 25
American Society of Certified Public Accountants, 21
Amortization, 261; of bond discount and premium, 300; of investments, 212, 215, 222, 281-284
Anticipation of profits, 9, 23-24, 42, 77-78
Appraisals, 162-163, 167-169, 204, 209-211, 226-228, 243, 322; impracticability of, 321
Appraiser, 75, 184
Appreciation, 32
Appropriated surplus, 286-287
Arabia, money in, 104
Arabic numerals, 60, 63-64
Aristotle, 85
Asia, 69
Assets, 22-23; capital, 27; concealment of, 27; current, 23-24, 42-43, 76; current ratio, 191; fixed, 23-24, 28, 32, 42-43, 74-76, 190; liquid ratio, 191; marketable, 134, 172, 183; nonmarketable, 152, 158, 172, 183-188, 242-243, 245; nonreproducible, 184-185, 187-189, 242-243, 245; reproducible, 183; special, 162, 167-168; standard, 162-163
Audit, 21
Austrian law, 38

Authority, accounting, 18, 25, 28, 32, 212, 223, 251
Axiology, 85-86

B

Babylonian tablets, 58
Bad debts, 301; reserve for, 286
Badwill, 273
Badham v. *Williams*, 292
Balance sheet, 24, 27, 32, 40; function, 232; 271-275; purpose, 24; suggested form, 269-270, 290-291; technique, 263; theory of values, 24-25, 28
Balancing the ledger, 61
Balch v. *Hallet*, 292
Bank of England, 25
Banker, 32
Banks, 29
Barbarigo, firm of, 61
Barter, 103-104, 160
Bennett, James, 65
Bethlehem Steel Corporation, 273
Bids and offers, 135-136, 138-139
Birth of public accounting, 73
Blue-sky laws, 17
Bolton v. *Natal Land and Colonization Co. Ltd.*, 200
Book value, 28
Bookkeeping entries, 303-304
Booms and depressions, 158
Bonbright, Professor, 81
Bonds, 280; amortization of premiums and discounts, 300; discount on, 280, 283-285; premium on, 281, 283, 285; reserve for retirement of, 287
Broad markets, 131
Brokers' commissions, 147-148, 150

Brown, Richard, 58
Buildings, 23, 30, 32, 204, 209
Business Advisory and Planning Council, 52

C

Capital, 193; account, 180, 279-280, 288; assets, 27; discount on stock, 276-277; premium on stock, 276; profits and losses, 193-196, 198-199, 267, 278, 298-299, 304; stock, 275, 278; surplus, 199, 288, 304.
Cash, 23-24, 229-230; book, 64
Certificate, accountant's, 20-22
Certified public accountants, number of, 69
Charges, transportation, 147-150, 169-171, 173, 272
Chinese money, 104, yuan dollar, 109
Christoffels, Ympyn, 63
Civilization, 177
Colinson, Robert, 64
Collegio dei Raxonati, 67
Commission, brokers', 147-148, 150; Federal Trade, 17, 20-21; Securities and Exchange, 17; stock salesmen's, 238
Commodity, dollar, 111, 113; index, 108, 116, 168
Competitive markets, 129
Concealment, of assets, 27; of profits, 42-43, 297
Concept of accounting function, 316-317
Concessions to expediency, 185, 188
Conditions, ideal accounting, 176
Congressional Library, 58

Conservatism, 9, 29, 38-39, 50, 77, 100, 204
Consolidations, 212-214
Consumer's surplus, 92-93, 201
Contingencies, reserve for, 287
Convenience of money, 105
Conventions, accounting, 20, 159
Conville v. *Shook*, 293
Coöperation between men, 177
Copyrights, 243
Cost, 27, 30, 33; counting the, 71; installation, 169-171, 173; of sales account, 314; original, 4, 23-24, 72, 78, 159-161, 167, 179, 243-244, 246, 304; replacement, 78, 155, 157, 161, 168, 244; reproduction, 161-162; system, 310
Cotrugli, Benedetto, 61
Creditor, 32, 180-181
Crichton's Oil Co. case, 293
Criticism of accounting, 315
Current, assets, 23-24, 42-43, 76; asset ratio, 191; profits, 198-199, 304
Customs, accounting, 20

D

Dafforne, John, 67; Richard, 64
Dark Ages, 177
Debits and Credits, 65-66
Decrement, 36
Defects of replacement cost as value, 157
Defense of present practices, 44
Deferred charges, 237
Demand and supply, 95
Depletion, 262
Depreciation, 70, 195, 205, 247-259, 264-266; declining value basis, 248, 256-257; flat basis,

248-256; production unit method, 258; reserve for, 286; sinking fund method, 258
Depressions and Booms, 158
Determination, of market prices, 135; of replacement cost, 161, 168
Dickinson, Arthur Lowes, 27, 30, 36, 38, 40, 66, 223
Dicksee, L. R., 66
Differential between market prices, 149
Discount, amortization of, 300; on bonds, 280, 283-285; on capital stock, 276-277; on notes, 281-282
Discretionary orders, 137
Displacement cost theory of value, 154
Dollar, commodity, 111, 113; yuan, 109
Domesday Book, 59
Double entry, 61
Dues, 237
du Pont, Pierre S., 52
Durability of money, 105

E

Early accountants, 67
Early operating losses, 238
Earned surplus, 199, 288-289, 30;
Earnings, 15, 37, 288-289; statement, 33
Earp's Appeal, 293
Economic, equilibrium, 156; value, 85, 87, 141-142, 145, 150, 180
Economic principles, 35, 39-40, 42, 295
Economist, 33

Element, of exchangeability, 89; of scarcity, 88; of utility, 91
Engineering fees, 238
England, 24, 59-60, 63-64, 72
Engraving bonds and stock, cost of, 238
Entries, bookkeeping, 303-304
Entry, double, 61; single, 36
Equipment, 210
Eras of accounting development, 70
Esquerré, Paul-Joseph, 28, 30, 33, 66
Europe, continental, 68-69
Excelsior Water & Mining Co. v. Pierce, 292
Exchange, mediums of, 103
Exchangeability, element of, 89
Expediency, concessions to, 185, 188
Expense, advertising, 178, 238; organization, 238-242; sales, 178
Eyster v. Centennial Board of Finance, 293

F

Fable, of two factories, 2; of two flour mills, 6; of two investment trusts, 9
Factories, fable of two, 2
False and misleading statements, 22, 42
Faulty concepts of value, 99
Federal Trade Commission, 17, 20-21
Fees, engineering, 238; incorporation, 238; legal, 238
Fiduciary institutions, 29
Financial position, 27, 32
Financial statements, 22, 42; interdependency of, 40, 323

Fisher, Irving, 111-112
Fixed assets, 23-24, 28, 32, 42-43, 74-76, 190
Flour mills, fable of two, 6
Fluctuations in value, 207-208
Form utility, 91-92
Frame of reference of gold, 108
Fraud, 26
Free markets, 129
French, Norman, 60
Function, of accounting, 295, 316-317; of balance sheet, 232, 271-275; of profit and loss statement, 297-299
Futility of Securities laws, 15
Future of accounting, 315, 323

G

General Electric Company, 189, 245
Genoa, 60
Gerisher, Charles, 65
German companies, 25
German law, 29, 38-39
Germany, 60, 63; money in, 104
Gibbons v. Mahon, 293
Gifford, Walter S., 52
Goal of accounting, 26
Goddard, J. H., 65
Going concern value, 4-5, 44-49, 75, 79, 99, 101, 201-202, 204
Gold, frame of reference of, 108; standard, 105; value of, 107-109, 202, 206
Goodwill, 230-237, 242
Gottlieb, Johann, 63
Gowghe, John, 63
Great Britain, 68-69
Green, Wilmer L., 58

H

Harriman, William A., 52
Harvard Graduate School, 52
Hastings, Senator, 21
Hatfield, Henry Rand, 25, 26, 28, 32, 35, 38, 39, 44, 50, 66, 223
Historical data, in balance sheet, 159
History of acounting, 58
Hoare and Co. case, 293
Holden's triennial directory of London, Westminster and Southwark, 68
Holland, 63
Hubbard v. *Weare*, 292

I

Ideal accounting, aim, 174-176, 179; conditions, 176; principles, 174-176
Imputed market prices, 151-152
Income and expenses, 288-289, statement of 33
Inconsistency, 32, 39
Incorporation fees, 238
Increment, 36
Index, alphabetical, 61; commodity, 108, 116, 168
Indigo, 102
Installation costs, 169-171, 173
Institute of Accountants (London), 68
Institute of Chartered Accountants in England and Wales, 68
Insurance, 237; companies, 29; reserve for self, 287; self, 302
Interdependency of financial statements, 40, 323
Interest, 237; legal in England, 72; nominal, 282; prepaid, 281-282;

real, 282; theoretical, 282-283
Interpreters, 1
Intrinsic value, 101-102
Inventories, 9, 23-24, 26-28, 29-31, 42-43, 146, 223, 225-226, 304; reserve for loss on, 286; speculative profits on, 308
Investment trusts, fable of two, 9
Investments, 30, 32, 212, 243; amortization of, 212, 215-222, 281-284
Investors, key to protecting, 53
Italy, 59, 68

J

Jones, Edward Thomas, 64
Jones, Thomas, 65

K

Kant, Immanuel, 85
Kelly, Dr. Patrick, 65
Key to protecting investors, 53, 55

L

Land, 23, 29, 32, 200, 204
Law, Austrian, 38; blue-sky, 17; German, 29, 38-39; of diminishing utility, 93; securities, 15
Ledger, balancing the, 61
Legal definition of profits, 292-293
Legal fees, 238
Liabilities, 271; money value, 285; real value, 285-286
Library of Congress, 58
Limited orders, 137
Liquid asset ratio, 191
Lisle, George, 66
Littleton, A. C., 58

London, accounts of, 60, Holden's directory of, 68

Losses (see profits)

Lotze, 85

M

Machinery, 210

Mair, John, 64

Managers, 180-181

Margin, profit, 197

Marginal, utility, 93-94; utility theory of value, 153; vendibility, 93-94

Market, 127, 177-179, 182; acceptable, 128, 134, 225; active, 133; broad, 131; competitive, 129; free, 129; orders, 137; prices, 127, 135, 143, 149, 151-152; restricted, 165; value, 23-24, 28-31, 33

Marketable assets, 134, 172, 183

Marsh, C. C., 65

Marx, Karl, theory of value, 153

Materials, raw, 29

Mathematical truth, 284

Mediums of exchange, 103

Melon, financial, 191

Merchandise, 32

Methods, 20

Mines, 243

Minot v. *Paine*, 293

Misrepresentation, 24, 42-43, 83, 305-306

Mitchell, William, 65

Mobile, etc., R. R. v. *Tenn.*, 292

Money, 103; convenience of, 105; durability of, 105; in Africa, 104; in Arabia, 104; in China, 104; in Germany, 104; in U.S., 104; representative, 104; stability of, 105; stabilization of, 111, 193-194; value liabilities, 285

Monopoly prices, 163-164

Montgomery, Robert H., 26, 29, 32-33, 35, 37, 39, 66, 224

Morrison, James, 65

Mortgage, 190

Mortgagees, 79, 190-191

N

National Bank of Wales, 293

Nederlands Instituit van Accountants, 68

Net worth, 31; account, 280, 288

New York State Society of Certified Public Accountants, 69

New York Stock Exchange, 317

Newton v. *Birmingham Small Arms Co.*, 24

Nietzsche, Friedrich Wilhelm, 85

Nominal interest, 282

Nonmarketable assets, 152, 158, 172, 184-188, 242-243, 245

Non-operating profits, 198

Nonrecurrent profits, 23-24, 43

Nonreproducible assets, 184-185, 187-189, 242-243, 245

Norman French, 60

Note discount, 281-282

Notes receivable, 229-230

Number, of public accountants, 69; of security holders, 82; of stockholders, 82.

Numerals, Arabic, 60, 63-64; Roman, 59, 62, 64

O

Obsolescence, 259-261

Offers and Bids, 135-136, 138-139

Oil wells, 243
Oldcastle, Hugh, 63
Operating, early losses, 238; profits, 198; surplus, 289
Orders, discretionary, 137; limited, 137; market, 137
Organization expense, 238-242
Origin of present practices, 58
Original cost, 4, 23-24, 72, 78, 159-161, 167, 179, 243-244, 246, 304
Overstatement, 28, 33, 73-74
Overvaluation, 25-26, 32, 41

P

Pacioli, Lucas, 61-63
Par value of capital stock, 278
Passchier-Goessens, 63
Patents, 243-244, 246
People v. *San Francisco Savings Union*, 292
Petrie, Nicolaus, 63
Philosophical value, 85
Pipe Roll, 59
Pixley, F. W., 66
Place Utility, 92
Platinum, 102
Plato, 85
Position, financial, 27, 32
Practicability, of present practices, 52
Practices, accounting, 20, 22; defense of, 44; origin of, 58; practicability of, 52
Premium, amortization of, 300; on bonds, 281, 283, 285; on capital stock, 276,
Prepaid interest, 281-282
Prestige of accounting, 323
Prices, 27; market, 127, 135, 143, 149, 151-152; monopoly, 163-164
Prince of Orange, 64
Principles, accounting, 18, 20, 42-43, 56, 174-176, 320; economic, 35, 39-40, 42
Profession, accounting, 21-22
Profit and loss statement, 23-24, 33, 37, 40, 181, 194, 199, 308; function of, 297-299; suggested form, 312-314
Profits, 23, 27, 31-35, 38, 40; anticipation of, 9, 23-24, 42, 77-78; capital, 193-196, 198-199, 267, 278, 298-299, 304; concealment of, 42-43, 297; correct definition of, 295; current, 198-199, 304; economist's definition of, 295; legal definition of, 292-293; margin of, 197; non-operating, 198; nonrecurrent, 23-24, 43; on inventories, 308; operating, 198, 238; present accounting definition of, 294; realized, 23; unrealized, 9, 15, 23, 34, 37-38, 42-43, 267, 295-297, 300, 305-306, 308
Profits and income, statement of, 33
Prophecy by accountants, 102, 141, 145, 215, 285, 300, 303
Psychological value, 85
Purpose of balance sheet, 24

Q

Quarries, 243

R

Railways, American, 25
Ratio, current asset, 191; liquid asset, 191
Raw materials, 29

Real estate, 25

Real, interest, 282; value, 101-102; value liabilities, 285-286

Realized profits, 23

Rent, 237

Replacement cost, 78, 244; defects as value, 157; determination of, 161, 168; theory of value, 155

Representative money, 104

Reproducible assets, 183

Reproduction cost, 161-162

Reserves, 286, for bed debts, 286; for bond retirements, 287; for contingencies, 287; for depreciation, 286; for loss on inventory, 286; for self-insurance, 287; secret, 26, 28, 74, 192

Restricted markets, 165

Revaluation accounts, 266

Richardson v. *Buhl*, 292

Ripley, William Z., 317

Roman Empire, 58, 177

Roman numerals, 59, 62, 64

S

Sales expense, 178

Sanders, T. H., 52

Scarcity, element of, 88

Scotland, 60, 67-68

Secret reserves, 26, 28, 74, 192

Securities, 29, 31, 243; number of holders of, 82

Securities and exchange commission, 17

Securities Act of 1933, 15, 20

Securities Exchange Act of 1934, 15

Securities laws, futility of, 15

Self-Insurance, 302; reserve for, 287

Single entry, 36

Snell, Charles, 67

Societies, accountants, 21, 68, 69

Society of Accountants in Edinburgh, 68

Soranzo and Brothers, 61

Sound value, 162

South America, 69

South Sea Company, 68

Special assets, 162, 167-168

Speculation, 159

Speculative profits on inventories, 308

Stability of money, 105

Stabilization of money, 111, 193-194

Stabilized accounting, 115; criticism of, 123; illustration of, 118

Standard, assets, 162-163; gold, 105; of accounting, 26

Stated value of capital stock, 278

Statement, earnings, 33; income and expenses, 33; profit and loss, 23-24, 33, 37, 40, 181, 194, 199, 308, 312-314; profits and income, 33

Stevin, Simon, 63-64

Stock, 243; capital, 275; discount on, 276-277; exchanges, 26; par value of, 278; premium on, 276; salesmen's commissions, 238; stated value of, 278; watered, 49-50, 192

Stockholders, 2, 32, 180-181; number of, 82

Subjective value, 91, 201, 205

Subscriptions, 237

Suggested form, of balance sheet, 269-270, 290-291; of profit and loss statement, 312-314

Sumerian documents, 58
Supply and demand, 95
Surplus, 23-24, 287; appropriated, 286-287; capital, 199, 288, 304; consumer's, 92-93, 201; earned, 199, 288-289, 304; operating, 289
Sweeny, Henry W., 115

T

Taxes, 237
Technique, balance sheet, 263
Theodosius the Great, 58
Theoretical interest, 282-283
Theory of balance sheet values, 24-25
Thomas v. *Gregg*, 293
Time utility, 92
Tools, 210
Towers v. *African Tug Co.*, 293
Trade, 176
Trademarks, 243
Transportation charges, 147-150, 169-171, 173, 272
Truth, 25, 28, 57, 203; mathematical, 284
Turner, Thomas, 65

U

Understatement, 24, 26, 28, 33, 73-74
Undervaluation, 24, 26, 32, 41
United States, 69; money in, 104
United States Department of Commerce, 52
United States Senate Committee on Banking and Currency, 317
United States Steel Corporation, 49
United States v. *Kansas Pacific R.R.*, 293

United Verde Copper Co. v. *Roberts*, 292
Unrealized profits, 9, 15, 23, 34, 37-38, 42-43, 267, 295-297, 300, 305-306, 308
Untruths, 18, 21-22
Use of market prices, 143
Utility, element of, 91; form, 91-92; law of diminishing, 93; marginal, 93-94; place, 92; time, 92

V

Valuation, 25, 26, 36; accounts, 247, 286-287
Value, 27, 29; actual, 101-102; asset, 22-23; balance sheet, 24-25, 28; book, 28; displacement cost theory of, 154; economic, 85, 87, 141-142, 145, 150, 180; expressed in money, 109; faulty concepts of, 99; fluctuations in, 207-208; to a going concern, 4-5, 44-49, 75, 79, 99, 101, 201-202, 204; intrinsic, 101-102; in use, 91; Karl Marx theory of, 153; marginal utility theory of, 153; market, 23-24, 28-31, 33; of a business as a whole, 233, 271-273; of gold, 107, 109, 202, 206; of goodwill, 233; par value of capital stock, 278; philosophical, 85; psychological, 85; real, 101-102; replacement cost theory of, 155; sound, 162; stated value of capital stock, 278; subjective, 9, 201, 205
Valuer, 24, 26, 84, 323
Vendibility, marginal, 93-94
Venice, 61-62, 67

Venture, basis of accounting, 71-72
Vernier v. *The General and Commercial Investment Trust Ltd.*, 292
Vernon, John, 64

W

Warren v. *King.*, 292
Watered Stock, 49-50, 192

Watson, George, 67
Wealth, 33, 36, 295, 296; of a business, 271-272
William the Conqueror, 59
Wittenborg, Herman and Johann, 60

X Y Z

Yuan dollar, 109

Date Due